BT 1/12

BATS

Revised Edition

BATS
REVISED EDITION

M. BROCK FENTON

Fitzhenry & Whiteside

Bats, Revised Edition

Copyright 2001, 1992 by M. Brock Fenton

Fitzhenry & Whiteside
195 Allstate Parkway
Markham, Ontario
L3R 4T8
godwit@fitzhenry.ca

National Library of Canada Cataloguing in Publication Data

Fenton, M. Brock (Melville Brockett), 1943–
Bats

2nd ed.
Includes bibliographical references and index.
ISBN 1-55041-482-8

1. Bats. I. Title.

QL737.C5F44 2001   599.4   C2001-930727-6

Previous pages: *The wings, their supporting structures and attachment to the body are clear in this male Pallid Bat. The red color band serves to identify the individual in behavioral experiments.*

You can find Fitzhenry & Whiteside on the World Wide Web at
http://www.fitzhenry.ca

Text design by Donna Sinisgalli
Jacket design by Joan M. Toro

Printed in Hong Kong

This book is printed on acid-free paper.

TABLE OF CONTENTS

Boxes

FOREWORD

B rock Fenton has devoted most of his life to the study of bats, and he
loves to explore and share their amazing world. In this book, he provides one of the most complete summaries of knowledge about bats
yet available, including insights that will create new interest and change many
readers' opinions from fear to admiration.

As you will learn in this book, bats are among the world's most fascinating
animals; they range in size from the Hog-nosed Bat, which weighs less than a
penny, to gigantic flying foxes with six-foot wingspans. Bats are the only mammals that fly, and their orientation systems are a scientific marvel. Many bats
have ears so sensitive that they can hear the footsteps of small insects. Others
have suction discs for climbing on slick leaf surfaces, huge feet and claws for
fishing, heat-sensing noses for finding prey, spectacular crests and epaulets for
courtship display, brilliant colors and designs for camouflage and attracting
mates, and much, much more.

Nearly a thousand kinds of bats comprise almost one-quarter of all
mammal species, and they live nearly everywhere except in the most extreme desert and polar regions. Bats are the primary predators of vast numbers of night-flying insects. They pollinate flowers and disperse seeds
essential to the maintenance of whole ecosystems, and bat-dependent
plants produce crops valued in the hundreds of millions of dollars annually
in cash-poor developing countries. Despite the fact that bats rank among
the world's most interesting and important mammals, they remain the most
scientifically neglected, frequently misunderstood and needlessly perse-
cuted by the public. Because many species produce only a single young
each year and live in conspicuous colonies numbering from thousands to
millions, they are exceptionally vulnerable to extinction. Like all animals,
they are increasingly threatened by habitat loss and pollution, but for many
bats, the single most important threat comes from people who kill large
numbers out of fear and ignorance.

The world of bats, so long neglected yet so important, provides a vast and exciting frontier for the student. Although bats play key roles in many ecosystems and in some economies, virtually nothing is known about the ecology, behavior, or conservation needs of most species. Alarming declines of bat populations are increasingly documented and the environmental and economic consequences, though largely uninvestigated, are potentially serious. Several species already have become extinct without even being listed as endangered, and many more are in serious need of help that cannot be provided without additional knowledge. It is my hope that Brock Fenton's personal curiosity and enthusiasm about bats will, through this exceptionally well organized and beautifully illustrated book, contribute to a new era of investigation and understanding of these unique and marvelous masters of the night skies.

Merlin D. Tuttle
Founder and Director
Bat Conservation International

PREFACE

Yeh yen, chauve-souris, flaggermaus, slepi misi, nycteris . . . bats by other names. Humans have a long fascination with bats, but some of our names for them suggest that we have not always known just what to make of these winged mammals. *Yeh yen,* one Chinese name for bats, means "swallow of the night." The French *chauve-souris* means "bald mouse," while the Norwegian *flaggermaus* translates to "flying mouse." The Serbo-Croatian *slepi misi* suggests blindness, while the Greek *nycteris* denotes obscurity. In other languages, the names for bats suggest evening (the Italian *pipistrello,* the Latin *vespertilio*), fluttering flight (the old French *ratapignata*), or an aberrant bird (the Scottish *gaucky bird* or the Irish *sciatham leathair*). Perhaps most revealing of people's attitudes toward bats is the Hungarian *denever,* meaning bat, which recognizes bats as distinct entities without relying on another animal or a single bat characteristic to classify these creatures.

Denever is closest to the mark because bats are distinctive and have been for more than 60 million years. *Pipistrello* and *vespertilio* are also appropriate, however, since most bats are nocturnal and emerge at dusk to begin their daily cycle of activity. Names associating bats with rodents, whether rats or mice, are inappropriate because although rodents and bats are mammals, they are in many ways quite different. But bats and many rodents are relatively small animals, and someone catching a fleeting glimpse of a passing mouse or bat might easily assume that all things small, furry and brownish are related.

Chiroptera, the scientific name for bats, identifies them by the structure of their wings. Chiroptera comes from the Greek *cheiro* (hand) and *ptera* (wing), suggesting hand wings, the feature that makes it easy to recognize bats and distinguish them from birds and the extinct pterosaurs, the other flying vertebrates. A bat's four elongated fingers give its wings an obvious hand-like structure. In birds, where the fingers supporting the wings are fused, or in pterosaurs where one digit was elongated, the basic hand structure is less obvious than it is in the Chiroptera.

While scientific names may reflect detailed knowledge of the animals and plants they describe, many people consider bats to be a paradox: a mammal that flies. Some common names reflect this view of bats. The French *Mitatarat* suggests that bats are part mammal and part bird, while *yeh yen* identifies them as birds of the night. These are recurring themes in popular names for bats in the folklore that surround them. The folklore of some American Indian tribes (the Cherokee, Seminole and Creek), Australian aborigines, some peoples of southern Nigeria and the ancient Romans and Greeks includes stories reflecting the dichotomy of bat characters. Often a ball game between the mammals and the birds is the setting for the tale. Fur suggests that bats should be on the mammals' team, while wings could mean they belong with the birds. The bats are sometimes portrayed as deceitful outcasts, adjusting their allegiance according to the score. Other times they emerge as heroes, rejected by the bird team and joining the mammals to score the winning points.

There are about 900 different species of bats and their diversity is reflected in their appearance, their dietary habits, their social organization and their choice of places to roost. While some bats use echolocation to "see with their ears, none of them is blind. To some people bats are symbols of fertility or of good luck and long life; to others they are frightening and symbolize evil. What is the truth about bats? With 900 species to consider, the truth about one species may not apply to others.

The purpose of this book is to introduce you to these extraordinary and varied creatures. They are even more amazing than you may think.

So what's changed since 1992 when the first edition of this book appeared?First, people are more aware of bats now thanks to the proliferation of information about them. In North America and in Europe "Masters of the Night," a traveling exhibit about bats has opened many people's eyes to these fascinating creatures. This change has been aided and abetted by exhibits about bats at zoos and museums throughout the world.Second, today there are many more books about bats. The list includes general books about bats (page 209) as well as story books and fact books for children (page 210). Then, of course, there are web sites that allow the curious to learn more about bats from the comfort of their own work areas.

Perhaps the most important change in the information readily available about bats is the appearance of books about the bats of specific areas (pages 211–217). Whether it's Texas or Ohio, Central America, Papua New Guinea, Borneo, Australia or the Indian subcontinent, it's much easier now to find out about the bats you may encounter on your travels.

And then, as we shall see, there have been many new discoveries about bats that simultaneously shed more light on these animals while raising more and more intriguing questions to which we still do not have answers.

M. B. Fenton
Toronto
April 2001

ACKNOWLEDGMENTS

I is a pleasure to thank the late professors R. E. Beschel and R. L. Peterson, who fired and fed my initial interest in bats, and then to acknowledge Professor D. R. Griffin and the late professor K. D. Roeder, who further stimulated and expanded it. Along the way, John D. Altringham, David H. M. Cumming, Gareth Jones, Tom H. Kunz, Gary F. McCracken, Don J. McQueen, H. Gray Merriam, Ulla M. Norberg, Paul A. Racey, I. L. (Naas)Rautenbach, Jens Rydell, and Clive M. Swanepoel made it easy to diversify my interests in bats. I am particularly grateful to G. Roy Horst, who maintained communication of information about bats by ensuring that the North American Symposium on Bat Research was an annual event.

I thank J. P. Balcombe, E. Bernard, E. Cholewa, J. Habersetzer, A. J. Harris, P. Kumarasamy, G. F. McCracken, M. E. McCully, C. Merriman, M. Obrist, P. A. Racey, J. Taylor and J. G. Woods for permitting me to use their photographs here. I am especially grateful to Max Licht and Sylvie Bouchard for their artistic contributions. The Royal Ontario Museum (J. Chileni, J. L. Eger, M. D. Engstrom and D. M. Pendergast) and the Gardiner Museum (M. Chilton) kindly allowed me to photograph material in their collections. My photographic efforts have been substantially assisted by advice from J. Rydell, G. Temple and R. A. Koehler.

My work on bats has been generously supported by grants from the Natural Sciences and Engineering Research Council of Canada; the Chautauqua Bird, Tree and Garden Club; and the World Wildlife Fund (Canada). The work, and some of the photographs in this book, would not have been possible without the kind cooperation of the Department of National Parks and Wild Life Management in Zimbabwe, the National Parks Board in South Africa, Madurai Kamaraj University in India and the Wau Ecology Institute in Papua New Guinea.

I am especially indebted to many students, graduate, undergraduate and postdoctoral, who have worked with me at Carleton University and York University. Of particular note (because they read all or parts of the text) are Lalita

Acharya, Doris Audet, Enrico Bernard, Sylvie Bouchard, Joe Cebek, Jenna Dunlop, Leesa Fawcett, Brian Hickey, Mark Hovorka, David Johnston, Jennifer Long, Cathy Merriman, Alison Neilson, Martin Obrist, David Pearl, Stuart Perlmeter, Dan Riskin, Bill Scully, Daphne Syme, Jason Taylor, Maarten Vonhof and Jane Waterman. I also thank D. H. Johnston for reading and commenting on parts of the text. For the first edition, Deidre Mullane, *the* editor at Facts On File, Inc., kept me on the straight and for this I am extremely grateful. I also thank Jeff Golick, her successor on the project, and Frank Darmstadt who looked after the revised edition.

My greatest thanks go to Anne and to the bats.

INTRODUCING BATS

Their Anatomy, Origins and Flight

Bats are the only mammals that can fly, and their wings make any of the 900 or so living species instantly recognizable. Whether the bats are modern species or those that lived 50 million years ago, and wherever they occur in the world, they all share the same basic structure. The wings of bats are folds of skin stretched between elongated finger and hand bones and attached to the sides of the body and the hind legs. This pattern distinguishes them from other flying vertebrates, the birds and the pterosaurs. In birds the wings are made of feathers supported by specialized hand bones, while in pterosaurs (now extinct) each wing consisted of folds of skin stretched from the side of the body, along the arm and one elongated finger.

But bats, like humans, are mammals, so most have fur or hair, give birth to live young, and feed their newborns milk until they are old enough to fend for themselves. Being warm-blooded is another feature we associate with mammals, but bats show some variation on this theme. Most warm-blooded (technically, "homeothermic") animals die if their internal body temperature falls too low. While many species of bats are warm-blooded, many others can survive periods when their body temperatures fall close to freezing. These periods may be short (daily) or long (seasonal) depending upon the species and the circumstances (see Chapter Six).

Although wings are the most distinctive characteristic of bats, their variety is a more striking feature. While most bats feed mainly on insects, others visit plants to obtain food in the form of leaves, fruit and/or nectar and pollen. Some bats eat fish and others take prey ranging from insects and frogs to other bats, fish and birds. The most infamous of bats, the vampires, feed only on blood. Their faces also reflect their variety. There are bats with long, narrow faces and others with short, rounded faces; some kinds have faces adorned with elaborate leaf-like structures, while others have simple, dog-like faces. Some species have enormous ears, others small ears. Bats' social lives also vary. Some kinds are solitary, while others live in tightly-knit social groups. In some bats the basic social unit is one adult male with several adult females and their current

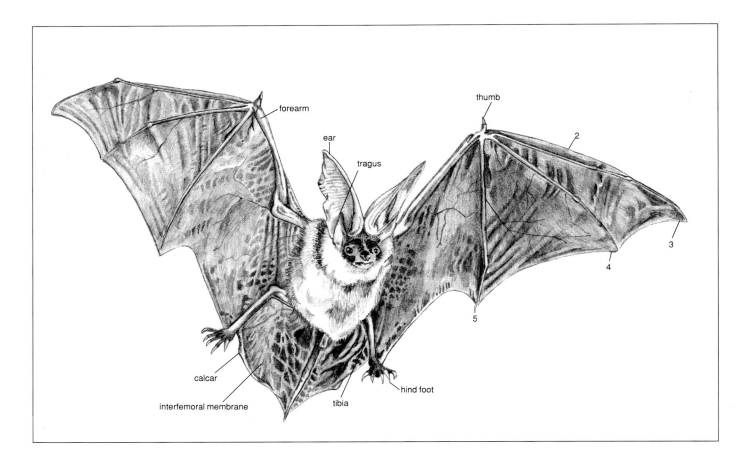

forearm

thumb

ear

tragus

2

3

4

5

calcar

hind foot

interfemoral membrane

tibia

This illustration introduces some external features of a bat, including the ear and tragus; the thumb and fingers 2, 3, 4 and 5; the forearm; lower leg (tibia); hind foot; and calcar. The membrane between the hind legs is the interfemoral membrane, which is missing or abbreviated in some bats. Drawing by Max Licht.

Opposite Page: *These drawings compare the basic wing structures of a bat (top), bird (middle) and pterosaur (bottom), the three groups of flying vertebrates. Note that the hand-like structure is clearest in the bat, although the basic support of the bird and pterosaur wings also is the forelimb and hand.* Drawing by Max Licht.

young (a harem). In other species the basic social unit is a female and her current offspring. The many variations in the basic structure of bats reflect different ways of life.

THE NAMES OF BATS

Knowing something about their names is the first step in exploring the world of bats. Bats comprise the mammalian order called Chiroptera, a name derived from the Greek and meaning hand wing. Within the Chiroptera, the living species are arranged in 19 different families identified in Table 1. Each of the 900 or so living species has a unique scientific name and is classified according to its relationships with other bats. The living bats are arranged in two major categories (suborders), the Megachiroptera, or large bats, and the Microchiroptera, or small bats.

The "common" names of species of bats are not standardized as they are in birds, probably because most people rarely encounter bats at close quarters and at a distance many of them look the same. While the common names "American Robin" or "Robin" identify two species of birds as precisely as their scientific counterparts (*Turdus migratorius* and *Erithacus rubecula*, respectively), the common name Little Brown Bat identifies one species in North America (*Myotis lucifugus*) and another in Australia (*Eptesicus pumilus*). Furthermore, in North America, some books refer to *Myotis lucifugus* as "The Little Brown Bat," and others call it "The Little Brown Myotis."

The scientific names of bats typically involve Latin or Greek roots, so most people find them intimidating because the names are unfamiliar and difficult to pronounce. To biologists, however, scientific names are comfortable because they precisely identify the species in question. Both the pair of words comprising the scientific name and international regulations about their use account for the precision. However, this does not mean that most biologists are any more familiar with the Latin and Greek roots or any better at pronouncing scientific names than are non-biologists. One can appreciate this by listening to the diversity of pronunciations uttered by biologists at any scientific meeting. In some cases, the scientific name describes the particular characteristics of the bat in question. For example, *Antrozous pallidus* is the scientific name for the Pallid Bat and these words identify a cave animal (*Antrozous*) that is pale in color (*pallidus*). Other scientific names provide information about the species' habits. For example, Roberts' Flat-headed Bat is called *Sauromys petrophilus*, which means lizard mouse (*Sauromys*) that loves rocks (*petrophilus*). This African Free-tailed bat commonly roosts under stones. Some scientific names appear nonsensical, such as the generic name *Tadarida*, which means withered toad. Part of the scientific name may identify the area where the species occurs, the person who captured the first specimen known to science, another scientist or a patron of science. So *Tadarida brasiliensis* is a species that occurs in Brazil; *Tadarida chapini* was first described from a specimen collected by an Ameri-

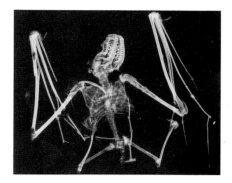

This fossil bat was found in Germany in rocks that are about 50 million years old. Known as Palaeochiropteryx tupaiodon, *this species is very similar in general structure to a modern bat such as the one whose skeleton is shown below. This well-preserved fossil had eaten some moths just before it died; notice that its left forearm is broken.* Radiograph courtesy of J. Habersetzerg, of the Senckenberg Research Institute in Frankfurt, Germany.

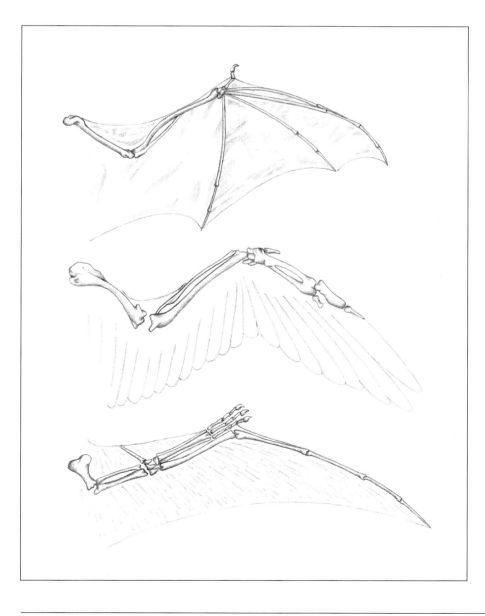

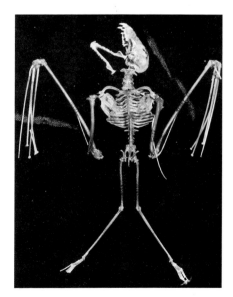

A view from beneath the skeleton of a Lesser False Vampire Bat illustrates the general similarity to fossil bats (above). The skeleton is dominated by the head, the forelimbs and the long, spindly hind limbs. Note that the ribs are also quite broad.

TABLE 1. THE DIVERSITY OF BATS: THEIR CLASSIFICATION, FOSSIL AGE, WORLDWIDE DISTRIBUTION AND DIET

The † denotes a family known only from the fossil record.

FAMILY	FIRST FOSSILS		DISTRIBUTION	VARIATION IN DIET	NUMBER OF LIVING SPECIES	PAGE NUMBER OF ILLUSTRATION
	EPOCH	YEARS AGO (MILLIONS)				
MEGACHIROPTERAMORPHA						
Suborder Megachiroptera						
Pteropodidae (Old World Fruit Bats; Flying Foxes)	Oligocene	30	Old World Tropics	Fruit, leaves nectar, pollen	150	6
MICROCHIROPTERAMORPHA						
Icaronycteridae†	Eocene	50	North America	insects		
Archaeonycteridae†	Eocene	50	Europe	insects		
Microchiropteraformes						
Palaeochiropterygidae†	Eocene	50	Europe	insects		
Hassianycteridae†	Eocene	50	Europe	insects		
Suborder Microchiroptera						
Superfamily Emballonuroidea						
Emballonuridae (Sheath-tailed Bats)	Eocene	50	Pantropical	insects	44	27
Infraorder Yinochiroptera						
Superfamily Rhinopomatoidea						
Craseonycteridae (Hog-nosed Bats)			Thailand	insects	1	124
Rhinopomatidae (Rat-[a.k.a. Mouse-]tailed Bats)			North Africa to Burma	insects	3	123
Superfamily Rhinolophoidea						
Nycteridae (Slit-faced Bats)			Africa, Java, Sumatra	animals	13	126
Megadermatidae (False Vampire Bats)	Eocene	50	Africa to Australia	animals	5	30
Rhinolophidae (Horseshoe Bats)	Eocene	50	Old World	insects	69	12
Hipposideridae (Old World Leaf-nosed Bats)	Eocene	50	Old World Topics	insects	56	29
Infraorder Yangochiroptera						
Phylididae†	Eocene	50	Africa			
Mystacinidae (Short-tailed Bats)			New Zealand	insects, nectar fruit, carrion	1	135
Superfamily Noctilionoidea						
Noctilionidae (Bulldog Bats)			Neotropics	insects, fish	2	128
Mormoopidae (Moustached Bats)			Neotropics	insects	8	131
Phyllostomidae (New World Leaf-nosed Bats)	Mid-Miocene	22	Neotropics	insects, fruit, leaves, nectar pollen, blood	123	5
Superfamily Nataloidea	Eocene		North America/Africa Madagascar			
Myzopodidae (Old World Disk-winged Bats)				insects	1	28
Thyropteridae (New World Disk-winged Bats)			Neotropics	insects, arthropods	3	28
Furipteridae (Thumbless Bats)			Neotropics	insects	2	28
Natalidae (Funnel-eared Bats)			Neotropics	insects	4	29

FAMILY	FIRST FOSSILS		DISTRIBUTION	VARIATION IN DIET	NUMBER OF LIVING SPECIES	PAGE NUMBER OF ILLUSTRATION
	EPOCH	YEARS AGO (MILLIONS)				
Superfamily Molossoidea						
Antrozoidae (Pallid Bats)			North America, Central America	arthropods	2	144
Molossidae (Free-tailed Bats)			Pantropical	insects	83	146
Superfamily Vespertilionoidea						
Vespertilionidae (Plain-nosed Bats)	Eocene	50	worldwide	insects, fish, other vertebrates	283	137

can zoologist, J. P. Chapin; and *Tadarida aloysiisabaudiae* honors the Duke of Abruzzi, who supported an early 20th-century expedition to East Africa that produced the first specimens of this species.

For simplicity's sake, in this book I will refer to bats by their common names. For clarity, the common and scientific names are shown together in the Appendix.

ANATOMY

The anatomy of bats clearly reflects their classification as mammals, whether one examines the skeleton and skull, the skin, the hair or the internal organs. Flight does impose some differences between bats and other mammals, which are most obvious in the skeleton or the cardiovascular system. The skeletons of bats are dominated by the wings and the work associated with flight means that the hearts of bats are proportionally larger than the hearts of other mammals. For example, the heart of a 30-g Mouse-eared Bat is three times larger than the heart of a 30-g laboratory mouse.

Bat skulls show considerable variation in shape, reflecting differences in lifestyle. The skulls and teeth of species that feed on insects and animals are shaped differently than those feeding on plant products (leaves, fruit, nectar and pollen) or blood. Furthermore, fruit-eaters show a much greater range in body and in skull size than do animal-eaters. While there are striking differences in skull shape and teeth between species in different families, there are some basic themes. As you would expect, bigger bats usually have bigger skulls than do smaller bats, if length of the skull is used as a measure of skull size. There are, however, some interesting exceptions. Vampire bats have shorter skulls than expected for their body size, reflecting their specializations for feeding on blood. Some of the New World Leaf-nosed Bats that eat fruit and leaves also have shorter skulls than you would predict from their body size. This could indicate a different approach to feeding. In Ghost-faced Bats shorter skull length reflects the overall shape of the skull.

In general profile bat skulls range from long and narrow to short and high or short and flat. Often these variations reflect feeding habits. Long and narrow skulls, for example, are typical in nectar- and pollen-feeding species. Differences in the thickness of the muzzle or the shape of the braincase reflect bite mechanics and the ability to chew hard food. Specializations for a powerful bite are known in both fruit- and animal-eating bats, while the flat, narrow skulls of some Plain-nosed and Free-tailed Bats are associated with the roosting habits of the species.

Following Page: The dog-like face of the Epauletted Fruit Bat from Africa indicates why some other Old World Fruit Bats are known as "flying foxes." This bat, photographed in Mana Pools National Park in Zimbabwe, weighs about 80 g, and the white tufts of fur at the bases of its ears appear to play a role in camouflaging the bat when it roosts. Epauletted Fruit Bats are clearly the models for the bat of Stellaluna, a successful children's book.

Common Yellow-shouldered Bats are 15-g New World Leaf-nosed Bats that feed on fruit and occur widely in South and Central America. The conspicuous leaf-like structure on the bat's nose is important in echolocation.

Western Big-eared Bats are Plain-nosed Bats that occur widely in North America. These 10-g bats feed on insects and are known to roost in caves, old mines and buildings.

This Large Slit-faced Bat (30–35 g) is widespread in Africa. It is an example of a bat with large ears that lack ridges and do not fold (as do those of Western Big-eared Bats).

Animal-eating bats, whatever their diet, have prominent canine teeth and two or three molars in each quadrant of the jaw. Variation in the lengths of their muzzles usually reflects the numbers of premolar teeth. In some species the rostrum is relatively long. Mouse-eared Bats (genus *Myotis*), with two small premolars behind each canine tooth in the upper jaw, are a case in point. In other species such as those in the genus *Eptesicus* or *Lasiurus*, these two small teeth are missing and the muzzle is shorter.

The front (incisor) teeth of animal-eating bats are quite variable in size and shape. The upper incisors of most animal-eating bats are small, but there are exceptions in two directions. The Free-tailed Bats depart in one way, having stronger upper incisor teeth. The species in the superfamily Rhinolophoidea go the other way, with tiny upper incisors (the Horseshoe Bats, Old World Leaf-nosed Bats and Slit-faced Bats) or none at all (False Vampire Bats). In most Free-tailed Bats, the lower incisor teeth are long and slender and are located beneath the expanded bases of the lower canine teeth. The appearance of the teeth and the behavior of Free-tailed Bats sug-

The Wrinkle-faced Bat is one of the most bizarre looking of mammals. Weighing about 20 g, these New World Leaf-nosed Bats occur widely in South and Central America. The white shoulder spot on this male is brighter than those on females.

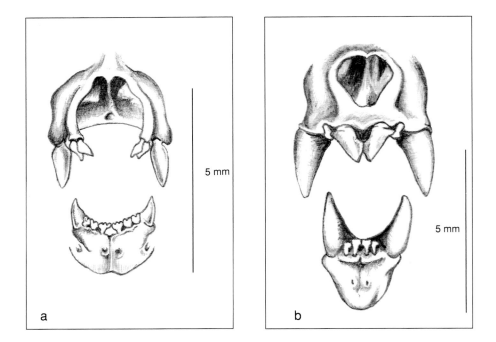

The canines and upper and lower incisor teeth are compared to illustrate the variety found in bats. The canines differ somewhat in form and size but the incisor teeth are more variable. The insectivorous Little Brown Bat (a) is typical, with medium-sized upper and lower incisor teeth. Although the lower incisor teeth of the fruit-eating Short-tailed Fruit Bat (b) are small and relatively uniform in size, the upper incisors are different. One pair is large and strong, flanked by smaller teeth. In the nectar-feeding Mexican Long-tongued Bat (c), the upper incisors are small, and there are no lower incisors. In Bemmeleni's Free-tailed Bat (d), there is one pair of upper incisors and two pairs of lower ones. The lower incisors are below the ridges of the canine teeth and are thought to be used in combing the fur. The scales are all 5 mm long. Drawing by Max Licht.

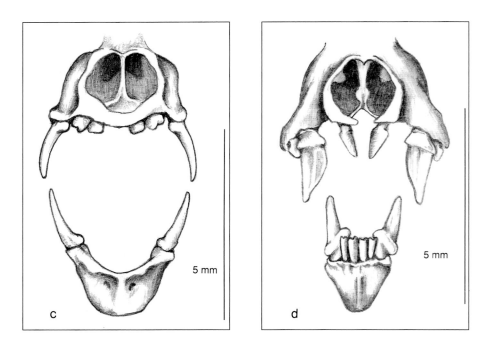

gest that the lower incisors are used for grooming and "combing" the fur. Many nectar-feeding bats' lower incisor teeth are absent in many species, while in other bats they vary in size and prominence.

The skeletons of bats generally resemble those of other mammals even though their wings make them distinct. As noted earlier, the arms and hands of bats are the main supporting framework for the wings. The collarbone (clavicle) is long and well developed and, as it does in humans, attaches the forelimbs to the body. The forearm is typically twice as long as the upper arm (humerus), reflecting specialization for flight. Unlike some other mammals such as humans, the forearms of bats are comprised mainly of one bone, the radius.

The posture of the legs of bats differs remarkably from that of other mammals. When bats are flying, their thigh bones (femora) stick out to the side and slightly back, while the lower leg bones (tibia and fibula) typically point to the rear. When bats are walking, their hind limbs splay to the side in a posture reminiscent of many lizards. In most species the femur is about the same length as the tibia and the fibula. Vampire Bats and some Free-tailed Bats are more agile on the ground than most other bats. In these species, particularly Common Vampire Bats, the femur is more robust than it is in most other bats, and their walking postures also are distinctive.

Although New World Disk-winged Bats roost with their heads up, many other bats hang upside down when they are not flying, anchoring themselves to their roosts by their toenails. The sharp claws on their hind feet enable bats to grip small surface irregularities. To hang by its toes from a perch, a bat does not need to expend energy. The arrangement of tendons in the foot means that the weight of the hanging bat keeps the claws firmly anchored. This specialization accounts for the macabre sight of dead and mummified bats still hanging from their last perches.

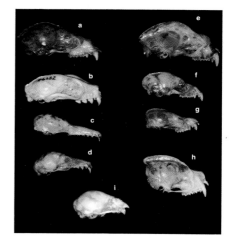

This illustrates variation in the general appearance of bat skulls by comparing two fruit-eating bats (a and b), two nectar-feeding bats (c and d), three animal-eating bats (e, f and g), a fishing bat (h) and a vampire bat (i). Skull A is 35 mm long, and skull i is 25 mm long. The skulls are those of a Greater Spear-nosed Bat (a), a Lesser Philippine Fruit Bat (b), a Mexican Long-tongued Bat (c), a Woermann's Bat (d), a Commerson's Leaf-nosed Bat (e), a Lesser False Vampire Bat (f), a Mouse-eared Bat (g), a Greater Bulldog Bat (h) and a Common Vampire Bat (i).

THE ORIGINS OF BATS

When did the first bat take flight? The answer to this fundamental question has eluded biologists and may continue to do so for some time because fossil bats are not commonly found. Bats are generally small and delicate with light bones, so they do not make good candidates for fossilization. Fossilized bats first appear in deposits of the Eocene epoch that are thought to be about 50 million years old. *Icaronycteris index*, the oldest fossil bat, was found in rocks in Wyoming, and other species are known from Eocene deposits in Europe and Pakistan. At least 13 species of bats lived in the Eocene and they are classified in 11 families. Six of the families (Sheath-tailed Bats, False Vampire Bats, Horseshoe Bats, Old World Leaf-nosed Bats, Nataloid Bats and Plain-nosed Bats) include species living today, but five other families are extinct (see Table 1).

Since these earliest specimens are clearly bats, and not part bat and part something else, it is difficult to say for certain just what kinds of mammals gave rise to the Chiroptera. Although vernacular names for bats often associate them with mice, fossil evidence makes it clear that bats did not evolve from rodents. Most biologists would agree that the shrews and their relatives (the order Insectivora) are as closely related to bats as they are to any other living mammals. Since the first known fossil bats are distinctly chiropteran and well developed, the group may have originated 70 to 100 million years ago.

We can guess that the evolutionary ancestor of bats was a small, nocturnal, forest-dwelling, shrew-like mammal that fed on insects. There are at least two theories to explain the origin of bats: the Insect Net Theory and the Top Down

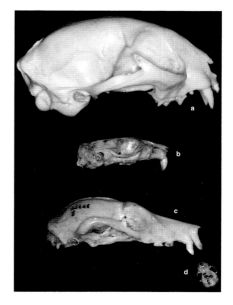

These skulls illustrate the small size of bats by comparing the skulls of a house cat (a), a Norwegian Rat (b), the world's largest bat, a Gigantic Flying Fox (c) and one of the world's smaller bats, a Greater Bamboo Bat (d). The cat's skull is 100 mm long and the skull of the world's largest bat is 75 mm.

Theory. The Insect Net Theory proposes that wings first appeared in proto-bats as webs of skin between the fingers used to catch flying insects. Like a similar explanation for the origin of flight in birds, the Insect Net Theory lacks mathematical support and is not widely accepted today.

The more popular Top Down Theory proposes that web-like membranes permitted proto-bats to glide. In this scenario, a proto-bat could scamper up the trunks and branches of trees searching for insect prey and from the top, glide to the next tree and begin again. This theory makes sense because it means that the proto-bat would not have had to climb down to the ground to move from one tree to the next.

We presume that at some point the gliding proto-bat began to take insects as it glided from one tree to another. The next stage would have involved flapping the gliding membranes, and evidence from mathematical models reveals that an ancestral bat could have generated lift during both the upstroke and the downstroke. Although the Top Down Theory is more credible to some biologists than the Insect Net Theory, we do not know which one is correct. The discovery of additional fossils could permit more realistic testing of theories about the origin and evolution of bats.

Are the flying foxes and other Megachiroptera (literally, large bats) close relatives of the other family of bats, the Microchiroptera (literally, small bats)? The question has preoccupied some biologists for at least 200 years. One proposed family tree of the living bats is shown below. It illustrates how the different families of bats relate to one another in an evolutionary sense. This family trees shows the Pteropodidae (Megachiroptera) more closely related to all other bats (the Microchiroptera) than either group is to any other mammals. Even so, the separation of the two suborders is an old one, and in 2000, some biologists still hold and vehemently defend the view that the Megachiroptera are more closely related to some Primates than they are to the Microchiroptera. Through the points of branching, this tree illustrates one view of how the different families of bats relate to one another. A more recent view based on analysis of DNA sequences, proposes that the

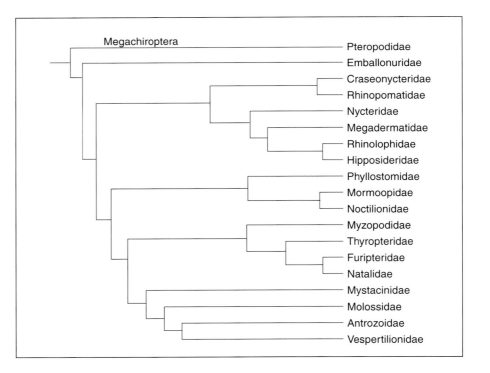

A family tree or phylogeny shows the presumed evolutionary relationships between the living families of bats. This presentation is modified from the work of Simmons and Geisler. The Rhinolophidae and the Hipposideridae are shown as separate families, as opposed to one family (Rhinolophidae) in other accounts. More details about the families appear in Table 1 and in Box 3.

BOX 1

CLASSIFICATION

Biologists use a system of classification to make it easier to appreciate the variety of organisms and the relationships between them. The first step in a classification is to give each kind of organism a unique name and then group the different kinds by evolutionary relationships. The levels of groupings represent hierarchies that are the building blocks of the classification. Most biologists accept the premise that classifications reflect the evolutionary relationships among organisms. Disagreements about classifications may reflect either a lack of fossil evidence or disputes about how to interpret different features.

The basic unit in a biological classification is the **species.** This label identifies a population of organisms that can interbreed to produce fertile offspring. We may call a species by its "common name," the one used by most people when referring to this kind or that kind of bat. While common names use words and terms that are familiar to most people, species also have "scientific names," more formal labels consisting of two words. For example, *Myotis lucifugus* is the scientific (species) name for the Little Brown Bat of North America. Scientific names are typically written in italics and in many cases are derived from Latin or Greek words. In this case, *Myotis* means "mouse-eared" and *lucifugus* "flees the light."

Species sharing common features are thought to be closely related, and are placed in the same **genus,** the next step up the hierarchy of classification. The first word in the scientific name is the name of the genus, in this case, *Myotis*. Two other species of bats in this genus are *Myotis septentrionalis*, the Northern Long-eared Bat of North America, and *Myotis daubentoni*, Daubenton's Bat of Eurasia. As we shall see, *Eptesicus, Pteropus, Tadarida, Natalus* and *Harpyionycteris* are the names of five of the 180 other genera of bats.

Proceeding up the hierarchy, genera with similar characteristics are placed in the same **family**. *Myotis lucifugus* belongs to the family Vespertilionidae, one of 19 families of living bats. In zoology, the names of families end in -idae. Families that are thought to be closely related are grouped in the same **superfamily**, identified by the ending -oidea. The Vespertilionidae are placed in the superfamily Vespertilionoidea.

Proceeding further up the hierarchy, living bats are placed in one of two **suborders**, the Megachiroptera or the Microchiroptera, which together comprise the **order** Chiroptera. The Chiroptera is one of 19 orders in the **class** Mammalia (mammals), and they, in turn, are part of the **subphylum** Vertebrata, animals with backbones. Vertebrates belong to the **phylum** Chordata, which is part of the Animal Kingdom.

Thus, tracing Little Brown Bats down through the classification hierarchy, we find the following arrangement:

phylum Chordata, the chordates; about 59,000 species
  subphylum Vertebrata, the vertebrates; about 58,000 species
    class Mammalia, the mammals; about 5,000 species
      order Chiroptera, the bats; about 900 species
        suborder Microchiroptera, the microchiroptera; about 750 species
          superfamily Vespertilionoidae, the vespertilionoids; about 283 species
            family Vespertilionidae, the Plain-nosed Bats; about 283 species
              genus *Myotis*, the Mouse-eared Bats; about 85 species
                species *Myotis lucifugus*, the Little Brown Bat

The families of bats are listed in Table 1, along with the numbers of living species in each and their arrangement by superfamilies in the suborder Megachiroptera or Microchiroptera.

Rhinolophoidea (Rhinolophidae, Hipposideridae, Nycteridae and Megadermatidae are more closely related to the Pteropodidae than either is to any other bats. This position does not support the idea that the Megachiroptera are more closely related to Primates than to other bats. Our knowledge about the evolution of bats has changed considerably since the first edition of this book was published (1992).

BOX 2

THE NECKS OF BATS

Bats and not giraffes should come to mind whenever people think of mammals with spectacular necks. When roosting, microchiropteran bats typically hang by their toes, upside down from a human perspective. From this posture these bats can lift their heads, arch their necks and look straight back. Just thinking about this contortion gives me a pain in the neck. When humans are standing or sitting in a normal position, their faces are oriented at 90° to their backbones and they look forward. Humans can arch their necks, turn their faces and look straight up. By comparison, microchiropteran bats can arch their necks so far as to face directly behind them.

While long necks of many birds are also flexible, microchiropteran bats have short necks and achieve flexibility in a different way. Like people, bats have seven neck (cervical) vertebrae. In the Microchiroptera, the cervical vertebrae are specialized. The top (neural arches) of most of the neck vertebrae are very slender arches, while the bottoms are expanded and interlock with one another. In some Free-tailed Bats adjacent neck vertebrae fit together by a system of ball and socket joints that are unique among mammals. It is the combination of these features that make microchiropteran necks so flexible.

This Hildebrandt's Horseshoe Bat is hunting, perched as it waits for a passing insect to come within range. In this posture, the bat is looking straight backward, 180° off the normal resting posture of a human being. Specialization of the bat's neck vertebrae gives it the flexibility to assume this posture.

To make the story even more interesting, neck vertebrae differ between the Microchiroptera and the Megachiroptera. The cervical vertebrae of the Megachiroptera resemble the general mammalian pattern and the necks of these bats are much less flexible than those of other bats.

There are some obvious differences between the two suborders of bats. Most megachiropterans have a claw on their second finger; none of the living microchiropterans has one. To complicate the picture, some fossil bats (now extinct) had claws on their second fingers. In the structure of their heads and teeth, the megachiropterans are more specialized than most of the microchiropterans, while the shoulder girdles (shoulder blades and collarbones) show the opposite trend and are less specialized. The details of neural connections of the eyes to the brains reveals that the Megachiroptera resemble species in the order Primates (which includes humans). In this feature, the Microchiroptera differ distinctly and are like all other mammals studied to date.

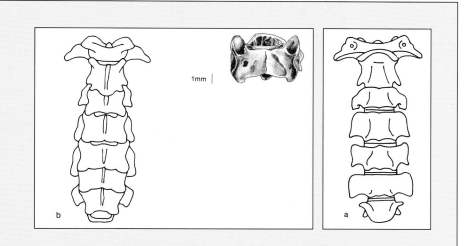

Shown here are the belly (a) and back (b) views of the neck vertebrae of a Hammerhead Bat, along with a detailed illustration of the top view of a single vertebra. These bats, like other Old World fruit bats, have necks that are about as flexible as those of humans. The scale is 1 mm long. Modified by Max Licht from a paper by Fenton and Crerar (1984).

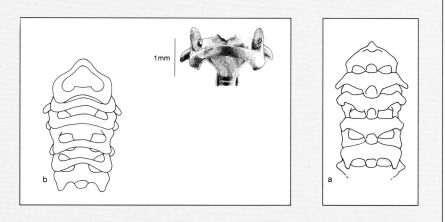

Compared to Hammerhead Bats, Pallas' Mastiff Bats have very flexible necks. Shown here are the belly (a) and back (b) views of the bat's neck vertebrae, along with a detailed illustration of the top view of a single vertebra. The neural arch, the part of the vertebra covering the spinal cord, is very thin in the Microchiroptera, giving them the great flexibility illustrated in the photo of the hunting Hildebrandt's Horseshoe Bat. The scale is 1 mm long. Modified by Max Licht from a paper by Fenton and Crerar (1984).

These and other differences may indicate that the Microchiroptera and Megachiroptera are not closely related to one another. But many other biologists find the strong similarity in wing structure and other features compelling evidence of a close relationship. Biologists defending other points of view interpret the same evidence in different ways. If bats did evolve from two different ancestors, the Megachiroptera from a primate stem, the Microchiroptera from an insectivore one, then flight has originated twice in mammals. The "right" answer remains elusive and may only come with the discovery of additional fossil material.

Questions about the classification of living bats extend beyond the fundamental differences and similarities between the two suborders. For example,

A Moluccan Naked-backed Bat is one of the larger species in the Chiroptera, weighing in at about 950 g. This fruit-eating species occurs in the East Indies and was photographed in Papua New Guinea being held by Professor H. F. Howden, a distinguished entomologist.

now the Short-tailed Bats of New Zealand (Mystacinidae) are close to the Noctilionoidea, but they have been moved back and forth between the Noctilionoidea and the Nataloidea. Recent research also suggests that Pallid Bats and Van Gelder's Bat, which had been included among the Vespertilionidae, constitute a separate lineage recognized as the Antrozoidae, a different family that is included among the Molossoidea. There is broad agreement that the Rhinolophidae and Hipposideridae represent a single evolutionary line and today many biologists treat them as one family. And yet, the bats in these two families are quite distinct from one another in the details of their faces and in their physiology, so I have treated them as two families.

In many books about bats, the blood-feeding vampires are identified as a separate family named the Desmodontidae. Here, the vampires are included as part of the New World Leaf-nosed Bats, the Phyllostomidae. As we shall see later, the three living species of vampire bats are highly specialized for feeding on blood. Some biologists find the distinctive lifestyle and specializations grounds for treating the vampire bats as a distinct family. The more conservative view, that vampire bats are part of the New World Leaf-nosed Bats, is based on comparisons of morphology, genetics and protein structure between vampire bats and the phyllostomids. For more information about vampire bats, see Chapter 10.

When classifying organisms, biologists must decide how to assess evolutionary relationships. Are differences more compelling evidence than similarities? In bats, discussions and disputes about classification involve the different levels of the classification hierarchy, from suborder to superfamily, family, genus or species. These controversies are one of the reasons that the study of bats (chiroptology) is interesting and exciting.

THE SIZE OF BATS

Perhaps the most deceptive characteristic of bats is their size. Many people think of bats as being large, even huge, but the reality is quite different. The largest bats in the world, the Gigantic Flying Foxes of Southeast Asia, may weigh 1.5 kg

At an adult weight of 3 g, the Banana Bat is one of the smaller species of bat. This one, photographed in Zimbabwe, occurs in many parts of Africa. It is a Plain-nosed Bat that feeds on insects.

and have wingspans of 2 m. At the other extreme are Hog-nosed Bats of Thailand, which weigh only 2 g and have wingspans of about 16 cm. As reflected by the size of their skulls, most bats are small compared to many other mammals.

How do you measure the size of a bat? Wingspan is an attractive method because it conveys an immediate impression of how the bat will look as it flies past. Judging the bat's wingspan, however, will depend upon how close to you it flies. Furthermore, it is difficult to accurately measure the wingspan of a bat, because the length you obtain will depend upon how hard you stretch the wings when you are measuring them. A more accurate measurement that is commonly used by biologists is the length of a bat's forearm, the distance from elbow to wrist. The forearms of bats range in length from a very small 25 mm to a very large 230 mm. To put these values in perspective, a human forearm may be 300 mm long. However, a bat with a forearm that is 225 mm long will weigh about 1.5 kg while a human with a 300 mm-long forearm will weigh closer to 80 kg. Bats are small compared to many other mammals, but they show considerable variation in size.

It is tempting to think of weight or body mass as a better indicator of size in bats. This measure also varies considerably, depending upon whether the bat you weigh is pregnant, has just eaten half its weight in food, or has just emerged from four months in hibernation. As adults, the vast majority of bat species weigh less than 100 g, and most weigh less than 50 g. None of the species of bats occurring in the United States of America, the United Kingdom, Kyrgyzstan, Tasmania or Chile weighs more than 50 g as adults; most weigh about 10 g. Most of the world's species of bats are small enough in body mass to be posted as a first-class letter.

FLIGHT

The true flight of bats differs from the gliding of mammals such as flying squirrels, flying lemurs or sugar gliders because it involves wings, the actions of

This Pallid Bat is turning toward the camera. Note the posture of the thumbs, the head and the fully spread fingers providing maximum wing area.

This flying Pallid Bat has just begun an upstroke to return its wings to the elevated position. In this situation, the area between the fifth finger and the body retains its airfoil section, while the wing membranes from the fifth finger to the wing tip collapse as the wing folds and is raised.

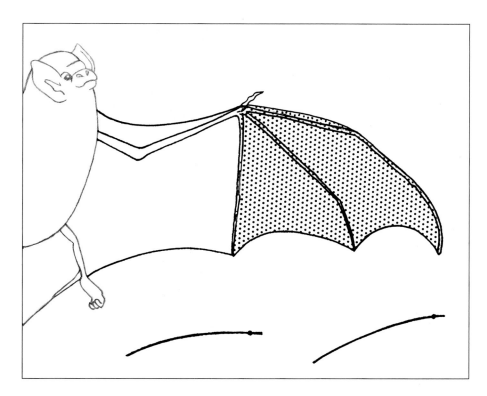

The stippled parts of this bat's wing generate thrust, while the clear parts closer to its body produce lift. Also shown are two diagrams illustrating airfoil section, one with a low angle of attack, left, the other with a high angle of attack, right. Drawing by Max Licht.

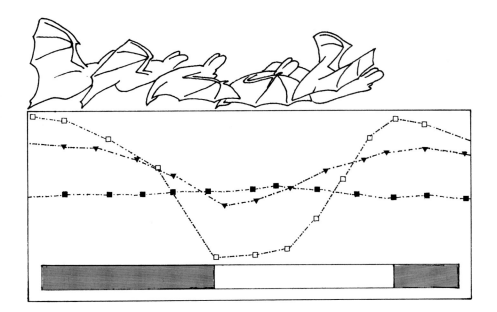

During flight, the parts of the wing farthest from the body move the greatest distances. This is illustrated by comparing the movement of the wing tip (open square), wrist (solid triangle) and elbow (solid square) of a bat's wing during one wing-beat cycle. The duration of the downstroke is shown across the bottom by the lined area, and the upstroke by the white area. Drawing by Max Licht.

which generate lift and thrust. Lift keeps a flying bat aloft, countering the pull of gravity on its body mass. Thrust propels the bat forward, countering the effect of drag, the friction generated by moving the bat's body through the air. Most of the lift comes from the airfoil section of the wing membranes between the sides of the bat's body and its fifth fingers. The thrust is generated by the movement of the rest of the wing, from the fifth finger out to the tip. The amounts of lift and thrust are influenced by the shape of the wing and the speed at which the bat is flying.

Lift is generated by the negative pressure created when air flows more rapidly across the upper surface of the wing than across the lower surface. The difference in rate of air flow depends upon the wing's curvature, technically its airfoil section or camber. By the actions of their wrists, thumbs and hind feet bats can change the camber of their wings and alter the amounts of lift that are generated. Between their hind legs, many species of bats have extensive interfemoral membranes that partly or wholly enclose their tails. These membranes may also generate some lift during flight. The very large ears of some bats are thought to generate additional lift.

Two other factors influence the generation of lift. The first is the pattern of air flow over the wing. A smooth wing surface affects the pattern of air flow across the wing by minimizing friction that disrupts air flow. Within the flight

This comparison of the breastbones and shoulder girdles of a bat (left), pterosaur (center) and bird (right) shows that bats lack the prominent keels (k) that dominate the breastbones of birds and pterosaurs. Drawing by Max Licht.

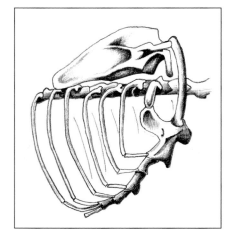
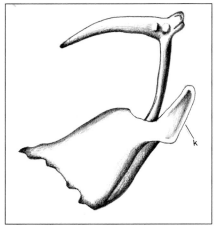
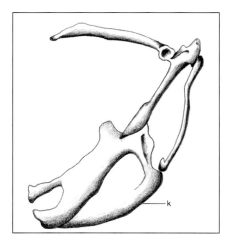

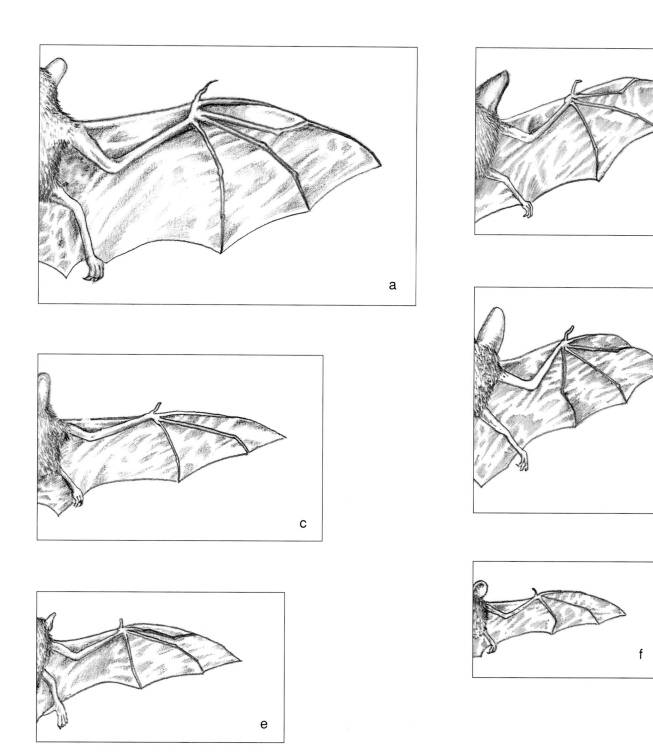

membranes of bats are layers of elastic tissue that keep the wing taut and its surface smooth. Sheets of muscles in the wing membranes of some species, notably Free-tailed Bats, help to maintain a smooth wing surface. The second is the angle at which the wing moves through the air, known as the angle of attack. The wings of a bat flying along parallel to the ground typically have a shallow angle of attack. As soon as the bat tries to rapidly gain altitude by making a steep climb, its wings take on a steeper angle of attack. When a flying bat (or bird, or aircraft) uses too steep an angle of attack there is a drastic decrease in lift until the animal stalls out. At the point of stalling, the pull of gravity on the bat's body is stronger than the lift the wings are generating.

Illustrated here are some variations in wing shapes of bats. Linnaeus' False Vampire Bat (a), Large Slit-faced Bat (b) and Hemprich's Long-eared Bat (d) have broad wings, while Martienssen's Free-tailed Bat (c), Greater Bulldog Bats (e) and Little Free-tailed Bats (f) have longer, narrower wings. Modified by Max Licht from Norberg and Fenton (1988).

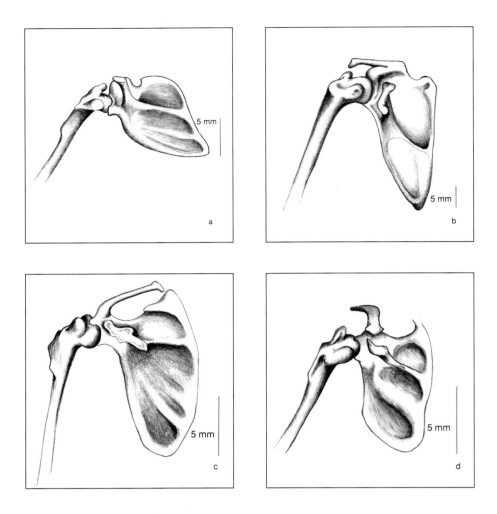

Since the lift-generating wing parts are closest to the body, their positions change less than the more distant thrust-generating wing parts during a wing-beat cycle. The magnitude and the precise details of these changes depend upon the flight posture of the bat and the maneuvers it is using. A bat in level flight, for example, will show less dramatic changes in wing position than one maneuvering to catch a flying insect. The actual pattern of flight will vary according to the role that flight plays in the life of the particular bat.

The amounts of lift and thrust generated in flight change as the wings move through a wing-beat cycle. At the beginning of a wing-beat the bat has its wings raised and extended slightly back. From here the wings are fully extended (palms down) and sweep forward and down until the bat's body is curved forward from nose to toes. At the bottom of the downstroke, the bat quickly turns its arms and wrists, changing the position of the wing by bringing its palms up and tilting them slightly to the rear. At this point large parts of the wing membranes fold up or collapse to minimize the drag as the wings are raised in preparation for another stroke. As they reach the top of the cycle, the wings return to the palms-down position.

The downstroke provides the power for flight and it is produced by the contraction of flight muscles located on bats' upper arms and chests. Since these muscles work against gravity, they are much larger than the muscles on the back that lift the wings in preparation for another wing-beat cycle. Three pairs of muscles are mainly responsible for powering the downstroke in bats, and three other pairs of muscles are involved in raising the wings.

The bat's flight muscles differ from those in birds. In birds, one pair of muscles is largely responsible for the downstroke and another pair for raising the wings. Both of these pairs of muscles are located on the chest, where they attach to the breastbone or sternum. A pulley arrangement in the bird's shoulder allows a pair of muscles on the chest to raise the wings. In bats the three pairs of muscles that power the downstroke are located on the chest and those responsible for the upstroke are on the back. In birds that can fly, the breastbone typically has a prominent ridge or keel that offers a larger area for attachment of the flight muscles. In most species of bats the breastbones rarely have keels. Differences in muscular arrangements and breastbone combine to make bats much thinner through the chest than birds. As we will see in Chapter 6, this has repercussions for bats' roosting behavior.

In their approaches to flight, bats and birds differ in other ways. Many species of birds soar and glide using hot air rising from the ground or wind patterns over the ocean. Bats do not soar in this way, as they are nocturnal and cannot take advantage of air heated by the Sun, although on some islands in the South Pacific, day-flying flying foxes often are observed soaring. Furthermore, bats do not fly over the open ocean as do albatrosses and some other soaring birds. But in southern India, one or two species of tomb bats soar on the air currents generated by wind blowing over huge rocky hills. This behavior, known as boundary soaring, is seen in either Black-bearded Tomb Bats or Naked-rumped Tomb Bats. Feathers may make birds' wings inherently better for gliding than the skin of bat wings.

The shape and size of bat wings vary considerably. Some species have wings that are long and narrow, while others have short and broad wings. Aspect ratio is a mathematical way of describing wing shape; it is calculated by dividing the wingspan squared by the wing area (b^2/S). A high aspect ratio indicates a long and narrow wing, a low aspect ratio a short and broad one. In bats, the highest aspect ratios occur in Free-tailed Bats such as the Madagascar Large Free-tailed Bat (14.3), while the lowest aspect ratios occur in Slit-faced Bats (e.g., the Hairy Slit-faced Bat, 4.8), False Vampire Bats (e.g., Yellow-winged Bat, 5.4) or New World Leaf-nosed Bats (e.g., Linnaeus' False Vampire, 5.4).

Another indicator of overall wing design is wing loading, calculated by dividing the bat's body mass by its wing area (Mg/S) and expressed as Newtons per square meter (N/m^2). Bat species with broad wings typically have the lowest wing loading, for example Hairy Slit-faced Bats (aspect ratio 4.3; wing loading 5.4 N/m^2), Ruppell's Horseshoe Bat (6.7; 7.7 N/m^2) or Small-footed Bats (6.1; 6.7 N/m^2). High wing loading typically occurs in species with high aspect ratios, such as the Madagascar Large Free-tailed Bat (aspect ratio 14.3; wing loading 20.0 N/m^2), or Martienssen's Free-tailed Bat (9.3; 14.9 N/m^2). Whether the subject is an aircraft, a bird or a bat, both aspect ratio and wing loading are essential for accurately predicting flight performance. Bats with broad wings and low aspect ratios tend to be more maneuverable in flight than those with narrower wings and higher aspect ratios. Broad wings and low aspect ratios are typical of species that fly more slowly. Biologists would not expect these bats to make long, nonstop flights because of higher flight energy costs. In comparison, species with higher aspect ratios and higher wing loading fly more rapidly and more economically. These are the species expected to fly for long periods each night and to make long-distance migrations.

Different species of bats make different use of flight. For some, flight is a means of getting from one place to another. Others hunt in flight, actively pursuing airborne prey in different settings. The shoulder girdles of bats reflect these differences, particularly where the shoulder blade (scapula) meets the upper arm (humerus). Plant-visiting bats tend to have less specialized shoulder blades and humeri than do species feeding on animals. In flying bats the shoulder blade rocks up and down, adding an additional functional joint to the wing.

Flight is the essence of bats. It directly affects their basic architecture and influences every aspect of their lives. But there is more to bats than flight.

STUDYING BATS

To appreciate what is known about bats and the many things left to discover about them requires some knowledge about how to study them. But the goal of a study affects both the approach and the techniques that are used. Some work involves live bats and other studies need preserved material such as museum specimens or fossils. Some research on bats cannot be accomplished with existing technology and other projects are impossible because the bats are either unavailable or inaccessible.

The first step may be finding the bats. This can be as simple as going up into the attic if you are lucky enough to live in a building that also houses a bat colony. It may be more difficult if the bats you want to study live on the other side of the world. Often bats are hard to find because they are relatively small and nocturnal. One reflection of this is the fact that in the mid-1970s 16 of 180 genera of bats were known from fewer than 10 specimens. Knowing something about their habits can simplify the task of finding bats. However, finding bats is one thing, catching them is another.

CATCHING BATS

How to catch a bat depends upon the situation. In 1972 I caught a Rusty Pipistrelle that was roosting behind a picture hanging on the wall of a pub in Zimbabwe. The bat was asleep and I just grabbed it. Grabbing bats also can work in a cave where bats are hibernating; in many such cases they can be plucked from the wall or ceiling. The bat flying around a bedroom in the middle of the night is more difficult because the animal now is alert and moving. In this situation the bat can more readily evade capture in the hand or in a net. When a bat is flying in the forest or over fields, catching it is even more challenging. The difficulty increases the higher the bat flies above the ground.

Fine-meshed, black nylon thread is the basis of Japanese mist nets, which are used to catch birds and bats.

Mist nets work by entangling their victims. This Egyptian Free-tailed Bat was caught in a mist net set beside the Limpopo River in South Africa. By looking closely, you can see the black mesh of the net.

Opposite Page: *The fur of young bats tends to be darker than the fur of adults, as shown in this comparison of an adult (left) and a young (right) Common Yellow-shouldered Bat.*

Shooting is one way to catch mammals, including bats. For studies requiring preserved specimens, shooting is an alternative as long as the bats are not too badly damaged by the shot (bullets).

Sometimes hand nets, also known as insect or butterfly nets, are very useful for catching bats. Inside a bat roost, hand nets may be the best way to catch flying or roosting individuals. This technique is more difficult when bats are flying in large rooms or outside because one's reach is limited by the length of the net's handle, and a flying bat can easily evade the net.

Catching bats as they fly in the open was revolutionized by the introduction of Japanese mist or fowling nets. These fine-meshed, black nylon nets come in a range of lengths (6 to 30 m) and widths (2 to 10 m). Originally developed for catching birds, mist nets are usually set between two poles and work because flying birds and bats fail to detect them until it is too late. Mist nets work by entangling their captives, so using them requires keeping a continuous watch to ensure that captured bats do not escape by chewing their way out of the net.

Mist nets have several disadvantages. First, they are labor-intensive, because each captured animal must be disentangled. Second, it is hard to get mist nets high enough into the air to catch bats flying well above the ground or the tree canopy. The third disadvantage is that being caught in a mist net is traumatic for many bats. This is obvious to anyone who has watched a bat frantically struggling to escape from a mist net. People have overcome these disadvantages in different ways. The ringing of a small bell fastened to a mist net indicates a struggling captive. This, in turn, makes it easy to quickly respond to a captured bat and a rapid response minimizes the time in the net and, perhaps, the trauma of capture. By suspending nets from the tallest branches of trees or by using very long poles (such as the masts of sailboats) biologists have put mist nets high above the ground. This approach has made it possible to catch some species of bats that previously had been seen alive only rarely.

Harp traps are another device for catching bats. These bat traps were first used in situations where thousands of bats flew out of cave roosts. The original harp traps were metal frames strung, like a harp, with vertical wires or lines. Suspended under the frame was a bag or container. Flying bats collided with the vertical lines, slid down them and ended up in the holding container. Harp traps were useful, for example, when biologists sampled populations of Mexican Free-tailed Bats at cave colonies in the southeastern United States.

In 1974 a new variation on the harp trap was introduced by Merlin D. Tuttle. Tuttle traps consist of a double frame with two sets of vertical lines. A canvas bag with plastic flaps receives the bats that slide down the lines. The narrowness of the bag prevents most bats from flying out of the trap, and the slippery plastic stops most from climbing to freedom. Tuttle traps can have legs and be free-standing. Biologists quickly discovered that Tuttle traps could be used to catch bats away from roosts. Since their introduction, Tuttle traps have appeared in many different forms, and they are widely used throughout the world.

The main advantage of the original harp traps or the Tuttle variation is that captured bats are not entangled. This makes it easier for the bat biologist to process bats, and, we presume, is less traumatic for the bats. Although some early Tuttle traps used lines made of piano wire, 3.2 kg test monofilament fishing line is an easier and less expensive alternative. Holding bags on Tuttle traps must have drain holes in the bottom to ensure that the bag does not fill with rainwater and drown the captured bats. Although the bags need plastic flaps to contain the bats, the main shell must be made of a breathable fabric such as canvas to ensure that captured bats do not suffocate. The frames of the newest Tuttle traps are made of plastics such as ABS or PCV which are light and easy to work with.

Biologists have used other innovative ploys to catch bats. In Finland, a clever trap baited with insects was used to catch several species of live Mouse-eared Bats. In many places biologists have lured flying bats down to mist nets by giving them targets to chase. Ever more inventive approaches to catching bats should appear as more biologists go forth in search of them, including swinging full or modified mist nets to capture flying bats.

IDENTIFYING BATS

Identifying captured bats can be more difficult than catching them. The first step is deciding whether your capture is a male or a female. In most bats, this decision is easy because the penises of bats are conspicuous. Some pteropodids are exceptions but in many bats, worn areas around the nipples make it easy to recognize adult females.

A second question is the age of the bat in hand. As we shall see (Chapter 7), young bats typically grow rapidly, so by the time they can fly, the forearms of the young are as long as those of adults. So, the difficulty is in telling an adult-sized young from an adult. Fur color can provide a clue. In many bats, young have dark, blackish fur compared to lighter colored fur in adults. Another indicator of age is found at the finger joints. Adult bats have knobby

Tuttle traps can be suspended from ropes. In this case the trap hangs in the gorge of the Sengwa River in Zimbabwe, where it caught two Lesser Yellow House Bats and a Hildebrandt's Horseshoe Bat. Note the "hip" joints for attaching legs. The frame of the trap is about 2 m high and 1.8 m wide.

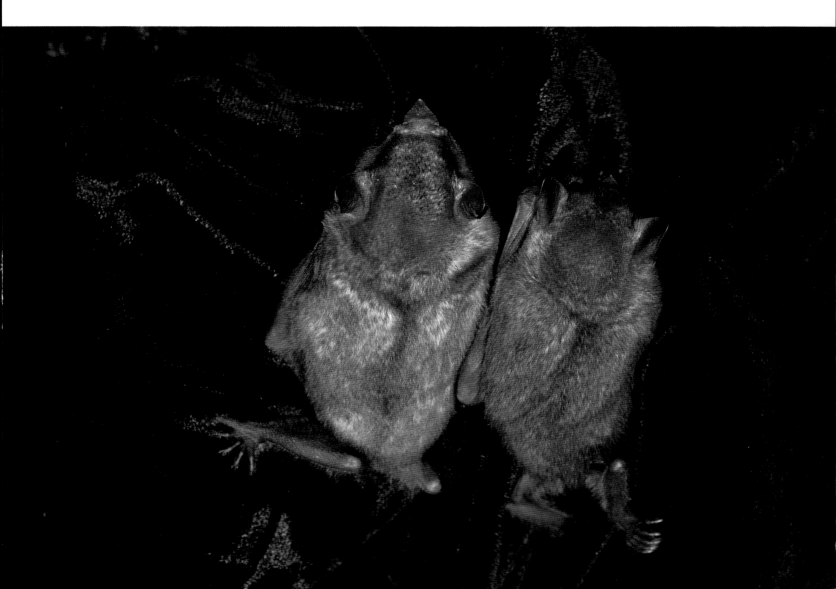

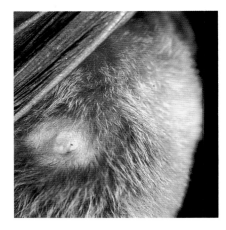

Adult female bats that have nursed babies usually can be recognized by bare areas around their nipples. The nursing action of the young wears away the fur, producing the bare areas. The nipple of this Common Yellow-shouldered Bat is conspicuous.

finger joints, while young bats have smooth ones. The adult finger joints are knobby because bone formation (ossification) and growth is complete. The smooth finger joints of young reflect incomplete ossification and still-growing finger bones. Differences in finger joints are easiest to see when the joints are back-lit.

Although it can be easy to tell adult bats from young born that year, biologists have not found a nonlethal way to determine the age of adult bats. Measurements of the lens in a bat's eye or examination of rings in its teeth may indicate age, but either technique is fatal for the bat.

After determining its gender and age, the next problem is deciding which species name goes with the bat. Identifying the bat depends upon the variety of bats living where it was caught. Identifying the bat caught in Hawaii is easy because only one species lives there. Two species make the problem more difficult in Newfoundland. But, compare this to more than 50 species in many parts of Africa, and more than 100 in some countries in South and Central America, and it becomes decidedly more difficult.

A first step in identifying a bat is deciding which of the 19 living families (Table 1) it belongs to. Sometimes the family names provide clues. For example, as implied by their names, New World Disk-winged Bats (Thyropteridae) have distinctive adhesive disks on their wrists and ankles and live only in the New World (the Americas). The Old World Disk-winged Bats (Myzopodidae) also have adhesive disks but occur in the Old World, only in Madagascar. Usually, the details of the bat's appearance are used to decide its family affiliations.

Biologists use "keys" to simplify the problem of identifying organisms, including bats. A key presents the features of the bat in a logical, stepwise sequence, making it easier for the user to determine the identity of the bat in question. The process is illustrated in Box 3, a key to the families of living bats. Keys work by focusing the user's attention on specific features and ordering the sequence in which different characteristics are considered.

Many features may be used to distinguish between species of bats (see Box 4). Wherever possible, keys rely on obvious, objective features such as size, numbers of teeth and sometimes color. Size usually is reported as length of the forearm (in millimeters), because it can be measured accurately and consistently. Relative or subjective features also are used. For example, the ears of one species may be slightly longer than those of another, or there may be subtle differences in the nature of their fur.

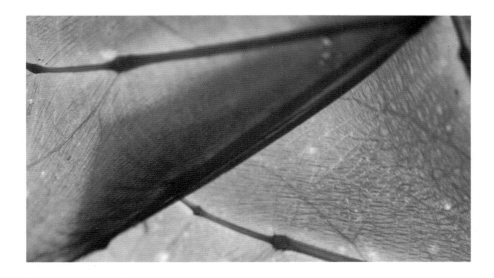

The finger joints of adult bats (bottom) are knobby, while those of young (top) are smooth. Again, Common Yellow-shouldered Bats are models.

For many areas in the world, books or other technical publications include keys for identifying local bats (see bibliography). In most cases, the identification process begins with a bat in the hand, although we shall encounter an exception to this in Box 8.

MARKING BATS

Since bats, like people, vary considerably between individuals, many studies are possible only if each bat carries its own distinctive tag. This labeling is routine and easy when the subjects are museum specimens of dead bats, because each specimen has a distinctive number and tag. Marking live bats is more difficult.

Tags for live bats must not interfere with their activities or make them more conspicuous to their predators or prey. Tags must be small enough to not hinder flight or prevent the bat from getting into its roost. Active tags, such as lights or radios, emit a signal to make it easier to find bats carrying them. Passive tags, such as bands, emit no signal and are evident only when the marked animal is in view.

Bands like those used on birds also work on bats. Although each band may carry a distinctive number or combination of colors, to read it the tracker must capture the bat. Since a band emits no signal, it is easy to overlook a banded bat. Some workers have marked bats with bands bearing different colors of reflective tape. Illuminating the bat in the beam of a spotlight makes it possible to read individual color codes from a distance. Reflective tape makes bands more conspicuous.

Light tags were made by injecting Cyalume fluid into gelatin pill capsules. Surgical cement is used to attach these lights to the bats. This picture shows the Cyalume stick and its wrapper (right), the surgical cement, the syringe and three light tags. Each light tag in this picture is 2.1 cm long, 0.8 cm in diameter and weighs 0.3 grams. Today tiny Cyalume sticks designed for fishing lures are much better light tags.

The signals from active tags may permit biologists to find bats they cannot see. Radio tags, for example, are miniature radio transmitters, each consisting of a battery and circuitry producing a signal. Biologists use special receivers to detect signals from radio tags and the procedure is known as radio tracking. Depending upon the local conditions, radio tracking can be used to follow bats over ranges of up to 5 km. The rate of pulse production allows some radio tags to indicate the bat's skin temperature.

BOX 3
RECOGNIZING THE FAMILIES OF BATS

Each of the 19 living families of bats can be easily recognized by its unique set of features. In some families, especially the New World Leaf-nosed Bats, the variation among the species makes them more difficult to identify than families with fewer species that are more uniform in appearance. The steps in this key direct the user to specific features on a bat that identify the family to which it belongs.

• • •

Step 1a. The bat usually has claws on its second fingers, and its ears are simple with their outer margins forming an unbroken ring. The face is generally dog-like and the forearms range in length from 40 to 220 mm. These bats occur in the Old World tropics.

the **Old World Fruit Bats**, the **Pteropodidae**

Step 1b. The bats never have claws on their second fingers, and their ears are often complex with tragi and their faces are not dog-like; go to Step 2.

Step 2a. The bat's tail ends in a T-shaped cartilage; there is a deep slit in the face and the ears are relatively large. The bats occur from Africa to the East Indies and their forearms range from 36 to 60 mm long.

the **Slit-faced Bats**, the **Nycteridae**

Step 2b. The bat's tail does not end in a T-shaped cartilage and its face has no deep slit; go to Step 3.

Step 3a. The bat's tail extends beyond the end of the interfemoral membrane; go to Step 4.

Step 4a. The bat's tail is long, slender and rat-like, extending well past the back edge of the interfemoral membrane. The forearms range in length from 55 to 70 mm. The bats occur from north Africa east to Burma and Sumatra.

The **Rat-tailed Bats**, the **Rhinopomatidae**

Step 4b. The bat's tail is short and thick and extends well beyond the back edge of the interfemoral membrane. The forearms range from 27 to 85 mm long and the bats occur in tropical and subtropical areas throughout the world.

the **Free-tailed Bats**, the **Molossidae**

Step 3b. The bat's tail protrudes through the interfemoral membrane at about the level of the knee; go to Step 5.

Step 5a. The bat's lips and chin have prominent leaf-like structures and the mouth is funnel shaped, particularly when opened. The forearms range from 35 to 65 mm long. The bats occur in the New World tropics.

the **Mustached Bats**, the **Mormoopidae**

Step 5b. The bat's lips are swollen and large, giving a bulldog-like appearance. The tail membrane is well supported by a long, robust calcar. The forearms range from 70 to 92 mm and the bats occur in the Neotropics.

the **Bulldog Bats**, the **Noctilionidae**

Step 5c. The bat's lips are not large and swollen and the lips and chin have no prominent leaflike structures. The forearms range from 32 to 80 mm, and the bats occur in the tropics throughout the world.

the **Sheath-tailed Bats**, the **Emballonuridae**

Step 3c. The bat is tiny (forearm 22–26 mm long) and has no external tail. The face is piglike and the bats occur in Thailand.

This Epauletted Fruit Bat has large eyes, simple ears and a claw on its second finger, all of which identify it as an Old World Fruit Bat, family Pteropodidae. These bats are widespread in Africa.

In Sheath-tailed Bats (Emballonuridae), the tail is short and blunt and protrudes through the interfemoral membrane. In this case the bat is a Black Bearded Tomb Bat from India.

In Free-tailed Bats (Molossidae), the tail is short and blunt, and extends beyond the interfemoral membrane. The bat is an Egyptian Free-tailed Bat from India. Drawing by Max Licht.

The T-shaped tail cartilage at the end of its tail identifies a bat as a Slit-faced Bat, family Nycteridae (in this case an Egyptian Slit-faced Bat). Drawing by Max Licht.

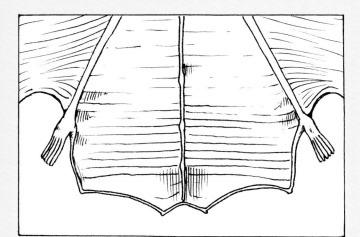

In Rat-tailed Bats (Rhinopomatidae), the long, slender tail extends well past the end of the inter-femoral membrane. Shown here is a Lesser Rat-tailed bat.

The leaf-like structures on the chin of the MacLeay's Mustached Bat clearly identify it as a Mustached Bat (Mormoopidae).

The Thumbless Bats (Furipteridae) have short thumbs that are almost completely enclosed in the wing membrane. Drawing by Max Licht.

Other bats have longer thumbs that are largely free of the wing membrane. Drawing by Max Licht.

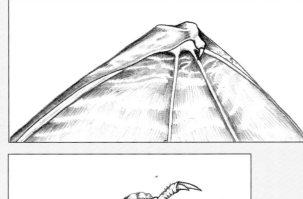

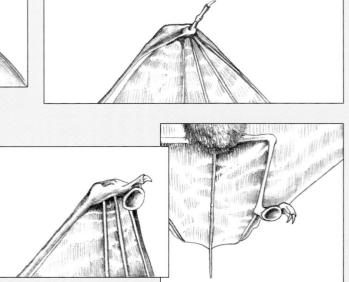

Claws on the thumbs of Short-tailed Bats (Mystacinidae) bear unique extra talons near their base. These distinctive claws always identify Short-tailed Bats. Drawing by Max Licht.

the **Hog-nosed Bats**, the **Craseonycteridae**

Step 3d. The bats are larger and, if present, their tails are fully enclosed in the interfemoral membrane; go to Step 6.

Step 6a. The bat has tiny thumbs with tiny claws and are entirely enclosed in the membrane in front of the forearm. Forearms are 30 to 40 mm long and the bats occur in the New World tropics.

the **Thumbless Bats**, the **Furipteridae**

Step 6b. The bat has large thumbs with strong claws and small talons at the bases of the large claws. These small talons are unique among bats and there are comparable features on the claws of the toes. The forearm measures 44 to 48 mm; the bats occur only in New Zealand.

the **Short-tailed Bats**, the **Mystacinidae**

Step 6c. The bat has normal thumbs bearing claws without basal talons. The thumbs are at least partially free from the membrane in front of the forearm. Go to Step 7.

Step 7a. The bat has sucker-like disks at the bases of its thumbs and on its ankles. Go to Step 8.

Step 8a. The bat's forearms range from 27 to 38 mm in length and the sucker-like disks at the bases of the thumbs are on short stalks. The bats occur in the New World tropics.

the **New World Disk-winged Bats**, the **Thyropteridae**

Step 8b. The bat's forearms are 44–48 mm long and the sucker-like disks at the bases of the thumbs are not on small stalks. The bats occur in Madagascar.

the **Old World Disk-winged Bats**, the **Myzopodidae**

Step 7b. The bat lacks well-developed suckerlike disks at the bases of its thumbs and on its ankles. Go to step 9.

Step 9a. The bat has spiral-shaped grooves around its nostrils (see page 137) and large ears. Its forearms range from 45-60 mm. The bats occur in parts of Central America and western North America.

the **Pallid Bats**, the **Antrozoidae**

Step 9b. The bat lacks spiral-shaped grooves around its nostrils, go to step 10.

Step 10a. The bat's ears are funnel-shaped, the forearm ranges from 27 to 41 mm. The bats occur in the New World tropics.

the **Funnel-eared Bats**, the **Natalidae**

Step 10b. The bat's ears are not funnel-shaped and their forearms range from 22 to 75 mm. The bats occur throughout the world.

the **Plain-nosed Bats**, the **Vespertilionidae**

Step 9c. The bats have leaflike structures on their noses and faces. Go to Step 11.

Step 11a. The noseleaf of the bat is as illustrated, the forearms range from 30 to 75 mm and the bats occur in the Old World.

the **Horseshoe Bats**, the **Rhinolophidae**

Step 11b. The noseleaf of the bat is as illustrated. The forearms range from 30 to 110 mm and the bats occur in the Old World tropics.

Ear shape identifies this Jamaican Funnel-eared Bat as a Funnel-eared Bat (Natalidae).

The horseshoe-shaped structure on the nose-leaf of this Hildebrandt's Horseshoe Bat is typical of bats belonging to the Horseshoe Bats (Rhinolophidae).

Old World Leaf-nosed Bats (Hipposideridae) have nose-leafs generally resembling the structure in Schneider's Roundleaf Bat. Some species, however, have tridentlike structures on the backs of the nose-leafs.

the **Old World Leaf-nosed Bats**, the **Hipposideridae**

Step 11c. The nose-leaf is as illustrated; the tragi are bifurcate and the bats lack upper incisor teeth. The bats occur in the Old World tropics. The forearms range from 50 to 115 mm.

the **False Vampire Bats**, the **Megadermatidae**

Step 11d. The nose-leaf ranges in structure and the bats vary in size (forearms from 30 to 105 mm). The bats are Neotropical.

the **New World Leaf-nosed Bats**, the **Phyllostomidae**

A closer view of the bifurcate tragus.

This Cozumel Spear-nosed Bat has a nose-leaf that is typical of many New World Leaf-nosed Bats (Phyllostomidae). Within this family, however, there is considerable variation in nose-leaf structure.

The nose-leaf and bifurcate tragus make this Indian False Vampire Bat easy to recognize as a False Vampire Bat (Megadermatidae).

Jamaican Fruit Bats have more typical nose-leafs.

The largest and most spectacular nose-leafs occur in Tome's Long-eared Bat.

In Common Vampire Bats, the nose-leaf is modified and is quite different from those of other New World Leaf-nosed Bats.

In 2000 the smallest radio tags for bats weighed about 0.45 g. Since tags weighing more than 5% of a bat's body mass interfere with its flight, technology limits the use of radio tags to bats weighing about 10 g.

Light tags were introduced for the study of bats in 1976. Then, light tags consisted of light-producing fluid injected into a clear receptacle such as a gelatin capsule, which was attached to the bat with surgical adhesive. Some light tags are small enough for use on bats weighing 5 g. In open areas on dark nights light tags can be seen from up to 1 km away. In forested habitats or areas with dense vegetation, visibility is much more limited. It is possible to mistake fireflies for light-tagged bats! The fluid in Cyalume light sticks was the light source commonly used for light tags. By 1995 tiny Cyalume sticks designed for fishing lures provided an excellent alternative. The tags were smaller and lighter, and unlike the gelatin capsules did not dissolve. Furthermore, even large bats could not chew them open.

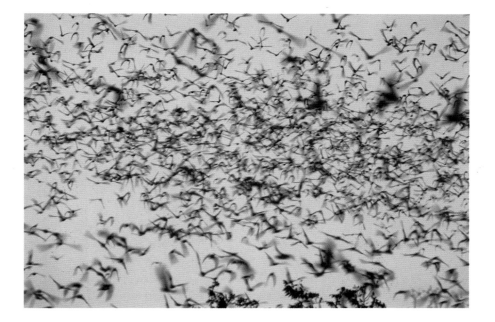

Photography is one way to count bats emerging from their day roost. The sheer numbers of Mexican Free-tailed Bats emerging from a cave in Texas makes counting them difficult even in the best of circumstances. Photograph by Jonathan P. Balcombe.

BOX 4

HOW TO IDENTIFY BATS

The first step in identifying a bat is knowing which species occur in your area. For example, if you are watching bats in Jamaica, you will not see Flying Foxes, and when you move to Australia, you will not encounter New World Leaf-nosed Bats. In some cases, species obviously differ in appearance. A key like the one in Box 3 tells you what to look for to recognize the differences. For example, Ruppell's Bat has dark wings and pure white underparts, while its back is dark and the fur frosted. Its forearms are 33–37 mm long. Rendall's Serotine is the same size, but its wings are white and its fur golden-colored.

Its pure white belly makes this Ruppell's Bat easy to recognize, particularly when compared to Rendall's Serotine.

Rendall's Serotine has golden-colored fur and white-colored wings, making it easy to distinguish from Ruppell's Bat.

Sometimes, when several similar species occur in an area, they can be distinguished by their size. This situation is illustrated by the four species of New World Leaf-nosed Bats show here. Although the bats differ in details of facial appearance and color, the differences are subjective. They are most obvious when all four are available for comparison. The size differences between the species are more obvious and can be more objectively collected and presented. This is illustrated by some information from the Province of Quintana Roo in Mexico.

Big Fruit Bat.

Intermediate Fruit Bat.

Jamaican Fruit Bat.

Pygmy Fruit Bat.

	BIG FRUIT Bat	INTERMEDIATE Fruit Bat	JAMAICAN Fruit Bat	PYGMY Fruit Bat
forearm in mm	69–71	64–67	51–67	36–41
mass in g	64–67	52–57	37–60	10–15

But it is clear that some of the species overlap in size, particularly the three larger bats. In this case, a key would draw attention to the conspicuous facial stripes in the Big Fruit Bat, the fainter stripes in the Intermediate Fruit Bat and the very faint stripes in the Jamaican Fruit Bat.

Other species can be identified by examining their teeth. For example, bats in the genus *Myotis* have two small premolars in their upper jaws, while those in the genus *Pipistrellus* have one, and those in the genus *Eptesicus* have none. The small upper premolars are the teeth just behind the canines. They are easy to see from the side when a bat opens its mouth.

Distinguishing one species from another is easier when the two can be directly compared using a key to identify the important diagnostic features. In other cases two bats may look quite different, but lack of knowledge leaves unanswered questions of distinguishing them and naming them.

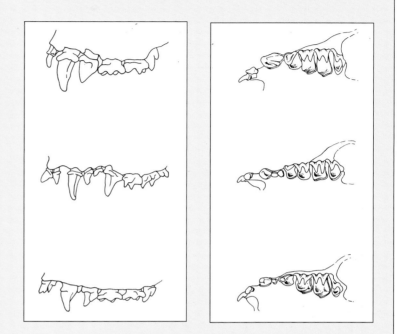

These drawings compare the upper left teeth of three bats. The presence of one, two or no small premolar teeth can be used to distinguish between bats in the genus Eptesicus *(no small premolars),* Myotis *(two small premolars) and* Pipistrellus *(one small premolar). While these teeth are reliable characteristics for some species in some areas, the distinction between* Pipistrellus *and* Eptesicus *is not always so clear. The topic continues to intrigue some bat researchers. Drawings by Max Licht.*

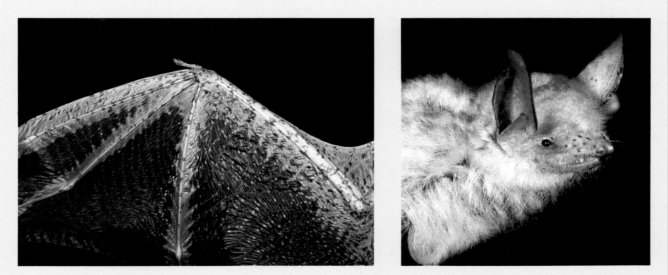

Some bats, like Welwitsch's Hairy Bat, are easy to recognize whether you look at their wings or faces. This distinctive species is widespread in Africa.

BOX 5

PHOTOGRAPHING BATS

Bats are small, fast on the wing and active at night. This combination of features makes them difficult to photograph. Fortunately, technology is available to deal with the problems these features present.

With a single lens reflex camera, different lenses can be used in different situations. This means that the same camera body can produce good bat photographs over a range of conditions. A macro lens is essential for taking pictures of roosting bats because it allows the photographer to get very close to the bat. Proximity ensures that a small bat fills the picture frame. A wide-angle lens, however, is necessary when the subjects are flying bats. This lens allows the camera to be close to the bat, showing its full wingspan without losing it against the background. Neither of these lenses is useful when the subject is a bat flying in its natural setting. This situation requires a lens of longer focal length. In some cases, a long (for example, 70 to 200 mm) zoom lens may work well. Carrying a selection of lenses is one way to offset some of the problems of photographing bats.

The left eye of this Short-faced Fruit Bat reflects the light from two flashes used to light up the bat for the picture. This portrait was taken with a 105-mm micro lens. Short-faced Fruit Bats weigh about 40 g and are widespread in India and Southeast Asia..

Light, too, can be provided by technology. Taking portraits of bats in bright sunlight usually produces well-lighted and exposed subjects with tightly closed eyes. By using an electronic flash as the main light source, however, the photographer can illuminate more relaxed subjects. A pair of flashes used together on either side of the camera gives more uniform lighting. In some situations, a third flash pointed upward gives the best illumination of flying bats. A ring flash is another way to achieve uniform lighting, but it leaves a peculiar reflection in the bat's eyes.

Whatever the combination of flash and lens, there should be enough light so that the photographs are taken with a lens aperture of f11 to f16. These settings will give enough depth of focus to ensure that most of the subject is sharply visible.

The choice of film also affects the quality of the pictures. Slower films (ISO or ASA of 64 to 200) are very useful for closeup work, because they are fine-grained and give detailed images. Faster films (ISO or ASA of at least 1000) are coarser-grained, but they require less light. They are more valuable for use in the field with longer lenses.

Light tags and radio tags have been instrumental in expanding our knowledge of bats.

OTHER APPROACHES

At some time almost everyone has watched a bat flitting about the night sky in pursuit of insect prey. This experience usually leaves the clear impression that watching bats is different from watching birds—if for no other reason than because most birds are active by day. Bat watching, as we shall see, is much easier if you have a bat detector for eavesdropping on their echolocation calls (Box 8).

Some studies use photography to explore the details of bat behavior. An excellent example is the high-speed photography that has revealed details of bat

The pattern in the eye of this Mauritian Tomb Bat shows the reflection of the ring flash used to illuminate it for the photograph. This portrait was taken with a 105-mm micro lens. These 15-g bats occur in savannah woodland in many parts of Africa.

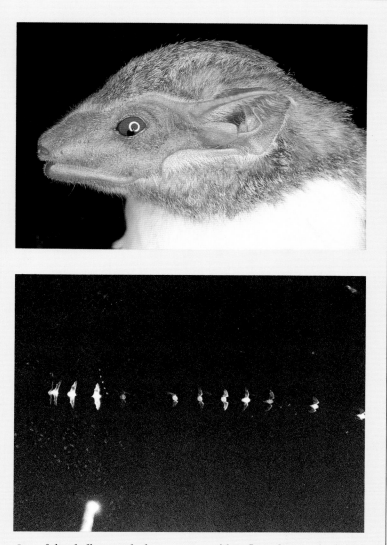

Background is another essential ingredient in bat photographs. A small dark-colored bat often will not show against a bright, light-colored background. Pieces of different-colored velvet can be good backgrounds for staged bat pictures. Using black velvet means that only light from the bat reflects back to automatic camera or flash units. This, in turn, can mean sharp, well-exposed pictures. By combining a black velvet background with natural props it is possible to take superior photographs of bats.

The best photographs of flying bats are usually of individuals trained to perform in a certain way. For example, a bat coming to get a food reward at a known place make it easy for photographers to adjust the setting to their advantage. In this case, the camera, lighting and lens angle can be carefully set up along with props and background. There are electronic devices that permit the photographer to get the bat to take its own picture. These may be part of the camera system, or may be used with light beam accessories. Either way, the apparatus can be set so that when the bat reaches a specific point, it takes its own photograph.

There is always room for more excellent pictures of bats.

One of the challenges of taking pictures of free-flying bats in the field is illustrated here. Here, a stroboscope presents 11 views of the same foraging Eastern Red Bat as it passes overhead. Differences in distances between image reflects changes in the bat's flight speed (it accelerated as it left the camera's view). Photographed by Martin Obrist.

flight. Biologists also rely on photography to measure the size of bat populations. In some cases, the numbers of bats leaving a roost can be estimated by counting the bats in photographs taken as they emerge. Photographs also have been used to count the numbers of bats hibernating together in clusters. For some hints about photographing bats, see Box 5.

The range of techniques and equipment used to study bats is quite extensive. Fine electrodes can reveal information about the contraction of muscles during flight or about how the brains of echolocating bats process information. Night vision or starlight scopes have permitted direct observation of the behavior of some bats under natural conditions. Scanning electron microscopes have revealed the fine surface details of structures such as hair and teeth (see page 107). Transmission electron microscopes provide pictures of the structure of different bat tissues. At another level, analysis of proteins and the molecular biology technique known as DNA fingerprinting have permitted the study of

Photographs also can be used to count the numbers of bats hibernating in clusters. In this case more than 50 Little Brown Bats are hibernating together in a cluster. At least two of them are banded. The banded bats were at least 15 years old when this photograph was taken in an abandoned mine in Ontario.

the genetic relatedness of bats that live together. It is safe to say that biologists have used almost every imaginable technique to study bats.

We have learned a great deal from captive animals. Work with captive bats may show the function of the circulatory, excretory or nervous systems. In other captive studies, bats are trained to do different tasks and their performances give us an idea of how they see the world. Biologists have found that some bats quickly learn how to solve problems in the laboratory under some circumstances. For example, research with Pallid Bats, Big Brown Bats and Little Brown Bats reveals that these bats will learn to fly across a room to a target when they get a food reward for doing so. When the trainer is a biologist the process takes about 14 days. Training time is just two days when the naive bats can observe a trained bat performing the task!

Although many species of bats adjust well to captivity, I do not recommend them as pets. Working with bats carries some special hazards that are outlined later (Box 15). There also are logistical problems. Insectivorous bats are difficult to feed in captivity and their voracious appetites (see Chapter 5) make them expensive to keep. Another complication is providing the captives with a balanced diet, because a steady fare of mealworms (the larvae of flour beetles, *Tenebrio*) usually does not contain adequate vitamins.

It is easy to be overwhelmed by the many things we know about bats. More exciting, however, is what we do not know. There are many opportunities to use new and innovative approaches and techniques in the study of bats.

ECHOLOCATION

The Sonar Sight of Bats

"Echolocation" describes how an animal uses *echoes* of sounds it produces to *locate* objects in its path. This method of orientation, sometimes also called "biosonar," is the animal equivalent of sonar which also depends upon pulses of sound (signals) and their echoes. Echolocation is best known from bats, but it is not characteristic of or unique to them. Some other mammals and birds also use biosonar.

Signal production makes echolocation, sonar and radar *active* processes because it involves spending energy to operate in otherwise impossible situations. In contrast, *passive* systems of orientation operate by collecting available information, through eyes, ears or nostrils.

People often resort to active orientation to extend their use of vision. Since our eyes need light to work, vision is useless in the dark and unreliable when light is faint and unpredictable. To remedy this we can use a flashlight. The energy required to produce the light makes the system active and allows us to see in the dark.

But echolocation differs from using a flashlight to extend your use of vision because it involves discrete pulses of sound rather than a continuous beam of light. Most echolocating animals produce a pulse of sound and receive the returning echo before producing the next signal. The differences between the original signal and its echoes contain the raw data necessary for echolocation. Some of the features of sounds and the information available to an echolocating animal are shown in Box 6.

Animals can use echolocation in several ways. Perhaps the most straightforward is relying on it to detect large obstacles, and to find nesting and roosting sites in caves. A more complicated task is using echolocation to locate, identify and track prey. This involves greater precision and smaller targets than general orientation within caves or other dark roosting sites. While the more precise echolocation systems can be used for general orientation, the reverse does not appear to be true.

BOX 6

SOME BASIC FEATURES OF SOUND

Several measurable features of sound are relevant to echolocation. They include pitch or frequency, which affects wavelength, as well as intensity and loudness.

The **pitch** or **frequency** of bat sounds normally is measured in kiloHertz, abbreviated as kHz. One kHz is one thousand cycles per second or 1000 Hertz. Sounds above 20 kHz are called "ultrasonic" because they are beyond the range of "normal" human hearing. The echolocation calls of most bats are ultrasonic and not audible to people. Higher frequency sounds have shorter wavelengths than lower frequency sounds. This means that to an echolocating bat, higher frequency sounds can provide more detailed information about a target. On balance, however, higher frequency sounds are more rapidly absorbed by the atmosphere, giving bats a shorter operational range by echolocation.

The strength of a sound can be expressed as loudness or intensity. **Loudness** is a perceptual measure reflecting how a signal sounds to a listener. **Intensity** is a physical measure of the energy or power in a sound. It usually is measured in decibels, abbreviated as dB. The echolocation signals of the Little Brown Bat measure 110 dB at 10 cm in front of the bat's mouth. The signals are slightly more intense than the sound from a smoke detector, a common fixture in many homes. The smoke detector sounds loud to us, while we cannot hear the echolocation calls of a Little Brown Bat, but the two different sounds have similar intensities. This comparison illustrates the difference between loudness and intensity. Not all intense sounds are loud.

An echolocating bat produces a pulse of sound and within half a second could theoretically receive echoes from objects up to 85 m away. The initial pulse is much stronger than the returning echo and the echo's strength depends upon the distance it has traveled. By measuring the time in milliseconds (ms) between the production of the original signal and the arrival of its echo, the bat learns the distance to the echo's source. Time is one important source of information for the echolocating bat.

Many bats produce echolocation pulses that cover a range of frequencies. The range of frequencies is the **bandwidth** of the signal. Often the bat puts more energy into some frequencies of its signal than it does into others. The **power spectrum** is one way of representing the distribution of energy across the frequencies in the sig-

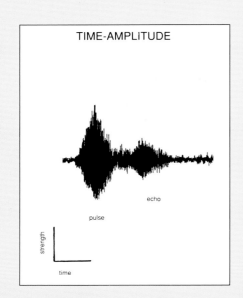

A time-amplitude display of a Big Brown Bat's echolocation call and its echo. The call lasted 2.5 milliseconds, and the echo followed 1.4 milliseconds after the end of the call. This means that the echo returned from an object 0.66 m in front of the bat.

THE ECHOLOCATORS

Echolocation is not a feature of all bats. With the exception of Egyptian Fruit Bats and perhaps another species of Dog-faced Bats, megachiropterans do not use it. In contrast, all of the species in the Microchiroptera are presumed to echolocate. Although the approaches of microchiropteran bats to biosonar vary, the details have been studied in few bats.

Other well-known echolocators are the toothed whales (Odontocetes), porpoises, dolphins, killer whales and their relatives. Research done mainly with dolphins has revealed that their biosonar is every bit as effective as that of

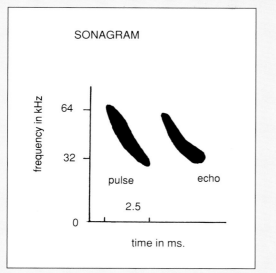

Sonagrams comparing the pulse and echo illustrated above. A sonagram shows how the call changes in frequency over time. Energy in the signal is reflected by the blackness of the display.

nal. Echolocating bats collect detailed information about targets by comparing the power spectra of the original signal and its echo.

Sonagrams show how frequency changes over time. Some sonagrams show the original pulse and the returning echo. Structured changes in frequency over time give bat echolocation calls a tonal feature absent from the echolocation clicks of Egyptian Fruit Bats, birds, dolphins and shrews.

By comparing pulse and echo, an echolocating bat uses differences in time and frequency structure to measure its distance from a target and to assess the details of the target.

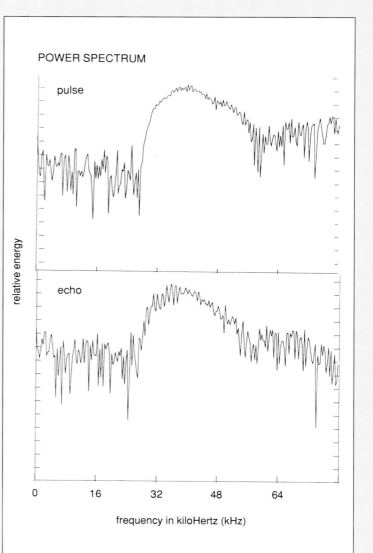

The power of the spectra of the echolocation call and its echo are shown above. The frequencies range from about 30 kHz to about 60 kHz. Note the differences between the original pulse and its echo. These differences provide echolocating bats with detailed information about target structure.

bats. It is likely that the baleen whales (Mystacetes) also use echolocation, but this remains unproven.

Some species of shrews and their relatives (order Insectivora) also echolocate. The Wandering Shrew and the Short-tailed Shrew are two North American examples of species that echolocate, especially when exploring unfamiliar areas. At least one species of tenrec, an Insectivora from Madagascar, uses echolocation under the same circumstances.

Echolocation by rats, pack rats, some seals and humans is less well documented. The evidence for rats and pack rats is inconclusive, and the same appears to be true of the situation in seals. Some sightless people appear

to use echolocation, which is the basis of sonar aids developed for the sightless.

The echolocating birds are the oilbirds of South America and several species of Swiftlets from Southeast Asia. These oilbirds and swiftlets nest in caves and rely on echolocation to orient themselves underground. Oilbirds belong to the order Caprimulgiformes along with the whippoorwills, goatsuckers, nightjars, frogmouths and their relatives. The echolocating swiftlets are relatives of swifts that occur in many parts of the world. Both swifts and swiftlets belong to the order Apodiformes, and all of them feed on insects. The nests of some species of echolocating swiftlets are used to make bird's nest soup.

THE HISTORY OF ECHOLOCATION IN BATS

The structure of the auditory bullae, the bones enclosing parts of the auditory system, of the first known fossil bats indicates that these animals could echolocate. As noted on page 9, these fossils are about 50 million years old, indicating that biosonar is an ancient trait in the Microchiroptera.

Although the anatomy of fossil Microchiroptera reveals that these bats used echolocation, we do not know if this was true of their ancestors. Some biologists have proposed that echolocation was one of the most important keys to the success of bats. It would have permitted the ancestors of bats to hunt flying insects at night, giving them access to food not available to predators using vision. Biosonar, therefore, might have been a key advantage in competition with birds and pterosaurs. This view assumes that the ancestors of bats were nocturnal and fed on insects.

Other biologists contend that the ancestors of bats fed on fruit and did not echolocate. These two alternatives involve questions about the evolutionary relationships between the Megachiroptera and the Microchiroptera (see page 10). If the two suborders did share a common ancestor that used biosonar, then this ability has been lost in the Megachiroptera and has reappeared in Egyptian

Fruit Bats. The explanation might be less complex if ancestors of bats did not echolocate or if the Megachiroptera and Microchiroptera evolved from different ancestors.

In 2000, the "right" answer about the origin of echolocation in bats remains unclear. Like other questions about the evolution of bats, additional fossil material may provide answers. For the time being, we do not know when bats began to echolocate. The same is not true of our own discovery of this behavior.

HUMANS DISCOVER ECHOLOCATION

About 1790, the Italian scientist Lazarro Spallanzani proposed that bats could see with their ears. He based this conclusion on the results of experiments demonstrating that when flying in a dark room, without the use of vision, smell or touch, Pipistrelles avoided obstacles. In some of the key experiments, Spallanzani and Charles Jurine (a Swiss) manipulated bats' hearing by inserting small tubes into the bats' ear canals. The bats with these tubes behaved normally. Using small stoppers, the bats' ears could be blocked and unblocked. Bats with both ears blocked avoided obstacles slightly less adeptly than bats with unplugged ears. When just one ear was blocked, however, the bats became totally disoriented.

Although Spallanzani's conclusion followed logically from his findings, they were not widely accepted by the scientific establishment of the time. In the next 135 years, several workers paid passing attention to "Spallanzani's bat problem," but the next major breakthrough came from Donald R. Griffin at Harvard University in the late 1930s. Using a microphone sensitive to sounds beyond the range of human hearing (ultrasonic), Griffin demonstrated that flying Little Brown Bats continuously produced pulses of high frequency sound. Furthermore, as these bats approached obstacles, they increased the rates at which they produced these pulses.

By repeating some of Spallanzani's experiments and adding embellishments of his own, Griffin showed that Little Brown Bats used echoes of sounds they produced to locate objects in their path. Further studies indicated that this mode of orientation was widespread in microchiropteran bats. Meanwhile, in Nazi-occupied Holland, S. Dijkgraaf had come to a similar conclusion by listening closely to flying bats. He observed that the bats produced faint pulses of sound and increased their rates of pulse production as they approached obstacles.

The story of human's discovery of echolocation is well documented in D. R. Griffin's 1958 book, *Listening in the Dark*. In the intervening period, biosonar has been the topic of a great deal of research, documented in the scientific and popular literature.

ECHOLOCATION IN BATS

As we proceed, bear in mind four important dichotomies in the echolocation of bats. First are differences in the site of call production (larynx versus mouth). Second are differences in call strength or intensity (intense versus weak). Third are differences in the ways that bats avoid deafening themselves (separating pulse and echo in time versus separating them in frequency; see also page 76). Fourth is the use bats make of echolocation, namely to detect flying prey (aerial-feeders) versus more general orientation.

BOX 7

DEAFENING AND JAMMING: TWO OPERATIONAL PROBLEMS

Echolocating bats avoid deafening themselves in one of two ways, by separating pulse and echo in time or in frequency. Consider the situation facing a Little Brown Bat flying in a room and using echolocation to detect wire obstacles placed there by an experimenter. At a distance of 30 cm, a 0.25-mm-diameter wire reflects a 45-dB echo from a 100-dB echolocation call. At 30 cm, the time lag between pulse and echo is 17.6 ms and the echo is 90% weaker than the original signal. The bat solves this problem and avoids the wires even if several other bats are echolocating and flying in the immediate area at the same time.

The bat's first problem is to ensure that the intense original call does not deafen it to the returning echo. But the challenge is maintaining enough hearing sensitivity to register the outgoing pulse for later comparison with its echoes. Little Brown Bats use specializations in their middle ears to resolve this problem.

About 6 ms before beginning to produce an echolocation call, muscles in the middle ear contract, reaching their full contraction during the production of the vocalization. After the call, the middle ear muscles begin to relax, and they are fully relaxed 2 to 8 ms later. The contraction of the middle ear muscles separates the three bones of the middle ear, the malleus, incus and stapes, reducing the transmission of sounds from the eardrum to the inner ear. In short, the contraction of muscles in the middle ear reduces the bat's hearing sensitivity but does not completely deafen the bat.

The action of the middle ear muscles is coordinated with the sound-production operation. This ensures that the outgoing pulse is registered without deafening the bat and that the bat's hearing is fully restored before the echoes return.

Little Brown Bats, like most other microchiropterans, separate pulse and echo in time. They cannot broadcast and receive at the same time because the intense outgoing pulses deafen the bat to the returning echoes. In one second bats that separate pulse and echo in time produce signals for less than 10% of the time. They are known as "low duty cycle bats."

The second approach to avoiding self-deafening is known from Horseshoe Bats, Old World Leaf-nosed Bats and Parnell's Mustached Bats. These species separate pulse and echo in frequency so they can broadcast and receive at the same time. The echolocation calls of these bats are dominated by a single frequency, and Doppler shifts of this frequency mean that the returning echoes are dominated by a different frequency than the emitted signals. In one second, bats separating pulse and echo in frequency produce signals more than 30% of the time. They are known as "high duty cycle bats."

Pulse and echoes from other bats should not interfere with echolocation because each individual is comparing each original pulse with its echo. Since the echolocating bat is listening for echoes of its own voice, it should not be disturbed by other sounds.

When flying in the immediate vicinity of other echolocating bats, however, several species adjust their outgoing calls. Rat-tailed Bats, Hoary Bats and Spotted Bats slightly change the frequencies of their calls. This may be the equivalent of changing channels to minimize interference. Big Brown Bats and Red Bats change the intensities of their calls and the rates at which they are produced. These approaches permit several animals to use the same channel while making it easy for each individual to recognize the echoes of its calls.

In situations where hundreds, thousands or tens of thousands of echolocating bats are pouring into or out of a roost, it is difficult to imagine how each individual keeps track of faint echoes of its calls against a din of other bats' calls and echoes. In this setting bats often orient by memory and not by paying immediate attention to objects in their path. This makes them vulnerable to capture in mist nets or harp traps (see page 22), structures they normally could detect and avoid.

Producing and transmitting the signals and receiving echoes from them are the two main components to the process of echolocation (see Box 7). Although these steps are fundamental to echolocation, the problems differ when used in air and under water. So although microchiropteran bats and odontocete cetaceans (toothed whales) use the same basic approach to echolocation, some variations reflect differences between air and water. Sound travels about 340 m per second in air, but moves over four times faster (1490 m/s) in water, which is denser and therefore a better conductor.

Echolocation in air is a relatively short-range operation because air absorbs sound, especially high frequency sound. For example, in the laboratory, an echolocating Big Brown Bat first detects a 19-mm-diameter sphere at a range of 5 m. Putting this in perspective, the average Big Brown Bat is 115 mm long, so the 19-mm-diameter sphere is 16% of its body length. Using echolocation, therefore, the Big Brown Bat first detects the sphere at 5000 mm (5 m), 43 times the length of its body. If our vision offered a similar range performance, a 2-m tall person would first see a stop sign at 86 m. It is obvious that in humans, vision gives better resolution over distance than does the echolocation of bats.

Are Big Brown Bats typical bats or are they "short-sighted"? As we shall see below, differences in echolocation call design influence a bat's perception of the world. Echolocating bats using longer calls may detect targets at 10 or even 20 m, but echolocation is a short-range orientation system because of the basic laws of physics that govern the movement of sound in air.

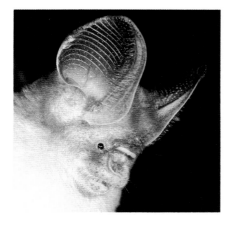

Old World Leaf-nosed Bats, like this Bicolored Round-leaf Bat, also emit their echolocation calls through their nostrils and have conspicuous facial ornaments. It, too, is a high duty cycle bat.

PRODUCING AND TRANSMITTING ECHOLOCATION CALLS

Microchiropteran bats all use vocalizations as echolocation calls. The sounds are called vocalizations because they are produced in the voice box, or larynx. Vocalizations are sounds made when vocal chords vibrate as air passes over them. Muscles in the larynx adjust the tension on the vocal chords affecting the

Bats that emit their echolocation calls through their nostrils often have elaborate facial ornamentation, like the nose-leaf of this Greater Horseshoe Bat, a high duty cycle bat.

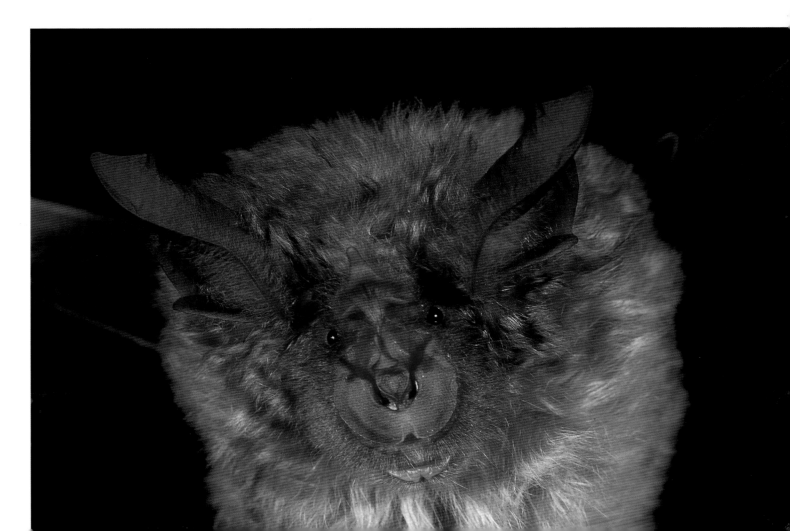

Like other New World Leaf-nosed Bats, this Pale Spear-nosed Bat emits its echolocation calls through its nostrils. In the related Short-tailed Fruit Bat, changes in the position of the noseleaf affect the pattern of sound radiation from the bat's nostrils. This is a low duty cycle bat.

rate at which the chords vibrate and thus the frequency (pitch) of the sounds produced. Differences in the vocal tracts and nasal chambers may enhance or alter the details of the sounds. The process is essentially the same as it is in other mammals, including humans.

Only one or two species of megachiropteran bats can echolocate, but the sounds they use are *not* vocalizations. Egyptian Fruit Bats roost in caves and rely on biosonar to orient themselves in the total darkness of their roosts. Egyptian Fruit Bats produce echolocation pulses by clicking their tongues, an approach to sound production that differs markedly from the microchiropterans. Like other megachiropterans, Egyptian Fruit Bats also vocalize, but not for echolocation.

Bats that use echolocation to detect, track and assess airborne targets adjust the features of their calls as they progress through an attack sequence. Calls a,b,c and d here were produced by one individual Mouse-eared Bat hunting over a pool in Israel. The bat changed the frequencies of its calls during the attack sequence. Calls e,f,g and h were produced by the same individual Bodenheimer's Pipistrelle as it hunted flying insects in the desert of southern Israel.

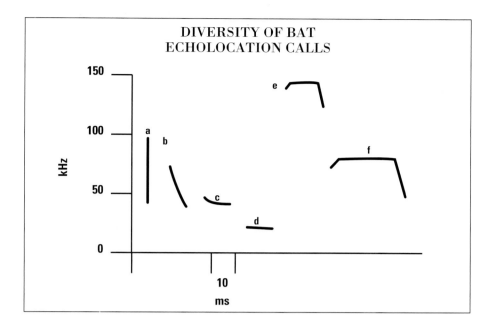

**DIVERSITY OF BAT
ECHOLOCATION CALLS**

Shown here are sonagrams—sound pictures—of a variety of bat echolocation calls. While some bats use short echolocation calls of broad bandwidth (a, b), others use longer calls of narrower bandwidth (c, d). High duty cycle species use calls dominated by a single frequency (e, f). The bats that produced these calls are a Northern Long-eared Bat (a), Little Brown Bat (b), Eastern Red Bat (c), Hoary Bat (d), Sundevall's Leaf-nosed Bat (e) and Greater Horseshoe Bat (f).

Whether vocalizations or tongue clicks, the signals used in echolocation must be transmitted from the bat. Most species appear to emit their echolocation signals through the open mouth, explaining why many photographs of flying bats show them with mouths open. Other species, notably Slit-faced Bats, False Vampire Bats, Old World Leaf-nosed Bats, Horseshoe Bats and New World Leaf-nosed Bats, emit their echolocation vocalizations through their nostrils. These bats fly with their mouths closed.

The species emitting their calls through their nostrils often have elaborate facial ornamentation. Typically the ornaments are leaflike, but the details vary from family to family and species to species. Work with the Short-tailed Fruit Bat, a New World Leaf-nosed Bat, has revealed that the nose-leaf is important in the transmission of echolocation calls. Temporarily changing the position of the nose-leaf with Krazy Glue® altered the pattern of sound radiation from the bat, directly affecting the bat's perception of its surroundings.

The position of the bat's head affects its view of the world through echolocation, or, for that matter, vision. By attaching small light-emitting diodes to the heads of Big Brown Bats, researchers have found that Big Brown Bats aim their heads at their intended targets. This discovery, made on sitting bats, was expected. It is more challenging to monitor changes in head position of a flying bat.

ECHOLOCATION SIGNALS

Echolocation sounds produced by tongue clicks differ in structure from those produced in a bat's larynx. The tongue clicks of Egyptian Fruit Bats are short, much, much less than one second long, and contain many frequencies, making them broad in bandwidth. You can make a similar sound by clicking your tongue against the roof of your mouth. Echolocation calls that are vocalizations are tonal, showing structured changes in frequency over time. You can make similar-sounding signals by whistling. The biosonar vocalizations vary considerably, reflecting different approaches to echolocation.

The echolocation signals of bats may be high or low intensity. The clicks of Egyptian Fruit Bats and the calls of many microchiropterans are quiet, and low in intensity. In absolute terms, these signals tend to be about 60 dB measured 10 cm in front of the bat's mouth or nostrils, the equivalent to someone whispering in your ear. New World Leaf-nosed Bats, Slit-faced Bats and False Vampire Bats typically produce quiet echolocation calls. Differences in call intensity correspond to differences in hunting behavior. Species producing high intensity calls hunt flying insects, while those producing low intensity calls take plant products or blood, or snatch animal prey from surfaces.

High-intensity echolocation calls contain more energy. In absolute terms they measure over 100 dB 10 cm in front of the bat's mouth or nostrils—the equivalent of someone screaming in your ear. Sheath-tailed Bats, Mouse-tailed Bats, Horseshoe Bats, Free-tailed Bats and many Plain-nosed Bats typically produce high-intensity calls. These bats probably achieve greater effective range than those using lower-intensity calls, reflecting the amounts of energy in the two signals (the dB values).

Whether broadband or narrowband, the vocalizations used in echolocation by microchiropteran bats can be grouped into several basic categories according to their general design. These calls sometimes consist of a mixture of broadband and narrowband components. The situation is complicated because the bats often change the design of their calls according to the situation in which they are operating.

Narrowband vocalizations tend to be long (20–50 ms) and make it easy for bats to detect targets because most of the energy is focused within a narrow range of frequencies. This design maximizes the chances of detecting echoes returning from targets, particularly small flying targets such as insects. Broadband vocalizations tend to be shorter (less than 10 ms) and give bats good facility for collecting fine-grained detail about their targets. The short, broadband design of these calls decreases their effective range. By combining narrowband and broadband components bats may achieve the best of both worlds: distance and accuracy. Most species that hunt airborne targets change from narrowband to broadband calls as they detect and close in on a prey, usually an insect.

As bats close in on insect prey, they typically increase the rate of echolocation call production. For example, a Hoary Bat searching for a target may produce 3 to 10 calls per second (330 to 100 ms between pulses) and may increase this rate to 200 per second (5 ms between pulses) during an attack on a moth. Bat biologists use the term "feeding buzz" to describe the high pulse repetition rates associated with attacks on prey.

This sequence of echolocation calls was produced by a Greater Bulldog Bat as it approached and then snatched a grasshopper from the surface of the water. As the bat closed with the target, it increased the rate at which it produced echolocation calls, shortening each call in the process. The high call rate has been called a "feeding buzz" because it represents an attack. Bats taking prey from surfaces often do not produce feeding buzzes, but the Greater Bulldog Bat is an exception.

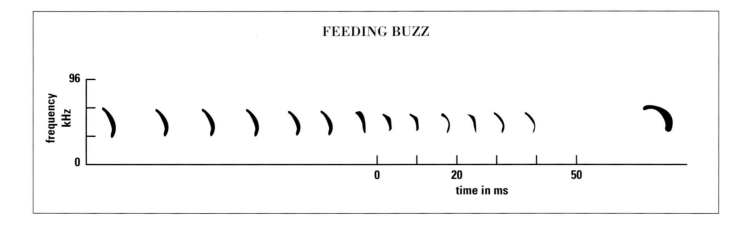

FEEDING BUZZ

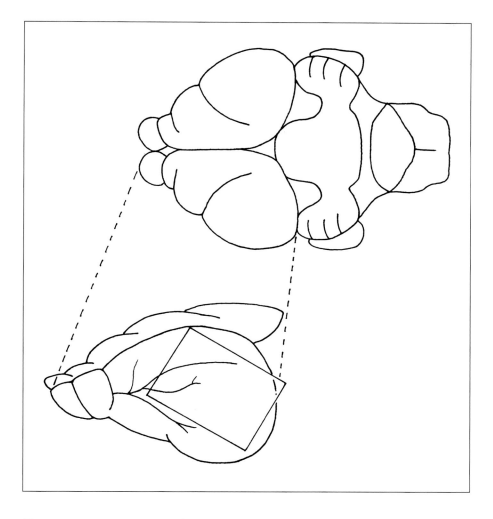

Looking down on the brain of a Parnell's Mustached Bat provides an impression of the basic structure. An expanded view shows the auditory cortex where some echolocation information is processed. The brain is about 10 mm long and the front end of the bat is to the left of the illustration. Drawing by Max Licht.

RECEIVING AND ANALYZING ECHOES

The early work of Spallanzani and Jurine demonstrated that ears are the important receptor organs for bats. The importance of ears is suggested by the prominence of the external ears, or pinnae, in most Microchiroptera. In shape, the pinnae of some bats are tuned to the sound frequencies dominating the echolocation calls and their echoes.

In Slit-faced Bats and False Vampire Bats—gleaners that take animals from surfaces—the ears are most sensitive to low frequency sounds made by moving prey. In Horseshoe Bats and Old World Leaf-nosed Bats, the ears are mechanically tuned to the narrowband frequencies that dominate the echolocation calls and their echoes.

At the eardrum, or tympanum, the echoes are converted from vibrations in air to mechanical vibrations. These are passed from the eardrum to the malleus, the incus and the stapes, the three bones of the middle ear. The stapes passes the echoes to the oval window where the inner ear begins. At the oval window, the mechanical vibrations are converted to vibrations in the fluid of the inner ear. The inner ear is housed in the cochlea or auditory bulla. There vibrations in the fluid of the inner ear affect the basilar membrane. Hair cells attached to this structure convert the fluid vibrations to electric signals that pass along the auditory nerve into the bat's brain.

The processing of the biosonar information takes place in the bat's brain. We know most about this operation in bats that use echolocation in aerial-feeding. Outgoing signals are registered in the bat's brain for comparison with

This pink moth hibernates in caves and mines with bats over much of its range, which includes North America, Europe and Asia. The moth has ears that are sensitive to the echolocation calls of bats.

returning echoes. In some species, for example Lesser Bulldog Bats and Greater Horseshoe Bats, the outgoing signals also prime the bats' auditory systems for receiving echoes.

The bat's processing includes the timing of the departure of the original signal and of the returning echoes, as well as comparison of the spectral features of the original sound and its echoes. From this information, the echolocating bat determines its range and position relative to the target. There is considerable evidence that echolocation permits bats to distinguish one species of flying insect from another.

Input from the auditory nerve is passed up through different parts of the brain to the auditory cortex. For the most part, the chiropteran auditory system is typical of mammals, although some echolocating bats have unique connections and pathways conducting impulses to the midbrain, specifically, the inferior colliculus. The auditory cortex of some echolocating bats is specialized for representing biosonar information. From the auditory cortex, echolocation information is relayed to the cerebrum.

Different information about targets is processed in parallel along parallel channels in the bat's brain. Echolocating bats provide excellent models for studying the processing of information by the brains of mammals.

THE ADVANTAGES OF ECHOLOCATION

Echolocation gives Egyptian Fruit Bats access to cave roosts where they enjoy some protection against predators. However, there is no evidence that these bats use biosonar to collect information about their food. Indeed, decisions about selecting the fruits on which they feed are based on aroma. Without echolocation, Egyptian Fruit Bats could roost only in places with enough light to permit them to orient by vision (passive orientation).

New World Leaf-nosed Bats that feed on fruit, nectar and pollen, and blood are accomplished echolocators. There is some evidence that species that are more dependent upon flowers have less echolocation acuity than those whose diets include more insects. Like Egyptian Fruit Bats, these New World Leaf-nosed Bats can use echolocation to exploit dark roost sites. However, one intriguing unanswered question is the role that echolocation plays in the lives of the New World Leaf-nosed Bats that feed on plant products or blood. Part of the answer to this question appeared in 1999 when experiments revealed that some New World night-blooming flowers pollinated by bats had "acoustic" nectar guides. The strength of the echoes of the bats' echolocation calls as they approached the flowers guided the bats to the appropriate feeding site.

For species of aerial-feeding Microchiroptera that take flying insects and some other prey (e.g., fish in the case of Bulldog Bats), echolocation is the prime means of detecting and tracking prey. For these species, biosonar means access to food—usually flying, nocturnal insects that are practically invisible to animals depending upon vision. The 100 or so species of nocturnal birds that feed on insects (owls and caprimulgiforms) are large and use specialized eyes or ears to find their prey. In terms of numbers of species and individuals, insectivorous bats outnumber nocturnal, insectivorous birds. Most of these bats locate their insect prey by echolocation. Specifically, Hog-nosed Bats, Mouse-tailed Bats, Sheath-tailed Bats, Horseshoe Bats, Old World Leaf-nosed Bats, Mustached Bats, many Plain-nosed Bats and Free-tailed Bats may depend entirely upon echolocation to find their prey—flying insects.

Like any other active system of orientation, echolocation offers clear advantages for roosting and feeding. At the same time, however, it makes its users conspicuous.

THE DISADVANTAGES OF ECHOLOCATION

Echolocation does for bats what radar does for people, posing benefits and costs. In many parts of the world, traffic police use radar to measure the speeds of vehicles. Since excessive speed is commonly identified as a leading cause of accidents, radar is a powerful tool in ensuring that speed limits are obeyed. In response, however, some motorists use "fuzz busters" to detect radar pulses and warn them of speed traps. Police with radar devices may catch more speeders than those using passive speed traps such as timing cars over known distances. Motorists with radar detectors, however, may evade radar traps and be caught in other kinds of speed traps.

This situation illustrates a major disadvantage of radar which also applies to echolocation. The problem is information leakage. The signals associated with active orientation are available to anyone that can receive them.

Who listens to the echolocation calls of bats? There are three obvious candidates and a fourth that is less obvious. The first candidates are other bats. It is clear that the echolocation calls of one bat may also permit it to communicate with others. The second candidates are potential prey. Many kinds of insects have ears that alert them to the echolocation calls of bats, warning them of approaching danger. The third candidate would be the predators of bats (see page 112). The fourth category is biologists who use bat detectors to study bats (Box 8).

Moths in many families, some mantids, crickets and katydids, some beetles, and lacewings are examples of insects that have bat-detecting ears. Their ears are especially sensitive to the ultrasonic echolocation calls of bats. The insects estimate the distance to the bat by the strength of the echolocation calls and adjust their defensive behavior accordingly. In response to a distant bat, perceived as a weak signal, moths and lacewings typically turn and fly in the op-

This photomicrograph shows the ear of the pink moth. Photograph by M. E. McCully.

Some tiger moths, like this one from Africa, produce evil-smelling froth when attacked by bats. The frothing is accompanied by clicking sounds which appear to warn the bat of the moth's bad taste.

BOX 8

BAT DETECTORS

Bat detectors convert the often-ultrasonic echolocation calls of bats to sounds clearly audible to most humans. Bat detectors have four basic components. The first is a microphone sensitive to high-pitched sounds, and the second is an electronic circuit that converts the input from microphone into a signal of lower pitch. A speaker system for broadcasting the converted signals is the third component, and the fourth is a battery to power the instrument. In some bat detectors, other circuits can transfer an electronic impression of the original signal at its original frequencies to a tape recorder.

There are three basic kinds of microphones (also known as transducers) in bat detectors. The first are crystal microphones tuned to one specific frequency, typically 40 kHz. The second are Electret microphones that respond to a broad range of frequencies both within and above the range of human hearing. Condenser microphones are the third kind, and they also respond to a wide range of frequencies (from about 5 to over 200 kHz).

Like the echolocation signals of bats, bat detectors may be narrowband or broadband. Narrowband bat detectors respond at any time to a small range of frequencies. Some bat detectors are narrowband because their microphones are sensitive to just one frequency. These are "leak detectors" originally marketed as devices for detecting leaks in high-pressure gas lines. They are also quite appropriate for eavesdropping on the echolocation signals of any bat that broadcasts in the appropriate frequency range. As noted above, tuned microphones are typically sensitive to sounds at 40 kHz.

Other narrowband bat detectors consist of a broadband microphone, either Electret or condenser, and use circuits that allow the user to tune in to one specific frequency at a time. Most models can be tuned from 10 to 180 kHz, making them flexible and suitable for listening to a variety of bats. The main drawback to this kind of narrowband detector is that one can listen to just one frequency at a time.

Broadband detectors can simultaneously scan a range of frequencies. By taking the frequencies in the incoming signal and dividing or counting them down, the circuitry in broadband detectors brings the sounds into our hearing range. Some models divide the incoming signals by 10, while in others the user can select countdown by 4, 8, 16 or 32. These bat detectors are very flexible because they allow simultaneous eavesdropping on a wide range of frequencies and a wide range of bats.

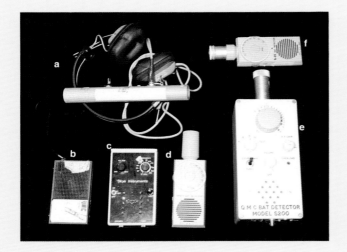

Shown here are six different kinds of bat detectors, including a leak detector with earphones (a), a QMC Mini detector (b), a Skye Bat detector (c) and an Ultra Sound Advice Mini-2 detector (d). The leak detector is tuned to 40 kHz, while the QMC Mini, the Skye and the Mini-2 have a broadband microphone and an electronically tuned output. The QMC S-200 (e) and the Ultra Sound Advice S-25 (f) Bat Detectors use broadband microphones and can produce broadband output.

The output of narrowband and broadband detectors can be recorded on cassette tape recorders for further analysis or review. The output also can be fed into a loudspeaker system, which is an effective way to make echolocating bats part of a public demonstration or interpretation event. Biologists or psychologists studying the details of echolocation signals record the direct output on high-speed instrumentation tape recorders, operated at tape speeds of 30 to 60 inches per second.

From the instrumentation tape recorder, bat echolocation calls (and other sounds can be analyzed by appropriate computer programs, for example Canary (available from the Cornell Laboratory of Ornithology at http://www.ornith.cornell.edu/brp/Candos.htm). The Anabat bat detector can be purchased with a module and software that allow presentation of the bats' echolocation calls on a DOS computer.

Bat detectors are available from several sources. Six companies or organizations that make and sell bat detectors are listed below:

- The Bat Conservation Trust, 15 Cloisters House, 8 Battersea Park Road, London, SW8 4BG United Kingdom. (Enquiries@bats.org.uk or www.bats.org.uk) produces the Magenta do-it-yourself kit, a tuneable, narrowband bat detector.
- Hertfordshire & Middlesex Bat Group (Dinah Harding), 2 Stonelea Road, Hemel, Hempstead, Hertfordshire HP3 9JY United Kingdom, produces a do-it-yourself kit for a narrowband detector.
- L. Pettersson Elektronik AB, Tallbacksvagen 51, S-756 45 Uppsala, Sweden, (www.bahnhof.se/~pettersson) produces several models of bat detectors and instruments and software for sound analysis.
- Skye Instruments Ltd., Unit 32, Ddole Industrial Estate, Llandrindod Wells, Powys LD1 6DF, United Kingdom, (skye.instruments@almac.co.uk) produces a range of bat detectors.
- Stag Electronics, 4 Esprit Court, New Road, Shoreham-by-sea, West Sussex BN43 6RB, United Kingdom, produces a variety of bat detectors.
- Titley Electronics, P.O. Box 19, Ballina NSW 2478, Australia, sells the Anabat bat detector with zero-crossing module and DOS-compatible software.
- Tranquility, 3 Suffolk Street, Cheltenham, Gloustershire GL50 2DH, United Kingdom, (courtpan@global-net.co.uk) producs a range of detectors.
- Ultra Sound Advice, 23 Aberdeen Road, London N5 2UG, United Kingdom, (www.ultrasoundadvice.co.uk) makes different kinds of bat detectors with either Electret or condenser microphones, as well as instruments for analysis of sounds.

Some bat detectors also may be purchased from Bat Conservation International (P.O. Box 2603, Austin, Texas 78715 (http://www.batcon.org)

Your choice of a bat detector will depend upon the use you plan for it and on your budget. A comparison of the ability of three kinds of bat detectors to pick up the echolocation calls of four species of bats reveals important differences between bats, but not between bat detectors. Leak detectors, the simplest ones, tend to be the least expensive while broadband detectors with countdown and direct output for recording the original signal are the most expensive.

With a bat detector you can eavesdrop on the echolocation calls of bats or any other sounds within the insturment's range. This means that when listening to the world through a bat detector you will hear electronic representations of echolocation calls, as well as scuffing sounds, jingling keys or change and sibliant hisses. The bat echolocation sound are usually distinctive because the rates at which they are produced change as the bats move about. In contrast, the scuffing and hissing sounds are more irregular. The ultrasonic mate-attraction calls of insects tend to be monotonously regular.

Perhaps the easiest of bat sounds to interpret are the changes in pulse repetition rate as the bat searches for, closes with, and attacks a flying insect. Feeding buzzes accompanying the attack are distinctive through the bat detector.

But since each species of bat produces characteristic echolocation calls, with a little practice you can learn to recognize different species by their calls. In most places in the United States and Canada, when your detector is tuned to 20 kHz and it produces chirplike sounds, it is announcing the presence of a Hoary Bat. Chirplike sounds from the detector tuned to 40 kHz suggest a Red Bat, while ticklike sound at 40 kHz suggest a species of Mouse-eared Bats (*Myotis*). In other parts of the world, the bat faunas change, but observers that have learned to use bat detectors can recognize many species by their calls.

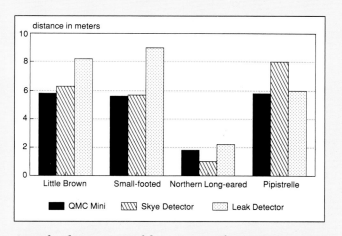

A graphical comparison of the sensitivity of a QMC Mini Detector, a Skye Detector and a Leak Detector to the echolocation calls of four species of bats. The minimum distance at which the different instruments detected the bats' calls are compared. The bats, Little Brown Bats, Small-footed Bats, Northern Long-eared Bats and Eastern Pipistrelles (Pipistrelle), were flying in a room during the experiment. Modified from a paper by Forbes and Newhook (1990).

posite direction. A close bat, perceived as a strong signal, causes moths and lacewings to stop flying and dive to the ground or to take other evasive action.

Moths, crickets and katydids, and lacewings have pairs of ears, and by comparing the signals received at each ear they can determine the direction from which the bat is approaching. Mantids, however, have a single ear and show no directional response to an attacking bat. Studies of moths and mantids suggest that the ability to hear bats reduces their vulnerability to these predators by 40%. Lacewings, mantids and most moths lack noisemakers, so it appears that their ears act as bat detectors. Male crickets and katydids, however, usually use sounds to attract mates. In these insects the ears can serve a dual function: finding a mate and detecting marauding bats. The bat-detecting ears of lacewings are located on the wings, while the crickets' and katydids' ears are on their forelegs. The mantids' ears are located on their chests between the third pair of legs. In moths the ears may be on the abdomen or the chest, or, in the case of some hawkmoths, next to their mouths.

Some of the Tiger Moths (family Arctiidae) use noisemakers when approached by echolocating bats. The noisemakers make clicks that affect the behavior of attacking bats. Bats hearing the clicks of tiger moths typically abort their attacks. There is some debate about the reasons for this behavior. One early suggestion was that the moth clicks interfere with the bats' echolocation, perhaps by mimicking echoes of the bats' biosonar calls. Studies of Pipistrelles, California Leaf-nosed Bats and Indian False Vampire Bats do not support this explanation as these species abort attacks on clicking targets whether they are using vision or echolocation.

Tiger Moth clicks could startle an attacking bat, surprising it and causing it to veer away from its intended target. Work with trained Big Brown Bats supports this view. But Big Brown Bats quickly learn to ignore moth clicks.

The caterpillars of many species of Tiger Moths feed on noxious or poisonous plants. The chemicals responsible for the bad tastes or toxic effects are taken into the caterpillars' bodies and passed along to the adult moths. The clicks of Tiger Moths could warn attacking bats that the moths are bad-tasting or poisonous. Animals with chemical weapons often advertise their armament to the apparent benefit of both predators and prey.

In Ontario, Eastern Red Bats and Hoary Bats have been observed while attacking Tiger Moths known as Painted Lichen Moths, which have effective noisemakers. Faced with an attacking Red or Hoary Bat, moths that can hear bats take obvious evasive action. Painted Lichen Moths do not alter their flight paths during attacks, and instead begin making clicks; as a result Red and Hoary Bats abort their attacks at an early stage. Red and Hoary Bats do attack Painted Lichen Moths with damaged noisemakers, but quickly spit them out. It's clear from this behavior that Painted Lichen Moths use clicks to warn Red and Hoary Bats that they taste bad.

There are direct parallels between bats and their insect prey and traffic police and motorists. The parallels depend upon the active nature of echolocation and radar and arise from information leakage.

SWITCHING OFF ECHOLOCATION

In the 30 years following Griffin's discovery of echolocation, biologists described the echolocation behavior of several species of bats and the calls they presumably used in echolocation. The late 1970s heralded a new set of results.

More and more studies showed that some microchiropteran bats eschewed echolocation and used passive cues to find their prey. The research involved a variety of species such as Long-eared Myotis in North America, Mouse-eared Bats in Europe, Fringe-lipped Bats in Panama and Large Slit-faced Bats or Egyptian Slit-faced Bats in Africa. The results revealed that although these species produced echolocation calls as they approached prey, they used other cues to find their targets. Fringe-lipped Bats provided a spectacular example, for they clearly used the songs of males to find the frogs on which they fed. These species all produced low-intensity echolocation calls which they appear to use to collect information about the background.

Other studies used Indian False Vampire Bats, California Leaf-nosed Bats and Pallid Bats. These species often stopped producing echolocation calls when relying on other cues to find their prey. The Indian False Vampire Bats and the California Leaf-nosed Bats would use vision or sounds coming from their prey to find their targets. Pallid Bats appeared to rely primarily on the sounds of prey.

It is important to note that any of these species of bats could use echolocation to find a sitting prey when all else fails. The bats are more efficient and effective, however, when they detect prey by passive means. So bats with well-developed echolocation abilities sometimes refrain from using this mode of orientation. It is tempting to predict that bats will do this when the costs of echolocation exceed the benefits. In this setting, the costs include alerting potential prey (or predators) and the benefit is more efficient location of prey.

Echolocation is one of the most amazing features of bat behavior and it pervades the lives of many species of Microchiroptera.

OTHER SENSES, ORIENTATION AND MIGRATION

THE OTHER SENSES

Because hearing is central to echolocation, it is easy to think of hearing as bats' main channel for collecting information about their surroundings. Indeed, the public perception of bats as blind is based partly on general knowledge of their biosonar. As we have seen, however, not all bats can echolocate. Furthermore, some echolocating bats use other ways to find out what is going on around them. Next to echolocation, heat detection is one of the more astounding sensory abilities of bats. Known only from studying Common Vampire Bats, heat detection will be discussed in Chapter 10.

Hearing

Because echolocation depends upon hearing, it is sensible to consider the role that hearing plays in the lives of bats in contexts other than echolocation. The hearing systems of bats are typical of mammals, although their external ears usually are more spectacular than those of most other mammals. (The relationship between the design of a bat's pinna, or external ear, and its echolocation signal has been explored [page 47].) In the high duty cycle bats (Horseshoe Bats, Old World Leaf-nosed Bats and Parnell's Mustached Bats), the auditory system is mechanically and neurologically tuned to the frequencies dominating the echolocation calls.

In other species of bats, such as Large Slit-faced Bats, Indian False Vampire Bats and Fringe-lipped Bats, the external ears are designed for maximum hearing sensitivity to sounds coming from their prey. For example, Indian False Vampire Bats hear very well across a wide range of frequencies (11 kHz–65 kHz). Their hearing is particularly acute between 16 kHz and 18 kHz and between 45 kHz and 50 kHz. These peaks in hearing acuity, partly due to the structure of their ears (pinnae), mean that the

When hibernating, this Western Big-eared Bat rolls its ears into tight balls and partly covers them with its wing. Pleats in the bat's ears allow them to fold up. Note the orange bat flies near the bat's elbow. Photograph by J. G. Woods in central British Columbia.

rustling sounds associated with their prey's movements on the ground are particularly obvious to Indian False Vampire Bats. In the laboratory, Indian False Vampire Bats listen for the footfalls of mice and use this information to locate and track these prey. The acute hearing and use of prey-generated sounds is similar to the behavior of barn owls.

Even species like Big Brown Bats that rely mainly on echolocation to detect and track their prey hear many other sounds. In the laboratory, Big Brown Bats learn to distinguish between the flight sounds of honey bees and beetles, but the importance of this behavior in their hunting remains unknown. In spring, hungry Big Brown Bats have been found to use the calls of frogs to find wetlands, areas where flying insects may be abundant. The ears of many species of bats have conspicuous pleats, which are absent in other species. Do these structures influence hearing sensitivity? Perhaps, but the pleats seem to allow bats to fold their ears. The most spectacular examples come from the bats with the largest ears, such as Western Big-eared Bats. One of these bats is shown with its ears erect on page 7. Hibernating Western Big-eared Bats fold up their ears, presumably to reduce the surface area exposed to the cold in their hibernation sites.

Bats hear very well and depend upon this sense in many different situations. Hearing is central to echolocation and some bats behave like barn owls, using their hearing to detect sounds coming from their prey. As we shall see in Chapter 7, bats also use sounds to communicate information, whether males are trying to attract females, or baby bats their mothers.

Sight

The eyes of bats vary considerably in size, from the large and conspicuous eyes of megachiropterans to the small inconspicuous eyes of microchiropterans such as Large Slit-faced Bats. Some Microchiroptera, however, have big eyes. Differences in eye size suggest that vision plays different roles in the lives of different species of bats.

At night when you catch the eyes of an Old World Fruit Bat in a bright light, they reflect conspicuous eyeshine, as do the eyes of many other nocturnal animals (e.g., cats, whippoorwills). Eyeshine comes from the "tapetum lucidum," a reflecting structure located behind the retina. The tapetum lucidum amplifies light, making it easier for the animals to take full advantage of whatever light is available. Although microchiropteran bats are not known to have tapeta lucida, I sometimes have seen what appeared to be eyeshine from Jamaican Fruit Bats caught in mist nets and flying Angola Free-tailed Bats.

In bats, only the Megachiroptera are known to see color. The pigments associated with color vision appear to be absent in the eyes of Microchiroptera. Like other nocturnal animals, bats are usually not brightly colored, and conspicuous patterns in fur or wings are most often high contrast black and white. Male Red Bats, however, tend to be brighter than females but the significance of this distinction remains unknown.

Some bats see very well. For example, the insectivorous California Leaf-nosed Bats see as well as any other bats studied to date, notably species of fruit-, nectar- and blood-feeding New World Leaf-nosed Bats and Gigantic

Greater White-lined Bats, 8-g Sheath-tailed Bats from the New World tropics, have patterns of high visual contrast on their backs. Like the Spotted Bats, the Greater White-lined Bats are insectivorous.

California Leaf-nosed Bats like this one have conspicuous eyes and see very well, particularly under conditions of dim lighting.

Flying Foxes. Like these other bats, California Leaf-nosed Bats see particularly well in dim light, better than do humans, and see much better in any light than do Big Brown Bats and Pallid Bats.

Some species of bats see much better than others, but there are no species of blind bats. An effective demonstration of vision in bats is replayed time and time again when a microchiropteran bat is released into a room during the day. The bat first flies about avoiding all of the potential obstacles, but within a few minutes will turn and fly directly into a window. This change in behavior corresponds to the use of different cues for orientation. Since echolocation reveals the window glass as a hard surface, the bat detects and avoids it. Vision, however, suggests that windows are openings and the bat using its eyes fails to detect the glass. Flying Foxes and their relatives (Egyptian Fruit Bats excepted), like birds, rely on vision and are often deceived by windows so they crash into the glass.

Smell

Odor plays many roles in the lives of bats and, as in humans, it is part and parcel of the sense of taste. All bats can collect information about odor through their nostrils. Variation in the facial appearances of bats partly reflects differences around the nostrils. As noted earlier, facial ornaments such as nose-leafs affect sound transmission in echolocating species. Other features may affect bats' perception of odor.

For example, there are tube-shaped nostrils in two groups of bats. About eight species of Tube-nosed Bats occur among the Old World Fruit Bats, and another 11 species among the Plain-nosed Bats. Tube-nosed bats live in Australia and the Malay Archipelago, with tube-nosed Old World Fruit Bats known from Australia, Papua New Guinea, the Celebes, Borneo and the Philippines. Tube-nosed species of Plain-nosed Bats (see page 136) occur in these areas, and in China and Japan. Other bats, such as Bulldog Bats and Short-tailed Bats, have nostrils that are somewhat tubelike, and some other Old World Fruit Bats show tendencies in this direction.

Since tubular nostrils occur in bats that eat fruit as well as species that eat animals, diet offers no obvious explanation for them. Similarly, tubular nostrils occur in echolocating and non-echolocating bats. Future observations of tube-nosed bats may suggest a function for these striking features, but for now, their functional significance remains unknown.

Laboratory and field evidence suggests that sense of smell is very important for fruit-eating bats. In West Africa, Dwarf Epauletted Bats and Buttikofer's Epauletted Bats take only ripe figs, which form the mainstay of their diet. These bats make brief hovering flights before figs and appear to use their sense of smell to identify ripe ones. They are better at this than even experienced biologists. New World Leaf-nosed Bats such as Jamaican Fruit Bats behave the same way.

While we now know that some flowers have ultra-sonic nectar guides presumably most effective for the flower-visiting New World Leaf-nosed Bats, nectar- and pollen-feeding bats also use their sense of smell to identify flowers with a supply of nectar (see page 69). On bat-pollinated plants such as Indian trumpet trees, only a few flowers on any stalk open on any night. Visiting Cave Nectar Bats force open flowers that are ready. The bats probably use odor to choose the "right" flowers.

Many bats use Jacobson's organs, specialized structures on the roof of the mouth, to help detect odor. The size of Jacobson's organs varies in bats. The largest occur in Common Vampire Bats, while some species lack them entirely. Large size suggests an important role for Jacobson's organs in the lives of Common Vampire Bats. In other vertebrates, Jacobson's organs are an additional channel for collect-

The striking black and white pattern on the back of this Spotted Bat is accentuated by the enormous pink-colored ears. Spotted Bats are Plain-nosed Bats, weighing 15–20 grams.

ing information about odor. Bulls, for example, use their Jacobson's organs to identify receptive cows. In Costa Rica, Common Vampire Bats sometimes feed on cows that are ready to mate. The bats are as good as bulls at identifying these cows, suggesting the bats use Jacobson's organs to identify preferred prey.

Bats that feed mainly on animals such as insects seem to depend less on odor for evaluating feeding opportunities than bats feeding on fruit, nectar or just blood. Still, smell and taste affect choice of food by insectivorous bats. Captive Big Brown Bats readily eat carrion beetles. Before eating them, however, the bats bite off and reject the tips of the abdomens which contain glands holding noxious-smelling substances. Brown Long-eared Bats also depend upon taste in making decisions about what to eat and not to eat. Near the town of York in England, one worker found a whole Garden Tiger Moth among the insect parts beneath a feeding perch used by a Brown Long-eared Bat. Garden Tiger Moths contain bad-smelling chemicals, but the rejected moth bore the bat's toothmarks. Apparently the bat had caught and killed the moth and then decided not to eat it. Odor could have affected the food choice of this insectivorous bat.

In behavioral experiments Big Brown Bats find the taste of quinine unacceptable. Big Brown Bats readily eat mealworms, the larvae of flour beetles, but spit out mealworms that have been dipped in quinine. Pallid Bats, however, readily accept and eat mealworms dipped in quinine, revealing that not all bats have the same standards of taste.

Odors also play important roles in the social lives of bats. Many species have conspicuous glands on their skin and the secretions of these glands may perform important social functions (see Chapters 7 and 13).

Tubular nostrils are a characteristic feature of this Lesser Tube-nosed Fruit Bat photographed in Papua New Guinea. Other bats also have tubular nostrils, but their function remains unknown.

ORIENTATION

Like humans, bats use hearing, vision and smell to collect information about their surroundings. At one level, these senses allow bats to locate and evaluate potential food. At another level, bats use some of these cues to orient themselves in their environment. Orientation means finding and recognizing important places such as roost sites. The challenge of finding a feeding or roosting area depends upon the life cycle of the bat. For a bat that spends its entire life within a few kilometers of where it was born, the problem of knowing where it is relative to its roost or roosts may be minor. In comparison, the bat that spends the summer in southern Ontario and the winter in Louisiana faces a bigger problem.

How do bats find their way from one place to another? When it comes to long-distance orientation, other animals use a mixture of cues. Terrestrial animals often use their sense of smell and their view of the sun to move toward "home." Birds, including many in the size range of bats, navigate using information about the sun and the stars that they collect by vision. Some species also use a magnetic sense, and others depend upon their sense of smell.

Although echolocation gives bats a picture of their immediate surroundings, its short operational range seems to make it of little value in navigation over long distances. Furthermore, there is little evidence that a sense of smell plays an important role in the general orientation of bats, although it may be critical when selecting a specific roost. Echolocation and sense of smell are good for short-range orientation, but over longer distances bats must use other information.

To study an animal's ability to orient itself, biologists use "homing experiments." As the name implies, these projects involve displacing marked animals from their homes, and recording the animals' ability to return home. There are sev-

A Garden Tiger Moth, which is distasteful to some bats.

eral elements to these studies. The animals must be marked to ensure that they can be recognized later. Active tags such as radio transmitters are better for this work than passive tags such as bands because they provide more details about the behavior of the tagged animal. The time it takes animals to return home is documented and the results are reported as percentage of homing success (number returning divided by number displaced x 100) over time. Once it has been established that the animals can find home, the experiments proceed to manipulations of the available cues. To investigate the role of vision, for example, some displaced animals are fitted with blindfolds, while others are not. If vision is important in orientation, blindfolded animals should home at lower rates than those that can see.

Several projects like these have found that some bats home effectively over considerable distances. The outcome of the experiments suggest that homing bats navigate by vision. One complication is that blindfolded bats could have trouble telling night from day. Since day-flying bats are easy prey for some birds, failure to home may reveal more about vulnerability to predators than it does about a bat's ability to navigate.

Homing experiments with Greater Spear-nosed Bats in Trinidad used radio tags, untreated bats, bats with goggles and bats with blindfolds. The untreated bats represented normal bats. Bats with blindfolds were deprived of vision, and bats with goggles had the physical discomfort of goggles but they could see. Any Greater Spear-nosed Bats that could see flew directly home whenever they were released less than 16 km away. From farther away, these bats took longer to get home and used more circuitous routes. When the home cave was more than 50 km from the release point, the bats showed little evidence of actively finding home. Blindfolded Greater Spear-nosed Bats usually found their home cave, but took much longer doing so. Furthermore, even at short distances their routes home were more circuitous. Vision is important for orientation and navigation by Greater Spear-nosed Bats, but we do not know what specific cues the bats used. They could have recognized landmarks or oriented their flight by the stars. Homing by blindfolded Greater Spear-nosed Bats reveals that bats also have well developed spatial memories. Deposits of magnetic materials in the brains of some Big Brown Bats suggest that, like many other animals, they are sensitive to magnetic fields. A magnetic sense is an additional navigational aid.

MIGRATION

Around the world, many species of bats make regular migrations, seasonal movements to and from specific sites. Two kinds of evidence support this view. The first is the seasonal absence of some species of bats from some areas. The second is information about the movements of banded animals.

In North America, Red Bats, Hoary Bats and Silver-haired Bats are widespread in summer and occur almost as far north as the tree line. In winter, however, these bats are absent from the northern parts of their range and live farther south, along the gulf states of the United States. Hoary Bats occur in northern Florida through the winter but not in the summer. In May, Silver-haired, Red and Hoary Bats first appear at locations in southern Canada. Near Delta, Manitoba and Grand Bend, Ontario, Hoary Bats arrive at their summer foraging areas in late May and begin to leave by the end of July. Most have left by the middle of August. No records of band recoveries document the specific movements of individuals between their summer and winter ranges. Near Grand Bend, Ontario, however, two banded Hoary Bats have returned in each of four summers to for-

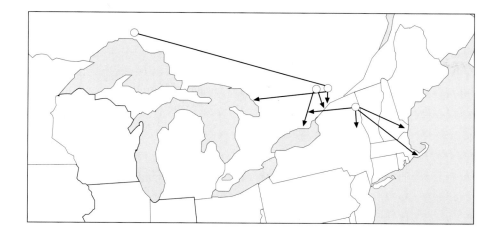

A map of eastern North America showing the movements of banded Little Brown Bats between hibernation sites (circles) and summer locations. Modified from Davis and Hitchcock (1965) and Fenton (1970).

age within 500 m of where they were originally caught and tagged. These bats know their way around.

The circumstantial evidence strongly suggests that Red, Hoary and Silver-haired Bats migrate. In some other species, band recoveries have documented the movements of individuals, providing clearer evidence of migration. Records of this nature are known from several species in different parts of the world, with most coming from temperate areas in regions where there are more people studying bats.

In different parts of their range in eastern and central North America, female Little Brown Bats form nursery colonies in May, June and July. In winter, male and female Little Brown Bats hibernate in underground settings, usually caves or mines. Since the nurseries are frequently situated in buildings, they have been convenient to study. Furthermore, a tendency for individuals to return to the same places year after year has provided a picture of seasonal movement between summer and winter sites. Many of the Little Brown Bats that summer in Cape Cod spend the winter in upper New York State. Some of the bats from these winter sites also have been found in southeastern Ontario, but more of the bats that summer there hibernate in caves or mines to the west and north. Little Brown

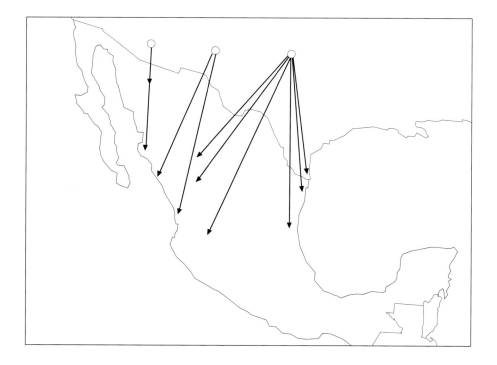

A map of the southwestern United States and Mexico showing the movements of banded Mexican Free-tailed Bats between their summer cave roosts (circles) and cave roosts where the bats spend the winter. Modified from Griffin (1970).

The comings and goings of large bats, like these Gray-headed Flying Foxes, are easy to monitor because the bats are loud and conspicuous.

Bats show similar behavior in Indiana and Kentucky, typically moving one-way distances of less than 500 km between summer and winter.

People in the northern hemisphere think of migrations to avoid winter as movements to the south; those living in the southern hemisphere have the opposite view, that you go north to avoid winter. Little Brown Bats and other species from temperate zones migrate to caves where they hibernate. They may fly west, east, north or south to find their wintering sites. Migrations to hibernation sites need not be flights toward the equator.

In other bats, seasonal movements to avoid winter are only southward. This is the case for Mexican Free-tailed Bats in North America or Noctules in Europe. Although band recoveries have documented these patterns of movement, few details are known about the routes taken by the bats or the times taken to cover the distances.

Tropical bats also migrate. For example, in Africa, Yellow House Bats vacate their summer (wet season) roosts in winter (cold, dry season), but their destinations remain unknown. Also in Africa, Straw-colored Fruit Bats migrate, with hundreds of thousands of bats covering hundreds of kilometers annually. The comings and goings of Straw-colored Fruit Bats are conspicuous because their day roosts are easy to find and the bats only occupy them at certain times of the year. Straw-colored Fruit Bats and Little Collared Fruit Bats show migrations synchronized to the seasonal patterns of the rains, moving northward with the rains and returning south at the end of the rainy season. Other Old World Fruit Bats in West Africa (Gambian Epauletted Bats, Buttikofer's Epauletted Bats and Dwarf Epauletted Fruit Bats) show no seasonal movements.

Changes in patterns of food availability govern the migrations of bats. Many species migrate, but we do not yet know enough about the routes they take and the cues they use for orientation and navigation.

WHAT BATS EAT

L ike all other mammals, bats consume milk as the first food after birth. It is produced by females in modified sweat glands, called mammary glands. The richness of bat milk varies among species, but it is always expensive to produce. Indeed, during lactation, the period of milk production, female bats have the highest energy consumption of any bats at any time in their lives. Lactating female bats consume vast amounts of food, partly reflecting the energy used in milk production.

For their size, bats, even non-lactating females, have big appetites. For a long time biologists suspected that bats consumed a great deal of food. Now studies of the energy budgets of bats have revealed that earlier estimates of 20 to 30% of body weight per day in food were conservative. Using water molecules labeled with two radioactive hydrogen atoms and one radioactive oxygen atom (isotopes), it is possible to measure the energy consumed by a bat over a known period. This approach, known as the "doubly labeled water technique," has produced startling results.

A baby Mexican Free-tailed Bat often consumes its own weight in milk every day, and during a night's foraging, its mother typically eats 1.2 times her body weight in insects. These figures are not exceptional. Lactating female Little Brown Bats also eat more than their own body mass in insects daily. Males and non-nursing females eat more than 50% of their body mass every day. Vampire Bats take about 60% of their body mass in food (blood).

FOOD PROCESSING

Eating large quantities of food is difficult for a flying animal because the food mass increases body weight, making flight more expensive and more difficult. Fruit Bats minimize the problem of excess food weight by processing the food before they eat it. Like other African fruit bats, the Dwarf-

A baby Little Brown Bat getting a drink of milk from one of its mother's mammary glands.

Epauletted Fruit Bat often handles about three times its body weight in fruits and leaves every night. By thoroughly chewing and crushing the food while sucking vigorously, these bats actually ingest only the juice and pulp—the parts they can digest. The rest, mainly fiber and pith, is spat out as a small, dry pellet. Fruit bats in the New World show the same behavior. To crush fruit, bats use flattened cheek teeth (usually their molars), tongues and ridges that run across the roofs of their mouths, their palates. The teeth crush the fruit while the tongue rubs the crushed fruit against the palatal ridges. By sucking during this operation, the bats remove and swallow only the juice and pulp. Recent studies have demonstrated differences in feeding behavior among New World Leaf-nosed Bats. Short-tailed Fruit Bats primarily use their incisors and canine teeth when biting into hard and soft fruits. Jamaican Fruit Bats and Common Yellow-shouldered Bats use the canines and cheek teeth on one side of their mouths when biting into hard fruits. Using the cheek teeth on one side of their mouth gives the bats a stronger bite. These differences suggest that some bats are better equipped than others to deal with hard food.

Bats that eat animals such as insects also process food before ingesting it. Many species bite off and drop the wings and legs of insect prey. Since these parts contain relatively little food value, the bats avoid taking on the extra weight of undigestible material. Insectivorous bats such as Hoary Bats bite off the wings of their prey as they fly along. Large Slit-faced Bats and other species use an alternate approach, taking their prey to a perch before processing it—culling the wings and legs from insects before eating the body.

The cheek teeth of insectivorous bats are "W" shaped for slicing and crushing food. These bats can chew very quickly, and a Little Brown Bat makes about seven complete chewing cycles per second. Chewing ensures that swallowed food is finely macerated and ready for the next stage in digestion.

Bats living on a liquid diet do not need to chew their food and many have teeth designed for other purposes. Baby bats have specialized milk teeth that help them to cling to their mothers' teats. Nectar-feeding bats have very long snouts and very small cheek teeth. The teeth of vampire bats are specialized for making wounds (the upper incisors), or for clipping fur and feathers (the canines and premolar teeth).

Whatever the diet, bats' digestive systems are specialized for rapid chemical breakdown of food. For example, just 20 minutes after swallowing a mouthful of insects, a Little Brown Bat passes their indigestible remains as feces. Rapid digestion of food is one reason that bats have such gigantic appetites.

Bats' abilities to process and eat vast quantities of food directly affects their importance in the ecosystems where they occur. Bats eat huge quantities of insects and may be important in biological control. Fruit-eaters handle so much fruit they disperse many seeds, and flower-visitors need so much nectar they visit and pollinate many flowers every night. The impact of leaf-eating remains to be determined. The details depend upon the food the bats actually take, whether it is animal material or plant material, insects, vertebrates, fruit, nectar or pollen.

ANIMALS AS BAT FOOD

Insects

The majority of species of bats feed mainly on insects (see Table 1). As a rule, bigger bats eat larger insects than smaller bats, but the actual choice of prey appears to depend upon its local abundance. This means that anywhere on any night what a Little Brown Bat, Hoary Bat, Greater Horseshoe Bat, or Noctule eats will depend upon the insects it encounters as it flies about hunting. For the Little Brown Bat, caddis flies, mayflies and midges may be staple items over the summer. Their actual proportions in the diet will change from night to night. For a Greater Horseshoe Bat, beetles known as cockchafers or June bugs are readily taken when they are abundant.

Insectivorous bats may hunt in concentrations of insects. For example, in southern British Columbia, Canada, Big Brown Bats hunt over the Okanagan River and for most of the summer caddis flies are the bulk of their diet. The caddis flies emerge by the tens of thousands from the river, feeding several other species of bats, as well as Common Nighthawks, insectivorous birds that hunt at twilight. Throughout the tropics many insectivorous bats regularly congregate to feed in swarms of flying termites. They usually are joined by other predators such as sun spiders, birds and mongooses.

In southern Ontario, Canada, Red Bats and Hoary Bats harvest insects that fly in clouds around spotlights. At some locations they take mainly moths, adjusting their selection according to the abundance of different species of moths. On some nights in July, Red Bats and Hoary Bats both feed mainly on forest and eastern tent caterpillar moths which emerge by the thousands. On other nights the Red Bats take smaller moths, and the Hoary Bats larger ones, reflecting the sizes of the two bats (12–15 g and 25–30 g, respectively). In some parts of Germany, Noctules forage on house crickets that emerge in large numbers from garbage dumps.

This Northern Long-eared Bat (6 g) has just caught and killed a 0.6-g underwing moth, which is more than a mouthful. The bat has just landed; after the picture was taken, it proceeded to remove and drop the moth's wings and legs. Note the moth scales in the bat's fur.

BOX 9

FROG-EATING BATS

In 1982 many people marveled at an article about frog-eating bats which appeared in *National Geographic* magazine. The spectacular photographs of Fringe-lipped Bats catching frogs were spellbinding and they revealed how the bats used their mouths to snatch calling frogs from land or water. Furthermore, by listening to the calls of male frogs, the Fringe-lipped Bats avoided the deadly arrowhead frogs and chose the good-tasting, non-toxic species.

The work on Fringe-lipped Bats on Barro Colorado Island in Panama made biologists more aware of some of the problems of sexual advertising. To attract a female, many male frogs sing to advertise their location and their vigor, but the song that attracts females also attracts foraging bats, and other potential predators. The results also revealed how bats would forsake echolocation and use other means to locate potential prey.

This captive Large Slit-faced Bat is eating a frog it caught during an experiment. Note that the bat cradles the frog in its partly opened left wing.

Fringe-lipped Bats use the calls of male frogs to find their targets. As they approach their prey, however, the bats produce echolocation calls, presumably to assess the background where the frog is calling. Since frogs do not hear the ultrasonic sounds of Fringe-lipped Bat echolocation calls, the bats' calls do not reveal their approach to the frogs. Calling frogs like the Tungara frog, however, are quick to respond to the silhouette of a marauding bat.

Meanwhile, in Africa and in India, other frog-eating bats have been discovered. In India, Indian False Vampire Bats often feed on frogs, while in East Africa, Heart-nosed Bats show the same behavior. In Zimbabwe, Large Slit-faced Bats make frogs a regular part of their diet. Frog-eating bats of any species typically attack the frog's head, grabbing their prey in their mouths and carrying it to a perch where they eat it from the head down. Indian False Vampire Bats and Fringe-lipped Bats eat the entire frog, while Large Slit-faced Bats always leave some of the frog

It is safe to say that around the world bats feed on almost any of the insects they might encounter at night. Although it is easy to find reports of a species of bat feeding only on one species of insect over a short period of time, this observation is not evidence that bats specialize on particular species of insect. Seasonal changes in the species of insects that are available makes it unlikely that bats can afford to specialize on any particular insect species over the long term. Furthermore, the insects available to the bats typically change over the course of a night. In southern Manitoba, Canada, for example, Hoary Bats take mainly beetles and moths in the first part of the night, but at dawn go out and hunt dragon flies.

Since some insectivorous bats occasionally emerge and forage during the day, their diet may also include diurnal insects such as butterflies and bees. Bats, such as the Mouse-eared Bat of Europe, that hunt only insects that walk along the ground, often prey on ground beetles.

Bats eat a lot of insects, as measured by numbers of individuals consumed or numbers of species. One indication of the affect bats have on insects is that many kinds of insects have ears for alerting them to echolocation calls which herald an approaching bat (see Chapter 3). As we shall see in uneaten; they drop the toes from one hind leg and the ankle and foot of the other.

Unlike the Fringe-lipped Bats, Indian False Vampire Bats, Heart-nosed Bats and Large Slit-faced Bats do not use the frogs' calls to locate and identify their targets. These three species rely upon the sounds of the frogs' movement to locate them on land and make their attacks accordingly. When there is sufficient light, Indian False Vampire Bats and Heart-nosed Bats use vision to find their prey, while Large Slit-faced Bats appear to depend upon the sounds of motion. The Large Slit-faced Bats, however, produce echolocation calls as they close with their frog targets, presumably, like the Fringe-lipped Bats, using echolocation to collect information about the background.

More recent research with Indian False Vampire Bats has revealed that a few of these bats tested in captivity use their echolocation to find frogs sitting in the water. These echolocating Indian False Vampire Bats oriented on objects protruding from the water, sometimes getting a mouthful of frog, other times a mouthful of water weeds.

Salivary glands provided an unexpected additional chapter to the frog-eating bat story. There is a strong resemblance in both general and detailed structure of the salivary glands located under the tongues of Indian False Vampire Bats and Fringe-lipped Bats. The bats belong to different superfamilies (Rhinolophoidea and Noctilionoidea, respectively) but have eating frogs in common. Perhaps, on further investigation, the Large Slit-faced Bats will be shown to have salivary glands like the other two species, further supporting the notion that some specializations are necessary when bats eat a lot of frogs.

An Indian False Vampire Bat about to take a frog from the surface of the water in a laboratory pool. This photograph was taken by P. Kumarasamy during experiments that revealed that in this setting Indian False Vampire Bats used echolocation to find the frogs.

Chapter 12, bat conservationists often argue that insectivorous bats are beneficial because of the vast quantities of insects they consume. If a lactating Little Brown Bat were to feed just on mosquitoes, she would eat more than 5,000 of them every night. In southeastern Ontario in August, Little Brown Bats regularly eat mosquitoes, but it remains to be seen if any of them feasts mainly on mosquitoes.

Other Arthropods

Insects belong to the huge phylum (group) of animals known as the Arthropoda, or joint-legged animals. Familiar arthropods are spiders, lobsters, shrimp, centipedes and scorpions. More exotic arthropods are sun spiders and whip-scorpions, which usually occur in warmer areas and are more familiar to biologists.

Bats eat many arthropods besides insects. In Australia, some small Dome-headed Bats spend parts of their nights taking spiders from their webs, while Spix's New World Disk-winged Bats appear to eat many jumping spiders. In the American southwest, Pallid Bats often hunt centipedes and scorpions, and in

BOX 10

CARNIVOROUS BATS?

Some biologists use the term "carnivorous" to describe the food habits of microchiropteran bats that often eat small terrestrial vertebrates such as frogs, lizards, birds, bats and mice. Others take the view that the carnivorous bats should not be treated as different from other bats that eat animals, because their food habits simply reflect the greater variety of prey available to bigger predators.

The species in question are in three different families—New World Leaf-nosed Bats, Slit-faced Bats and False Vampire Bats—and they occur around the tropics from South and Central America, to Africa, India, Southeast Asia, and Australia. The New World bats on this list are Linnaeus' False Vampire Bats, Woolly False Vampire Bats and Fringe-lipped Bats. In Africa, the list includes Heart-nosed Bats and Large Slit-faced Bats, while in India and Southeast Asia there is one species, the Indian False Vampire Bats. In Australia, another species of False Vampire Bats, the Ghost Bats, fill this role.

This Woolly False Vampire Bat is one of the larger (85 g) New World Leaf-nosed Bats that often eats small, terrestrial vertebrates such as lizards and geckos, bats and birds.

Most is known about the diets of Large Slit-faced Bats and Indian False Vampire Bats. When the prey of these two bats are examined in detail over a year, it is evident that small terrestrial vertebrates are more important in some seasons than in others. Furthermore, at most times of the year for both species, large arthropods are a staple part of the diet. The bats eat many sun spiders, scorpions, large moths, grasshoppers, cicadas and beetles. Large Slit-faced Bats seem to adjust their diet according to the availability of prey in the habitats where they hunt. Furthermore, both species sometimes hunt from perches, other times from continuous flight. This flexibility also affects their selection of prey.

All of these bats have four things in common. First, they are large, the smallest weighing at least 20 g, and the largest, Linnaeus' False Vampire Bat and the Ghost Bats (see pages 132 and 125), over 100 g. Second, they have broad wings. Size and wing shape well equip these bats to catch and kill larger prey and carry them off to a feeding perch. Third, these bats all use their vision or sounds made by their prey to find vulnerable targets. Fourth, they all eat arthropods as well as small terrestrial vertebrates.

Other species of microchiropteran bats with only some of these features do not eat small terrestrial vertebrates. For example, several species weigh at least 20 g but are aerial feeders. Included here are some species of Sheath-tailed Bats, Old World Leaf-nosed Bats, Horseshoe Bats, Plain-nosed Bats and Free-tailed Bats. Although they are probably big enough to manage small vertebrate prey, species such as the Blackhawk Bat (90 g), the Naked-rumped Tomb Bat (33 g), Midas' Free-tailed Bat (40 g) or Naked bats (100 g) are aerial feeders with long, narrow wings and hunt well above the ground, apparently using echolocation to find their prey. At 150 g, Commerson's Leaf-nosed Bat

Africa, Large Slit-faced Bats regularly eat sunspiders. Although there are no records of bats taking lobsters and shrimp, some, like Greater Bulldog Bats and Mexican Fishing Bats, eat small shrimp-like crustaceans (often called "krill" when the predator is a baleen whale). On Colubra Island, off of Puerto Rico, Great Bulldog Bats often eat fiddler crabs.

is big enough to take small vertebrates, as is Hildebrandt's Horseshoe Bat at 25 g. But these two species are high duty cycle bats, using flutter-detection to locate flying targets and apparently do not have access to more terrestrial prey.

Any large, broad-winged bat species that does not depend upon echolocation to find its food may occasionally eat small vertebrates. For example, there is a record of a Pallid Bat (18 g) taking a small pocket mouse. These bats (see page 143 and 178) weigh as much as 20 g, have broad wings and use sounds of prey to find their targets. There are more records of Greater Spearnosed Bats (90 g) taking small vertebrates, although this species seems to eat mainly fruit and leaves.

In the Yucatan Peninsula in Mexico in 1991 a 22-g Cozumel Spear-nosed Bat was caught flying along with a 1.5-g lizard it had caught. Later, a 23-g Cozumel Spear-nosed Bat was caught carrying a 1.4-g grasshopper. The size and broad wings of this bat, and its ability to listen to its prey, give it access to larger prey, and Cozumel Spear-nosed Bats probably take the biggest prey they can handle. What matters to the bat is the size of its prey rather than whether the victim is a grasshopper or a lizard.

Based on its size (20–30 g) and wing features, Hemprich's Long-eared Bat was predicted to be another species that could eat small terrestrial vertebrates. Studies in Kyrgyzstan revealed that when light-tagged, these bats flew continuously while hunting, taking arthropod prey from the ground. The same findings were obtained from radio-tagged Hemprich's Long-eared Bats in Israel. Apparently, not using feeding perches limits the upper size of prey that Hemprich's Big-eared Basts can handle.

Bats take almost any prey available to them. Bigger bats with broad wings and the ability to listen to sounds coming from prey will take bigger prey. Sometimes their diet will include small terrestrial vertebrates, but it also will include arthropods. Ghost Bats and Linnaeus' False Vampire Bats are big enough that they may feed more on small vertebrates than the other "carnivorous bats."

Carnivorous bats are not a distinct lifestyle in the Chiroptera, but merely another reflection of the theme of flexibility and variation that recurs in bats.

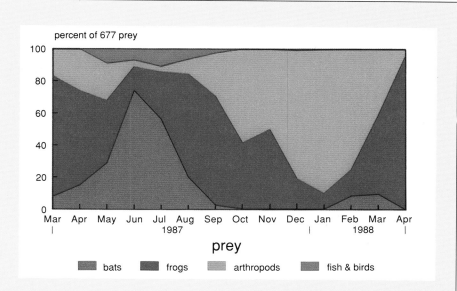

This graph illustrates the variation in the diet of Large Slit-faced Bats in Mana Pools National Park in Zimbabwe between March 1987 and April 1988. The cold, dry season (winter) is June and July, the time when the bats eat many bats and some birds and fish. Based on data presented in a paper by Fenton and colleagues (1990).

A Cozumel Spear-nosed Bat about to eat a 1.5-g lizard which it has caught.

Whether they fly or walk on the ground, most joint-legged animals are potential prey for some bats. For the many insectivorous bats that take only airborne prey, insects and the occasional ballooning spider are the staple food. Bats that also take prey from the ground, the trunks of trees or foliage are exposed to a more varied selection of food, including many non-insect arthropods. The picture of what any bats eat seems to depend upon what is available when and where they are hunting.

Fish

Since bats eat almost everything else, it should not be surprising to learn that some of them eat fish. Several species forage over the water, taking flying prey or snatching morsels from the surface. The Greater Bulldog Bats of the West Indies, Central America and South America (see page 128) and the Mexican Fishing Bats of Central America are examples of fishing bats. Both of these species have enlarged hind feet bearing long, sharp claws that are used to gaff fish swimming near the water's surface. The feet are specializations for fishing, but are not basic equipment for all fishing bats; other fishing bats lack the spectacular feet. A tendency to feed over water may predispose some bats to eating fish, and the open space over water may make it easier for these bats to detect prey and maneuver to catch it.

In Europe, Daubenton's Bat feeds over the water, catching flying insects and some other prey from the water's surface. In Australia, the Large-footed Myotis shows the same behavior, as do Little Brown Bats in much of North America. Some other species in the genus *Myotis* have large hind feet and, like Pallid Large-footed Myotis of the East Indies or Rickett's Big-footed Bat from China, are also presumed to hunt over water. Analysis of stomach contents has revealed that Daubenton's Bats sometimes eat fish, the other species named here may also do so from time to time.

Indian False Vampire Bats and Large Slit-faced Bats occasionally eat fish. These bats have normal feet and presumably grab their prey in their mouths. No details of the fishing behavior of Indian False Vampire Bats and Large Slit-faced Bats are available.

Terrestrial Vertebrates

Larger species of False Vampire Bats, Slit-faced Bats and New World Leaf-nosed Bats often eat small vertebrates that live mainly (or partly) on land. Included on the menu are other species of bats, birds, mice, lizards and frogs. Some details of frog-eating behavior are considered in Box 9, and the general nature of this "carnivorous" habit is explored in Box 10.

The general biology, diet and feeding behavior of some of the better-known "carnivorous bats" are presented later, specifically Ghost Bats from Australia (page 125), Large Slit-faced Bats from Africa (page 126) and Linnaeus' False Vampire Bats from South and Central America (page 132). There have been relatively few studies of the foraging ecology and prey selected by the larger species of New World Leaf-nosed Bats, False Vampire Bats and Slit-faced Bats, but what is known suggests flexibility in foraging behavior (see below) that coincides with a varied diet.

Blood

The blood-feeding vampires are the most notorious bats. The three species of vampires feed only on blood; they are the topic of Chapter 10. Vampire bats live in South and Central America, but the notion of vampire bats is more widespread. For example, the False Vampire Bats which occur in Africa, India, southeast Asia and Australia are neither blood-feeding nor closely related to the real vampire bats.

This Short-faced Fruit Bat is just beginning to feed on a large piece of banana. By the time the bat is finished, the fiber in the banana will have been sucked dry and spat out on the ground. The bat weighs about 40 g.

PLANTS AS BAT FOOD

In the tropics and subtropics some bats feed on plants, specifically on leaves, fruit, nectar and pollen. In South and Central America these are New World Leaf-nosed Bats, while in Africa, India, the East Indies and Australia, they are Old World Fruit Bats, some known as flying foxes. As noted earlier, the former belong to the Microchiroptera, the latter to the Megachiroptera. The general behavior and specializations are similar between the two groups of plant-feeding bats, providing an example of parallel evolution.

Bats cannot digest cellulose, the main nutritive and energetic component of leaves and stems. Many mammals, from cows to rodents and rabbits, can digest cellulose. They do so with the help of bacteria and fermentation; their digestive tracts have specialized fermentation chambers. The process, however, is time-consuming and has not been adopted by flying animals such as bats and birds, presumably because of the time it takes and the weight it adds.

Fruit

Fruit bats eat many different kinds of fruit, including some grown as cash crops. Obviously, larger species of fruit bats tend to take bigger fruits than smaller species. Furthermore, the details of which kinds of fruit are eaten and when usually reflects the fruiting seasons of different plants. As noted earlier, some African fruit bats migrate from place to place following the rains and the fruiting times of different species of plants.

Whether the setting is the New World tropics or the Old World tropics, most fruit bats visit a plant, select a ripe fruit, and take it elsewhere to eat it. This pattern of hit-and-run foraging is usually called an antipredator behavior: it permits the bats to avoid predators waiting at fruit trees. Some larger flying foxes remain in the trees bearing their preferred fruits. In Malaysia, for example, Large Flying Foxes often feed on the fruits of the Durio tree. These bats usually arrive at the trees about 7:30 P.M. and defend the chosen tree vigorously against other bats. Perhaps their large size (body mass about 1 kg) gives these fruit bats some protection against predators that would threaten a smaller bat.

Fruit bats have an unerring talent for selecting ripe fruits, and throughout the world figs are the fruits of choice for many of these bats. In the West African forest, figs are the staple diet of Buttikofer's Epauletted Bats, Gambian Epauletted Bats, Dwarf-Epauletted Fruit Bats and Hammerhead Bats. Since, on any given night, a fig tree bears relatively few ripe figs, each bat must visit several trees to get enough food, following the hit-and-run foraging pattern. Each ripe fig contains relatively little protein, an important commodity for bats, particularly lactating females. The low protein content in each fig obliges protein-hungry bats to process at least twice their body weight in figs every

At about 6 g, this Commissaris' Long-tongued Bat is a typical nectar-feeding, leaf-nosed bat with a long snout. Not shown here is the remarkably long tongue which is used for obtaining nectar from deep-throated flowers.

night. The low incidence of ripe figs per tree means that the bats visit several trees every night. When eating figs, bats ingest only juice, pulp and seeds.

Together, these factors have important consequences for the bats, the fig trees and the habitats where the interactions take place. The bats eat more carbohydrates than they require to maintain themselves, presumably giving them extra energy for long flights. Ingested fig seeds pass quickly through the bats and are deposited as components of bat droppings in the areas traversed by the bats. Since each bat must visit several trees, each covers a lot of ground, widely dispersing the fig seeds. This results in the wide dissemination of fig seeds and contributes to the regeneration of forests.

Leaves

While bats do not appear to be able to digest cellulose, they do eat leaves, using an approach called "fractionation." Bats approach leaf-eating as they do fruit-eating. Leaves are taken into the mouth and thoroughly chewed while the bat sucks out and swallows the liquid portion of the leaves, spitting out the indigestible fibrous material. This approach to leaf-eating explains why leaves do not appear in bat feces and makes it easy to understand why it was only in the mid-1990s that biologists began to appreciate the importance of leaf-eating to bats. Quite simply, the digestive tracts of many fruit-eating bats are specialized to deal with a largely liquid diet and rapid food passage. This means that the liquid portion is separated from the fiber before swallowing—making bats well suited for this approach to leaf-eating. Leaves may prove to be an important source of protein for plant-visiting bats.

At this time it is not clear how bats deal with some of the problems associated with leaf-eating. One of the most important ones is exposure to chemicals which plants use in defense and that may be toxic to the bats. Leaf-eating may be nothing new to bats, but it is still relatively new to biologists, leaving the potential for many exciting new discoveries.

Nectar and Pollen

Nectar attracts bats, birds and insects to flowers. In return for drinks of nectar, the visiting bat usually gets its head and shoulders covered with pollen. As noted above, some flowers have been ultrasonic nectar guides to assist echolocating flower bats in their quest for nectar. Since each flower provides a small amount of nectar, flower-visiting bats must go from flower to flower to fill their stomachs. On any plant on any night, relatively few flowers are open, obliging the bats to move between plants. The system ensures that pollen from one flower is moved to others and minimizes the chances of inbreeding—that is, one plant fertilizing itself. By outbreeding, plants are thought to maximize genetic variation and plant vigor.

For bats and many other animals, a complete diet involves a mixture of carbohydrates and proteins. Since nectar is basically sugar water, high in carbohydrates and lacking protein, flower-visiting bats must seek their protein elsewhere. Some species, particularly among the flower-visiting New World Leaf-nosed Bats, supplement their diets with insects, a rich source of protein. An acute sense of echolocation may permit these New World Leaf-nosed Bats to detect and catch insects, while allowing them to take full advantage of ultrasonic nectar guidelines.

Pollen also is a rich source of protein, but it is tough and difficult to digest. Species of New World Leaf-nosed Bats, such as Sanborn's Long-

The very elongated skull and small teeth are among the specializations of Mexican Long-tongued Bats associated with a diet of nectar and pollen. As illustrated earlier (page 8), this species lacks lower incisors. The long snout houses a long tongue. When feeding, the bat pumps blood into its tongue, lengthening it to reach deep into flowers. The absence of lower incisor teeth minimizes the chances of inadvertently cutting its tongue and bleeding to death. The bat's skull is 3 cm long.

The flowers of this baobab tree also are pollinated by bats. These flowers, which last one night, are easily accessible to the bats in the open canopy of the tree.

tongued Bats, get their protein from pollen. In the American southwest, these bats visit agave flowers. In southern Arizona, Sanborn's Long-tongued Bats forage in flocks of at least 25 bats. Each bat visits a flower for about 0.3 seconds and over a night must get about 4 g of nectar. So on any night each bat in a flock visits many flowers.

Agave flowers remain open for several nights, switching from the production of pollen to the production of nectar. Pollen is produced by the stamens, the male parts of the flower. During pollen production, the female part of the flower (the pistil) is not fertile. During nectar production, the flower does not release pollen and the pistil is fertile. This strategy minimizes the chances of a flower being fertilized by its own pollen and keeps the bats coming back to the flowers over several nights.

Sanborn's Long-tongued Bats collect large quantities of pollen when they visit pollen-bearing flowers. After a period of flower-visiting, the bats hang together in a cluster and groom themselves and one another. During the grooming they ingest pollen. Roosting bats also drink some of their own urine, a behavior that helps to create very acidic conditions in their stomachs. The acidic conditions, in turn, are necessary for digestion of the pollen they have eaten.

The skulls of bats such as Sanborn's Long-tongued Bats are more specialized for visiting flowers than those of Pallas' Long-tongued Bat and some other New World Leaf-nosed Bats. Increased morphological specialization for exploiting flowers coincides with a decrease in echolocation acuity. Together this evidence suggests that New World Leaf-nosed Bats that are more specialized for eating nectar and pollen depend less on insects as their source of protein.

Less is known about the interrelations between flowers and the flower-visiting Old World Fruit Bats. Nectar-feeding Old World Fruit Bats occur from Africa to India, Southeast Asia and Australia. Species such as Queensland Blossom Bats, Cave Nectar Bats, Northern Blossom Bats or Woermann's Bat are not known to echolocate, presumably limiting their access to insects as a source of protein. Furthermore, the flowers they visit should not have ultrasonic nectar guides.

"Chiropterophily" (literally, "bat loving") is the name given to the syndrome of bat-pollinated flowers. Chiropterophilous plants have flowers that open at night and are pale or reddish in color, and strong smelling. In many species, the odor resembles that of fermenting fruit. In plants such as agave, the flowers may remain open for several nights, while the flowers of others such as baobab trees and African sausage trees are open for just one night. The flowers on bat-pollinated plants are easily accessible to a flying bat. In plants such as India trumpet-flower trees, the flowers are borne on long stalks that protrude well beyond the canopy of the tree. In African sausage trees, the flower stalks hang down below the canopy. The terms flagelliflory and penduliflory, respectively, describe these two conditions. The open crowns of baobab trees, which also are pollinated by bats, give the bats easy access to the flowers.

In Malaysia, the flowers of the India trumpet-flower tree are specialized for pollination by Cave Nectar Bats. There, Cave Nectar Bats, weighing about 60 g, are the largest of the flower-visiting species; the rest weigh less than 20 g. The flowers of the India trumpet-flower trees open about two hours after dark, after the Cave Nectar Bats arrive in the area. Earlier in the evening, smaller nectar-feeding bats are active around the trees, but they weigh too little to force open the flowers.

Nectar-feeding bats may make long commuting flights from their day roosts to the plants they visit. Near Hermosillo in Mexico, some Lesser Long-nosed Bats roost by day in caves on an island about 25 km off the coast. Some of these bats fly every night to the mainland to visit the flowers of organ pipe and barrel cacti. The energy the bats spend in their commuting flight to and from the mainland is paid for by the nectar collected in visits to just seven flowers.

FINDING FOOD

The process of finding food has three stages. The first involves finding the general location of the food. The second is detecting specific food items and deciding which to pursue. The third stage is catching and eating the chosen prey. For bats and other animals, stages two and three are complicated when the food is mobile and able to take evasive action.

The Search

Our knowledge of the first stage comes from radio-tracking studies. Fruit bats use one or two basic strategies for hunting. Species such as Short-tailed Fruit Bats from Central and South America fly out from their cave roosts and search generally for fruits. These 15-g bats often feed on the small, slen-

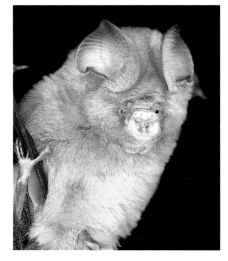

High duty cycle Old World Leaf-nosed Bats, like this Sundevall's Leaf-nosed Bat, listen for fluttering targets, often depending upon Doppler shifts to detect vulnerable prey.

der, podlike fruits of plants in the genus *Piper*. The *Piper* plants grow in the understory and are randomly dispersed. The bats quickly find them and other fruits.

The other strategy is represented by Jamaican Fruit Bats or Gray-headed Flying Foxes. Both species are larger (50 g and 800 g, respectively) and depend more on the rich patches of fruits such as fig trees. These bats tend to fly directly to fruiting fig trees, and rarely detect fruits that are less predictably available.

Aerial-feeding bats that feed on insects and other animals use one of two basic strategies when searching for prey. Some fly continuously while they are hunting, and others alternate between hunting in continuous flight and waiting on a perch for suitable prey to come within range. Hoary Bats Noctules, Little Brown Bats or Tomb Bats are examples of those hunting from continuous flight. Some Horseshoe Bats and Old World Leaf-nosed Bats also hunt from perches. The same dichotomy applies to gleaners, the bats that take prey from surfaces. Mouse-eared Bats from Europe or Pallid Bats from North America or Hemprich's Long-eared Bats fly continuously while hunting for arthropods on the ground. Gleaners that hunt from perches or from continuous flight include Yellow-winged Bats, Large Slit-faced Bats and Indian False Vampire Bats.

Detection

As we have seen in Chapter 3, many animal-eating bats use echolocation to detect prey, while others rely more upon vision or on sounds produced by their prey. We lack comparable information about the systems that fruit-eating or flower-visiting bats use for detecting suitable food. The color and aroma of bat-pollinated flowers suggest that vision and odor are important. For fruit bats such as Jamaican Fruit Bats or Gray-headed Flying Foxes that visit rich patches of fruit, spatial memory is probably a key to finding fruiting trees, although this begs the question of how the bat found the tree in the first place. Biologists suspect that by living in groups, bats can share information about food. In the United States, by following roost mates that had fed, other Evening Bats located good foraging grounds.

Some animal-eating bats locate their targets by detecting the fluttering wings of a flying insect. Egyptian Slit-faced Bats, among others, listen for the actual sounds of the wings beating and then home in on a vulnerable target. The high duty cycle bats, Horseshoe Bats, Old World Leaf-nosed Bats and Parnell's Mustached Bat use a specialized form of echolocation for detecting fluttering targets. As noted earlier, the ears of these bats are shaped to maximize sensitivity to sounds of certain frequencies. These bats are sensitive to small fluctuations in the frequencies of echoes returning from the fluttering insects. The fluctuations, called Doppler shifts, come from the movement of the insect's wings, alternately toward and away from the bat as the wings go up and down. The auditory systems of bats, like those of humans, perceive frequency or pitch as the numbers of sound waves passing the ear in a given time. This means that wings moving toward the ear generate waves of higher pitch, while those moving away produce lower-pitched ones. The changes in frequency are slight because the insect's wings move a relatively short distance during each wing stroke. The number of Doppler shifts per second is determined by the numbers of times the insect beats its wings. Twenty wing beats per second produces 20 Doppler shifts in this time. In the laboratory, Big Brown Bats and Narrow-winged Pipistrelles, which are low duty cycle bats, also use their echolocation to detect fluttering insects.

Horseshoe Bats, Old World Leaf-nosed Bats and Parnell's Mustached Bat use a combination of specializations to detect Doppler shifts. Involved in this process are the design of the echolocation calls, the structure of the basilar membrane inside the cochlea in the ear and the arrangement of nerves going from the inner ear to the brain. Most of the energy in the echolocation calls is at one frequency and each call tends to last at least 10 milliseconds in Old World Leaf-nosed Bats, 20 ms in Horseshoe Bats and Parnell's Mustached Bats. All of these bats produce a constant stream of calls. In engineering terms, they have a high duty cycle because they are producing calls 80–90% of the time they are echolocating. (By comparison, other echolocating Microchiroptera produce calls 10–20% of the time, a low duty cycle.)

The auditory systems of bats specialized for detecting Doppler shifted echoes are tuned to the frequency that dominates the echolocation call. For Greater Horseshoe Bats in Europe this means about 80 kHz; for the same species in Japan, 70 kHz. The Short-eared Trident Bat has an auditory system tuned to about 212 kHz, while the Rufous Horseshoe Bat's system is tuned to around 70 kHz. Parnell's Mustached Bats are tuned to about 60 kHz. The tuning is partly mechanical because of the design of the basilar membrane inside the cochlea. In addition, the array of nerve cells concentrated in the frequency range in question contributes to the tuning. The specialized tuning of the auditory system gives Horseshoe Bats, Old World Leaf-nosed Bats and Parnell's Mustached Bats the ability to detect flying insects. The bats do this using very small frequency changes generated by the insect's wingbeats. These specializations give these bats a special approach to echolocation.

The high duty cycle bats have an excellent mechanism for locating flying insects and distinguishing them from the background. Why is this approach not more common among echolocating bats? The 69 species of Horseshoe Bats, 56 species of Old World Leaf-nosed Bats, and Parnell's Mustached Bat make a total of 126 species of flutter-detecting bats. Just one New World Bat (Parnell's Mustached Bat) uses this approach to echolocation. Still, as noted above, at least two low duty cycle, aerial-feeding species of bat can use flutter detection. The diversity of approaches to echolocation makes bats particularly fascinating subjects of research.

Flutter detection by echolocation has a major weakness. If the insect target stops beating its wings, it disappears from the bat's sonar screen. It is the wing beats and the varied pitch they produce that reveal the insect's position and course to the bat. Does this flaw explain the incidence of this strategy among echolocating bats? We do not know, but the fossil Horseshoe and Old World Leaf-nosed Bats from the Eocene had cochleas with the mechanical specializations for flutter-detection. Exploiting Doppler shifted echoes was something that bats began to do a long time ago.

As we have seen in Chapter 3, some insectivorous bats use their senses of smell and taste to make the final decision: to eat or not to eat.

WATER AND WASTE

Many of the bats living in arid parts of the world obtain their water from their insect food. For most of the year, bats living in deserts have no direct access to water. The kidneys of desert bats are highly specialized for conserving water, and the bats produce small amounts of very concentrated urine. The same approach to water balance and the same general kidney structure occurs in Mexican Fishing Bats that feed over saltwater and in Common Vampire Bats.

Many other species of bats, perhaps most of them, regularly drink water. These species have less specialized kidneys that produce more dilute urine. Bats with these excretory systems need regular access to water. To drink, bats fly down and dip their mouths into the water of streams, ponds or agricultural tanks. The size of the bat usually determines the size of the water body it needs for drinking. Some small *Myotis* bats can adroitly touch down and drink at pools of water that are less than a meter in diameter. Larger fruit bats are less maneuverable in their flight and need a longer stretch for safe drinking.

Bats eliminate body wastes as carbon dioxide, urine and feces. Carbon dioxide is exhaled and presents little problem to a flying or roosting bat. Bats also can rid themselves of urine and feces by just letting go as they fly along. Roosting upside-down, however, could make the elimination of urine and feces a hygiene problem for bats. By turning upright—upside-down for the bat—they urinate and defecate without soiling themselves.

WHERE BATS ROOST

Secure roosts are essential to bats which are vulnerable to many predators. Small bats are bite-sized for small birds of prey or weasel-sized mammals. At 1.5 kg, even the largest bats would be easy victims for many other birds and mammals. Bats avoid many predators in three ways: by being nocturnal, by flying and by choosing secure places to spend the day. Roosts also protect bats from extreme environmental fluctuations such as overheating in the hot sun, being drenched by rain or freezing in the winter cold.

Bats excel at finding secure roost sites where they are easily overlooked. Therefore, we do not know the roosting places of perhaps half of the world's species of bats. This is not surprising because being unnoticed in their roosting places is key to bats' survival. The need for secure roosts probably has prevailed since before the ancestors of bats took to the air. This is plausible because the arrangement of flight muscles and the supporting bones retains bats' thin profiles through the chest, allowing them to squeeze into narrow openings and find secure roosts.

Day roosts, as the name implies, are places where bats spend the day. Bats may use roosts for different purposes. Many species, such as Indian False Vampire Bats and Short-tailed Fruit Bats, use night roosts, locations providing shelter while the bats are eating or resting between bouts of foraging. Sometimes, for example in Commerson's Leaf-nosed Bats, the night roosts serve a dual function: as perches from which to hunt, and as places to sit and eat or digest prey. Bats living throughout the year in temperate parts of the world use other roosts as places to hibernate.

Bats can be placed in four broad categories according to the kind of day roost they occupy. Some species make their day roosts among the foliage of plants, others in hollows that may be inside trees, within rocks or buildings. Still other species roost in narrow crevices which can be in trees, rocks or buildings. Still others have adopted special roosting habits.

BOX 11
ROOSTING BUTTERFLY BATS

Many bats roost in the foliage of trees, bushes or vines, where they are inconspicuous and difficult to find. When groups of bats roost together and squabble they become conspicuous to alert observers. Audible squeaks and squawks revealed some roosting Butterfly Bats in Mana Pools National Park in Zimbabwe in November 1987. The bats roosted about 7 m above the ground among some leaves of a Natal mahogany tree. After the bats had been detected, they were difficult to see even through binoculars, for they are relatively small (forearms 41–45 mm; 10–15 g) and well camouflaged.

These roosting Butterfly Bats were sitting between the leaves of a Natal mahogany tree, about 7 m above the ground.

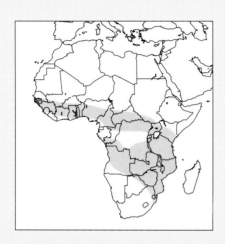

The stippled parts on the map of Africa indicate that Butterfly Bats are widespread in savanna woodland there.

Careful observation with binoculars suggested that five bats roosted together. By catching the roosting Butterfly Bats in a bucket trap (a plastic bucket on the end of a long pole) we found that there were actually 12 bats in the roost, six adult females each with a small, naked baby. Butterfly Bats have beautifully colored fur, which is more obvious when you see them close up.

Elsewhere in Africa, Butterfly Bats have been found roosting among the leaves of trees or shrubs and in the thatch roofs of some buildings. These bats are not known to roost in caves, and, although they have a large range in the savannahs of Africa, they rarely have been found in their roosts. North of the equator they bear their young in June, as do many mammals of the northern hemisphere. Farther south, the young are born in November, like many mammals of the southern hemisphere.

Like the Butterfly Bats, most bats are difficult to find in their roosts, especially when they spend the day among leaves.

Butterfly Bats are beautiful and colorful when seen up close.

Catching the Butterfly Bats in a bucket taped to the end of a long pole revealed that 12 bats occupied the roost, six females, each with a baby.

FOLIAGE

The foliage of plants provides bats with abundant opportunities for roosting. Most species are difficult if not impossible to spot as they sit quietly in their foliage roosts (see also Box 19). This is particularly true of smaller bats, which are inconspicuous at the best of times. Larger bats, such as flying foxes and their relatives, may be very conspicuous as they roost because they are large, and they often flap about and squawk at one another. Their raucous squawking makes the 500 or so Gigantic Flying Foxes in a banyan tree near the town of Piliangulam in southern India (see Box 19) conspicuous from at least 500 m away.

But most bats roosting in foliage are difficult or impossible to see. Even when you know the specific tree in which a bat is roosting, it may be next to impossible to actually see the bat among the leaves. On many occasions we have followed radio-tagged Hoary Bats and Red Bats to their roosts in trees but have yet to actually spot one of the bats in its roost. The same is true for radio-tagged Common Yellow-shouldered Bats, Heller's Broad-nosed Bats, and Wrinkle-faced Bats.

Although foliage can conceal bats from their predators, it does not insulate them from the daily changes in temperature in the environment around them. Depending upon the bat's position and size and the sizes of the leaves, foliage roosts may provide very little or a lot of protection against rain.

The specific foliage sites occupied by roosting bats typically offer shelter from above. Roosting under a thick canopy of leaves and branches shades the bats from the sun, protects them from all but heavy downpours and screens them from the view of birds of prey passing overhead. The specializations for roosting in foliage appear to be mainly behavioral, although, as noted in Boxes

By sitting motionless suspended from a small branch, this female Eastern Red Bat makes a secure roost in the foliage of a sugar maple tree. Like many other species, Red Bats roost in foliage where their small size (12–15 g) makes them inconspicuous.

BOX 12

BAT WINGS

Some of the variety in the wings of bats relates to flight patterns (see page 16), but bats use their wings for other purposes. Wings may be tightly wrapped around the body or used to fan an overheated bat. Some foliage-roosting bats in temperate regions (e.g., Red Bats or Hoary Bats) have thick fur on parts of their wings, while the wings of other bats are naked.

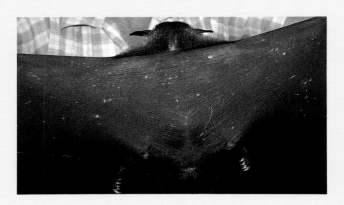

In some species, such as this Moluccan Naked-Backed Bat, the wings meet along the middle of the back.

While the wings of most bats attach to the side of their bodies, in some species they meet in the middle of the back. These "naked-backed bats" occur in the East Indies, New Guinea and Australia, and in the New World tropics. The naked-backed bats of the Old World are species in the pteropodid genus *Dobsonia*. In the New World, there are two species in the genus *Pteronotus*.

Since naked-backed bats include both insect- and fruit-eating species, diet does not account for the distinctive wing attachment. In fact, there is no obvious explanation why most bats have wings attached to the side of their bodies and a few have naked backs.

Their variegated wings make Butterfly Bats distinctive and easy to recognize. It is tempting to think that the variegated wing pattern camouflages these bats when they are roosting. The theory is that these bats

In most bats, like this Parnell's Mustached Bat, the wings join the side of the body.

envelop themselves in their wings and look like dead leaves. Under some conditions, roosting Butterfly Bats do not do this, so the bats' behavior does not support the theory.

In most species of bats the wing membranes are dark in color. In many parts of the tropics, however, some species of Sheath-tailed Bats, Plain-nosed Bats and Free-tailed Bats have wings that are translucent or white. White-winged Bats occur in the tropics, but at any location there are more species with dark wings. White wings may make the bats more conspicuous than dark-winged species and could play some role in communication. Both males and females in white-winged species have the same general appearance.

In the New World tropics, Wrinkle-faced Bats and Visored Bats have wings that are generally dark with two interesting variations. In Wrinkle-faced Bats, the first variation is a clear membrane between the second and third fingers. The second variation is stripes between the third and fourth fingers and just on the body side of the fifth finger. Either variation is more obvious when the wing is backlighted. In some circumstances, roosting Wrinkle-faced Bats do not hold the clear membranes in front of their eyes. However, virtually nothing is known of the roosting behavior of Wrinkle-faced or Visored Bats, so the eye shade function theory remains untested.

A roosting Butterfly Bat with wings partly flexed.

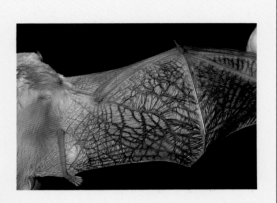

Variegated wings contribute to the beauty of Butterfly Bats. Although the bats are thought to envelop themselves in their wings, this is not always the case.

Rendall's Serotine Bats, like many other tropical insectivorous bats, have white-colored or translucent wings.

Wrinkle-faced Bats from the New World tropics have wings that include some translucent areas, as well as other parts that are striped.

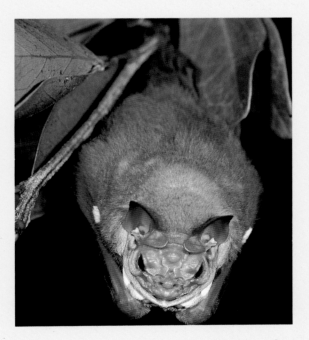

Wrinkle-faced Bats do not necessarily envelop themselves in their wings when roosting.

The entrance to St. Clair Cave in Jamaica is a mass of swirling bats twice each day. First, when the 100,000 or so resident bats leave for their night's foraging, and again when they return at dawn.

11 and 12, different patterns on fur or wings may contribute to making bats less conspicuous. Behavioral specializations include selecting appropriate roost sites and remaining inconspicuous in them.

HOLLOWS

Humans associate bats with caves and many species use the hollows of caves as day roosts. It is safe to say, however, that most species of bats never venture into caves and do not use them as roosts. The darkness of caves offers protection against many predators. Echolocation is essential for a flying animal that roosts in caves, otherwise it would certainly collide with the walls or ceiling as it flew in the total darkness. The echolocation of Egyptian Fruit Bats gives them access to cave roosts. As noted in Chapter 3, echolocation also allows some birds (oilbirds and some species of swiftlets) to nest in caves.

But hollows occur in other settings that bats use as roosts. Many species occupy cavities in trees or those offered by buildings. Indeed, many species of bats that roost in hollows may be found in any of these settings (caves, trees, buildings) or in mines. The hollow is what seems to be important, whether the bat hangs from the ceiling or clings to a wall.

In addition to the protection foliage offers from sun, rain and predators, hollows also insulate bats from changes in outside temperatures. In some settings, hollows protect bats from high air temperatures. For example, in Mana Pools National Park in Zimbabwe, Egyptian Slit-faced Bats pass the day in cavities in the trunks of acacia trees or hollows in military bunkers. When the outside air temperature is 45°C, the air temperature in these roosts is less than 40°C, and the concrete outside surfaces of the bunker are over 60°C!

Just as often, however, hollows protect bats from cooler temperatures, allowing them to save energy they might have spent shivering to keep warm. One example is provided by California Leaf-nosed Bats roosting in disused mine tunnels of southeastern California. In other cases, large numbers of bats clustering together benefit from their collective body heat. One example of this is Gray Bats in the southeastern United States. These bats establish nursery colonies in the ceiling of bell-shaped hollows in caves, and the body heat of the roosting bats raises the temperatures in these roosts well above those of the surrounding cave. In other parts of the world other species of bats use the same approach to roosting, whether it is Schreiber's Bent-winged Bats in Africa or Australia, or Cave Bats in the American west.

Often bats enter hollows through small openings. Whether the entrance is a 5-mm-wide crack along the eaves of a building, or a similar-sized rock crevice, the small size of bats allows them to enter the hollows. The small openings exclude larger predators and give the bats some measure of safety.

High concentrations of ammonia in its roost cave have given the fur of this Sundevall's Leaf-nosed Bat a varied appearance. (Compare with an unbleached bat shown on page 76.) The bat is just shy of 4.5 cm long.

The numbers of bats roosting together in a hollow will depend, in part, on the available space. Huge populations of active bats roosting in hollows can create three kinds of problems. First, in Switzerland, their droppings have filled the tree hollow roosts used by some populations of Daubenton's Bats. Second, the crowd can generate an important problem of air quality which is acute when hundreds of thousands of bats roost in a dead-end passage. Similar problems may arise when fewer bats occupy hollows ventilated by small openings. The accumulation of guano and urine and the chemical breakdown of urine often produces high levels of ammonia. One indication of this is bats with bleached fur, showing the chemical effect of the ammonia. High concentrations of ammonia are fatal for many mammals, including humans. Third, the concentration of bats itself can, in turn, attract predators (see Chapter 8).

An extreme example comes from caves in the southwestern United States that are occupied by over a million roosting Mexican Free-tailed Bats. The levels of ammonia in these caves makes the air uncomfortable and dangerous. Mexican Free-tailed bats survive concentrations of ammonia that will disable and even kill humans, partly by the production of large quantities of mucus. Caves harboring colonies of Common Vampire Bats also are prone to high concentrations of ammonia—more than enough to bring tears to the eyes of a human visitor or clear congested sinuses.

Large numbers of bats roosting in a confined or poorly ventilated area can also reduce oxygen levels. In some kaolin mines in Tanzania, the presence of tens of thousands of Triple Leaf-nosed Bats means that there is not enough oxygen to keep a pressure (Coleman®) lantern burning. It is not clear how bats cope with such low levels of oxygen.

CREVICES

Many bats wedge themselves into small crevices that they use as day roosts. Since crevices typically house fewer bats, they do not pose the same problems of air quality and high ammonia concentrations found in hollows. The population of bats may be limited by the size of the crevice because each bat's body may fill the width of the crevice. Roosting in crevices provides protection against predators. Bats tend to occupy crevices that slope downward so that during rainstorms the crevices remain dry. Deep crevices give bats a selection of temperature conditions, either warmer or colder as they move toward or away from the entrance. The sun beating the rock face around a crevice may, for example, heat up the air and rock at the entrance. On a cold day, bats may congregate near the entrance to exploit the warmth. On a hot day they may retreat farther into the crevice where it is cooler and, presumably, more comfortable. In the Negev Desert, in southern Israel, Hemprich's Long-eared Bats roosting in crevices during the heat of the summer were hotter than the temperature of the surrounding air.

In Africa and in South America, three species of Free-tailed Bats roost in the crevice spaces under stones. Compared to Free-tailed Bats that roost in more open settings, Roberts' Flat-headed Bats, Peters' Flat-headed Bats and South American Flat-headed Bats have very flattened skulls. Moreover, wart-like protrusions on the forearms of Peters' Flat-headed Bats and South American Flat-headed Bats protect the bats' skin from abrasion where it contacts the rocks.

This bridge over the Letaba River in South Africa's Kruger National Park contains expansion crevices that are the roosting sites of thousands of Little Free-tailed Bats and Angola Free-tailed Bats. Visitors who stop mid-bridge are usually aware of the aroma of the bats, particularly on hot days. Several species of birds of prey also know about these bats, often ambushing them as they leave.

Special Roosting Habits

Many environments appear to offer bats almost unlimited roosting opportunities. For species that roost in foliage, the presence of trees and bushes with leaves appears to be the important factor, although some foliage-roosting species, such as Butterfly Bats, may roost in the thatched roofs of buildings. For species roosting in hollows or crevices, the natural environments offer many appropriate places in and around trees and rocks. Moreover, throughout most of the world, human activities have provided buildings, tunnels and bridges that offer many crevices and hollows that can be and are used by bats.

In spite of what appears to be a plethora of roosting opportunities, some bats have more specialized habits. These include occupation of the hollows in bamboo stems, spaces in the unfurled leaves of some plants, and tents made by bats from leaves.

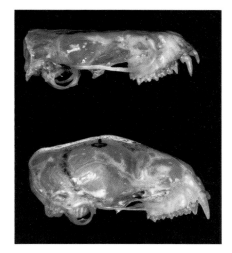

Compared to Pallas' Mastiff Bat that roosts in hollows in trees or buildings, Peters' Flat-headed Bats have very flattened skulls. Both species are Free-tailed Bats, the first from South and Central America, the second from Africa.

Bamboo Stems

In Southeast Asia, Greater Bamboo Bats and Lesser Bamboo Bats roost in the hollows between the nodes in the stems of bamboo. The bats enter the hollows through holes bored by bruchid beetles. These tiny bats have flattened skulls, similar in general appearance to those of the Free-tailed Bats that roost under stones.

Unfurled Leaves

The new leaves of plants such as bananas are long and tubular and open by unrolling. As they unroll, the tube-like hollows offer shelters that are used by several species of bats. These roosts, however, are limited in time. The bats cannot occupy the hollows until there is an opening at the tip, but when the leaf has opened too much, it no longer provides any shelter. In some species of plants, the leaves open so rapidly that the bats can use them as roosts for just one day. In Africa, Rufous Hairy Bats and Banana Bats sometimes roost in unfurled banana leaves. Five to seven Rufous Hairy Bats occupy one unfurled leaf. Such groups usually include a single adult male with a group of females and young.

In South and Central America, two species of New World Disk-winged Bats roost only in unfurled leaves (see also page 183). These bats have adhesive disks on their wrists and ankles, and they use suction to gain traction on the slippery leaf surfaces. Captive Spix's New World Disk-winged Bats often lick their disks, apparently to improve suction on the smooth leaves. Every child knows that licking makes suction-tipped arrows stick much better, especially to smooth surfaces like glass. Spix's New World Disk-winged Bats frequently licked their adhesive disks when moving about on a sheet of glass provided by an inquisitive biologist (see page 183). In Madagascar, Old World Disk-winged Bats have similar adhesive disks on their wrists and ankles, but nothing is known of the roosting habits of these bats. In southeast Asia, some Plain-nosed Bats have structures on their wrists that resemble adhesive disks. Again, nothing is known of their roosting behavior.

Tent-making Bats

At least 17 species of bats construct tents to use as day roosts: 15 species of New World Leaf-nosed Bats, one Old World Fruit Bat (Short-faced Fruit Bat), and

A Honduran Ghost Bat, a tent-making species from the New World.

one plain-nosed bat (a House Bat). The tents are made from the leaves or other parts of several species of plants. Bat tents fold along the lines where bats have bitten the leaves. Palm leaves, which consist of many leaflets, are usually bitten in a wedge-shaped pattern near the tip. Longer, broader leaves are bitten along either side of the main stem. In either case the bats roost beneath the folded part of the leaf.

The tent roosts protect their occupants from direct sunlight, which would cause the bats to overheat, and rain which could cool them too much. Like

Lesser Yellow House Bats roost in hollows in mopane trees in many parts of southern Africa. Although the bats consistently roost in mopane trees, they switch roosts, rarely using the same hollow two nights in a row.

other foliage roosts, however, the tents offer little insulation from local temperature conditions. Tents made in leaves on the end of long stems tend to vibrate easily, giving warning of a predator trying to scale the stem and attack the bats in the tent. However, as we shall see later (Chapter 8), tents do not make their occupants immune to predation.

There are many more questions than answers about tent-making bats. In spite of concerted efforts by several American researchers, there are few published records of bats making tents. In southern India a male Short-faced Fruit Bat was observed making a tent in a vine. In this operation the bat severed up to 300 small to medium-sized stems by biting. Does the same behavior occur in tent-making New World Leaf-nosed Bats? This remains one of the more interesting questions about bat behavior. For more about tents, see page 181.

These Wahlberg's Epauletted Fruit Bats roosted suspended from the ceiling of a small shelter cave. They are thought to normally roost in the foliage of trees, but radio tracking led to the discovery of this roost, about 7 km from the fig trees where the bats fed.

VARIATIONS IN ROOSTING BEHAVIOR

How consistent are bats in their selection of roosts? This is a question that biologists have only begun to answer, whether they consider the habits of a species or the habits of individuals. Although it is convenient to distinguish between species that roost in foliage and those roosting in hollows or in crevices, our interpretation may not reflect the behavior of the bats.

Like other Epauletted Fruit Bats, Wahlberg's Epauletted Fruit Bats are thought to roost in the foliage of trees and shrubs, under thatched roofs, or beneath a vine-covered arbor. In Kruger National Park in South Africa, radio tracking revealed, however, that some Wahlberg's Epauletted Fruit Bats roosted in a shelter cave. Suspended by their toes from the rough granite sur-

These female Big Brown Bats are roosting in the attic of an old farmhouse near Ottawa, Canada. The photograph was taken at the end of the first week of June, just before these females each had twins.

face, the bats were separated from one another by the same distances observed in traditional foliage roosts. The shelter cave was about 7 km from the fig trees they visited for feeding. Many other Wahlberg's Epauletted Fruit Bats, some also carrying radio transmitters, roosted in large trees about 2 km from the preferred fig trees.

Gray-headed Flying Foxes in Australia and Straw-colored Fruit Bats in Africa show similar variations in their selection of roosts. Both species form conspicuous "camps," typically in the crowns and upper branches of large trees. Near the town of Chillagoe in north Queensland, Australia, one colony of Gray-headed Flying Foxes roosts in the open part of a limestone tower. At several places in west Africa, Straw-colored Fruit Bats also occupy cliff-like roosts in lieu of trees.

In Canada, Big Brown Bats make their summer day roosts in the attics or eaves of buildings in southeastern Ontario, while in southern British Columbia, the same species roosts in hollow ponderosa pine trees. In Puerto Rico, I have seen nursery colonies of Big Brown Bats in caves. In peopled areas of North America, female Little Brown Bats typically make their nursery colonies in the attics of buildings, but elsewhere they may occupy hollow trees.

These records demonstrate the folly of associating any species of bats with a particular kind of roost. Quite simply, many species of bats quickly identify and exploit good roosting opportunities. As we shall see in Chapter 12, this behavior may put them in conflict with humans.

What do the records suggest for individual bats? Are the bats living in a given hollow tree or attic today the same ones that were there yesterday? Radio tracking has shown that species such as Lesser Yellow House Bats often roost in the chambered hollows of mopane trees in southern Africa. Each bat, however, has a repertoire of roosts and moves between them from day to day in random fashion. In contrast, Hildebrandt's Horseshoe Bats and Midas' Free-tailed Bats tend to return to the same hollow baobab roost day after day. In eastern North America, individual Big Brown Bats tenaciously return to the same building day after day and year after year. In parts of western North America these bats move unpredictably between a selection of hollow tree roosts.

The question about an individual bat's roost fidelity may require answers specific to the species and the setting. When Large Slit-faced Bats in Zimbabwe are disturbed in one roost, they will temporarily abandon it and return a few days later. Different patterns of roosting behavior can affect the plans for conservation of bats.

BATS AND TEMPERATURE REGULATION

Mammals are said to be warm-blooded, able to burn energy to keep themselves warm even when it is very cold. Fur, hair and body fat often are the insulation that makes it possible for mammals to be warm-blooded, or, technically, endothermic. Birds also are endothermic, while reptiles, amphibians and fish are said to be cold-blooded (ectothermic). Most bats are warm-blooded but the picture is varied.

Quite simply, bats are either too hot or too cold. A flying bat produces a great deal of heat, because of the work done by its flight muscles. The heart of a flying Little Brown Bat beats about 1,300 times a minute, indicating the energy cost of flight. Flying bats use their wings as radiators to shed the heat this work generates. Hot blood leaves the body and enters the wings in small arteries which connect directly to small veins. Such connections are rare in mammals, where arteries and veins are usually separated by capillary beds. In bats, the connections are one way to keep cool while flying.

Roosting bats usually face a different problem, namely a shortage of heat. By their selection of roosts, bats strive to ensure that the temperatures where they spend the day are within a few degrees of their preferred body temperatures, say between 25°C and 35°C. Roosting in a warm (or cool) place relative to the environment means that bats do not have to spend energy to stay cool (or warm). When the air temperature drops, most bats shiver to keep warm, using muscle contractions to generate heat. Shivering uses energy, and if the temperature is too cold for too long, the bats use up all their energy and perish; they run out of fuel.

Bats that roost in the open exposed to direct sunlight sometimes have a problem of overheating. For example, Gigantic Flying Foxes roosting in the sun in the topmost branches of a tree use two strategies to keep cool. They salivate, drooling on their chests and wings, and use their wings like fans, flapping to create a cooling breeze. In this situation the bats burn energy to keep cool, and, like the bats working to stay warm, they can only do this for a short time. An overheated Gigantic Flying Fox uses both body water (saliva) and energy to cool down. This bat is apt to exhaust its water supply if forced to actively cool itself for a long time.

Humans use the same strategies to keep their body temperatures constant. We shiver to keep warm; we perspire and fan ourselves to keep cool. The shivering and fanning cost energy, and perspiring uses water. In either case the behavior keeps our core body temperature within a narrow range. Humans face a comparable problem in controlling building temperatures. We use energy to keep buildings at comfortable temperatures. In winter, this means heat-

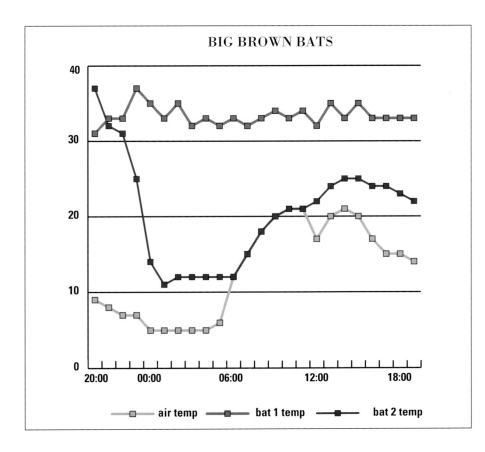

This graph compares the body temperatures of two pregnant Big Brown Bats with the air temperature over a 12-hour period on May 5, 1986. One bat remained active, the other entered torpor. The whole colony was situated just outside Ottawa, Canada. Modified from Audet and Fenton (1988).

Two Big Brown Bats hibernating in an old mine in southern Ontario.

ing, whether by fireplace, furnace or stove. In summer it means cooling by air conditioners or fans. Keeping a constant body temperature is exceptionally expensive for small animals (like bats) with small energy reserves.

Bats that roost under foliage may suffer in two ways. First they are shaded from the heat of the sun. Second, unlike bats roosting in hollows, they do not enjoy any insulation from changes in the air temperature. The growth rates of young Hoary Bats underscored the dilemma faced by bats that roost in foliage. In southern Manitoba, young Hoary Bats were not weaned until nearly 7 weeks of age. Compare this to Little Brown Bats and Big Brown Bats that roost in hollows or crevices and are weaned by 3–6 weeks of age. During cold weather, however, lactating Hoary Bats enter torpor (see below) conserving their own energy. The cost of this savings appears to be growth of the young.

The wings of bats mean that they have a huge surface area for their weight and volume. This makes it very easy for them to lose heat. By tightly folding its wings, a roosting bat can reduce its surface area, but it still loses heat rapidly, particularly when its surroundings are much cooler than its body. Bats use roosts to minimize this problem (as noted above). Some bats, species of Horseshoe Bats and Plain-nosed Bats, as well as some species of Free-tailed Bats, and Pallid Bats, have another strategy for cutting their heating costs. They have a variable thermostat so that their body temperature drops to the prevailing air

These Eastern Small-footed Bats were hibernating in an abandoned mine near Ottawa, Ontario. When the photograph was taken, the bats' body temperatures were 1°C, the same as the air and the rock.

temperature when it is cool. This is the equivalent of our turning down the thermostat to save energy.

The temperature regulation behavior of some female Big Brown Bats reflects some of the costs and benefits of this strategy. On the accompanying chart, three temperature records track the changes in air temperature and the body temperatures of two bats over one day in early May 1986. The bats roosted together in the attic of an old farmhouse near Ottawa, Canada. The body temperature of one bat quickly dropped to the air temperature when it returned from foraging, and it stayed cool until the roost heated up the next day. This bat had turned down its thermostat and spent no energy trying to keep warm. The second bat kept its body temperature quite high over the same period, spending energy to keep warm.

Why should the two bats differ in their energy expenditures? Both bats were pregnant. These results indicate that Big Brown Bats actively adopt different strategies of temperature regulation. This means that a cool Big Brown Bat in summer is not the victim of a primitive temperature regulation system. Rather the bat has opted for an energy-conserving strategy.

A Plain-nosed Bat or a Horseshoe Bat with a lower body temperature is said to be in a state of torpor, or deep sleep. During the warm season Horseshoe Bats and Plain-nosed Bats use torpor on a day-to-day basis to minimize the costs of periods of inclement weather. The variable thermostat strategy, also known as heterothermy, appears in winter as hibernation.

This hibernating Little Brown Bat is completely covered with large water droplets, the result of condensation and the high humidity in the underground sites where the bats pass the winter.

HIBERNATION

As noted in Chapter 4, some species of Horseshoe Bats and Plain-nosed Bats migrate long or short distances to sites where they hibernate through the winter. Hibernation in bats is a period of prolonged torpor when the body temperature stays very close to the temperature of the bat's roost. In caves and mines where bats hibernate along the St. Lawrence River in eastern North America, the midwinter temperatures usually vary between 1°C and 5°C. In these sites, Little Brown Bats choose places with this temperature range and high humidity. Big Brown Bats and Small-footed Bats may hibernate at drier sites where temperatures drop below freezing. Farther south in North America, Little Brown Bats hibernate at sites in caves and mines where the temperatures range from 5°C to 10°C, reflecting the generally warmer climate.

Hibernating bats must conserve energy. The bats enter hibernation carrying about 25% of their body weight as fat. The fat represents their energy reserves for the winter. Unlike hibernating ground squirrels or other rodents, bats do not cache winter snacks in their hibernation sites and must make it through the winter on a single tank of fuel.

Conserving energy means roosting in a place where the air is cold but not too cold. If a Little Brown Bat, for example, were to try to hibernate in the walls of a building, the temperatures on the warm side of the insulation would be so high that the bat would quickly exhaust its supply of fat. Were it to roost on the cold side of the insulation, it would quickly burn its fat shivering to keep its body from freezing. Many caves and mines provide excellent hibernation sites, because below the frost line, the temperatures are stable and just above freezing.

Other hibernating animals periodically wake up, stretch, urinate and defecate, groom themselves and go back to sleep. Waking up is the most expensive

Other hibernating Little Brown Bats, like this one, have smaller water droplets in their fur.

part of hibernation because the animal burns fuel to raise its body temperature from just above freezing to about 35°C. For a hibernating ground squirrel this is not a major problem because the animal has a cache of food in its burrow. Having aroused, the ground squirrel eats enough food to cover its costs of waking up. Hibernating bats do not eat, so they need not wake up to defecate. But since they have no caches of food, they must pay for the cost of arousal from their supply of fat. All of this means that hibernating bats survive by minimizing the number of times they arouse during the winter.

High levels of humidity also are important for hibernating bats. Little Brown Bats lose water by breathing, even when the humidity is high in the caves and mines where they overwinter. To minimize water loss, Little Brown Bats hibernate in sites where the air is nearly saturated with water. Now it is clear that clustering by hibernating Little Brown Bats reduces the rates at which individuals in the cluster lose water.

Where winters are less severe, some species of bats hibernate in hollow trees. There they are exposed to changes in air temperature. One cost of these sites is the energy burned to stay above freezing during cold snaps. A benefit is being able to wake up and hunt insects on a winter evening when it warms up enough for insects to be flying. Usually this happens at temperatures above 10°C.

Not all species of bats have the same hibernation site requirements. Big Brown Bats, for example, will hibernate in buildings and tolerate temperatures below freezing at sites that are dry. Little Brown Bats must have stable, above-freezing temperatures and high levels of humidity.

A variable thermostat (heterothermy) allows Plain-nosed Bats and Horseshoe Bats to thrive in cooler areas, well away from the equator and sometimes north of the Arctic Circle (see Box 18). Hibernation is one form of heterothermy, but energy-saving torpor during the day is another. But heterothermy is not a characteristic of all bats. It appears to be restricted to the four families mentioned above (Plain-nosed Bats, Horseshoe Bats, Pallid Bats, and some species of Free-tailed Bats).

AESTIVATION

In some tropical areas, particularly those with prolonged hot, dry seasons, bats are faced with the same shortage of insects brought on by winter in colder places. Some Mouse-tailed bats, Sheath-tailed Bats and Free-tailed Bats put on large deposits of fat when the conditions are favorable. These bats are thought to spend the hot, dry periods resting in their roosts. The process is called aestivation and it differs from hibernation because the bats' body temperatures do not fall.

By selecting roosts that insulate them from extremes of temperature, aestivating bats can increase their chances of surviving long, hot, dry periods. As we shall see, however, the survival of both aestivating and hibernating bats is jeopardized when these animals are disturbed. Disturbances cause them to increase their fuel consumption, minimizing their chances of survival (Chapter 12).

SOCIAL ORGANIZATION, FAMILY LIFE AND COMMUNICATION

Dusk at the entrance to one of the large Mexican Free-tailed Bat caves in the American southwest is an impressive sight as millions of these bats emerge to begin their night's hunting. Similar scenes, in many cases with fewer bats, are repeated at other sites around the world, making it easy to think of bats as the most social of mammals.

But are they? It is true that some caves in Texas harbor more than 5,000,000 Mexican Free-tailed Bats, or that St. Clair Cave in Jamaica probably shelters more than 100,000 bats. But, like the people at a sporting event, or the group emerging from a high-rise apartment building, a crowd of animals does not necessarily reflect a society or even a social unit. More often, a large crowd of animals is an aggregation related to some localized resource. Many bats use caves as roosts, but this does not mean that all of the bats in a cave "know" one another.

ROOST ASSOCIATIONS AMONG BATS

The most basic social unit among bats and other mammals is the group comprising a mother and her dependent young. In Red Bats this unit roosts among the foliage of trees or vines, and it may consist of the adult female and two,

A harem of female Greater Spear-nosed Bats in a hole in a cave ceiling in Trinidad. Each of the bats, including the harem male (bottom center), is wearing a distinctive combination of colored bands. Photograph by Gary F. McCracken.

The harem male shown close up. Photograph by Gary F. McCracken.

three, or even four babies. Most female bats, however, have just one baby at a time, so the basic social unit may be two animals. Female bats frequently form nursery colonies—that is, aggregations of females and their babies. Some of the huge Mexican Free-tailed Bat colonies are examples. The nature of the social interactions between the females in most bat nurseries remains a matter of speculation.

In temperate species and in some tropical ones, adult males are not part of the nursery colonies. In India, for example, some male Schneider's Roundleaf Bats roost in the entrances to caves that also house females and their young. In North America, female Little Brown Bats establish nursery colonies of anywhere from 50 to 5,000 individuals, but the summer whereabouts of the adult males remain largely unknown.

In other tropical species, the kinds of aggregations reflect differences in reproductive status. In Trinidad, some individual male Greater Spear-nosed Bats roost with groups of females and their dependent young. Genetic analyses have revealed that most of the young born to the females in these groups are sired by that one male. This is a typical harem. The caves housing these harems are also the roosts of immature males and females, and sexually mature males who have not established themselves as harem males. Harems are also known from bats roosting in tents, hollow trees, on the trunks of trees or in foliage.

Hibernating bats sometimes cluster together in large numbers, although there is considerable variation in the patterns within and between species. Some individual Little Brown Bats or Big Brown Bats, for example, hibernate alone, not in physical contact with other bats. Others of these species form clus-

ters that may number tens of individuals (Big Brown Bats) or hundreds or thousands (Little Brown Bats). Greater Horseshoe Bats and other species of Horseshoe Bats hibernate out of contact with other individuals. Populations of hibernating bats may include males and females, or a preponderance of one gender or the other. The social significance, if any, of hibernating assemblages of bats remains to be determined.

As we shall see, there are groups of bats with long-term relationships between individuals. These associations certainly deserve the term "society." One example is provided by the female Greater Spear-nosed Bats in a harem, the other by Common Vampire Bats (see Chapter 10).

REPRODUCTION

Reproduction is a main organizing factor in the social lives of bats. In most species, one litter is born each year, and the number of young per litter is usually one or two. Red Bats, as noted above, with three or even four young in a litter, are exceptional among bats. Some New World Leaf-nosed Bats bear young twice a year, as do some Old World Fruit Bats living in lush habitats. Female Wroughton's Pipistrelles, 4-g bats from India, bear twins, and some of the females may breed three times each year. Little Free-tailed Bats in Africa are also more prolific than most other bats, perhaps having up to five litters per year.

For most species of bats, there is little information about age at sexual maturity. Female Wroughton's Pipistrelles may be exceptional, reaching sexual maturity at five months. At the other extreme, male Hammerhead Bats are sexually mature at 18 months, females at six months. The local climate and conditions may affect the timing of maturity, as female Little Brown Bats can bear their first young when they are just a year old in the southern parts of their range, and at two years old farther north.

Climate also affects the reproductive patterns of bats in other ways. In most species, fertilization of the egg or eggs follows mating; the females become pregnant and bear their young. But there are some noteworthy exceptions. California Leaf-nosed Bats and many Plain-nosed and Horseshoe Bats have a long delay between mating and birth of the young. In California Leaf-nosed Bats, the egg is fertilized at mating but the initial development of the fetus is very slow. The process is called "delayed development" and it is one way to separate the mating season and the birthing season.

In many Plain-nosed and Horseshoe Bats the long delay between mating and birth is achieved by delaying fertilization. In these species, the female bats store sperm in their uteri for periods ranging from five days (Bamboo Bats) to 190 days (Little Brown Bats or Noctules). This pattern of sperm storage prevails among species of bats living in the temperate zones and also occurs in some tropical vespertilionids and rhinolophids. The strategy seems well suited to species that hibernate, for the period of storage coincides with hibernation.

Mating in the late summer or early autumn means that sexual activity takes place when the bats are in prime condition. Adult Little Brown Bats, for example, weigh 10–12 g in late August and early September, and on evenings when the weather is good, there are still many insects flying about. If the bats postponed mating until the spring, their energy supplies would be at a low ebb. When Little Brown Bats leave hibernation, they weigh 6.5–7.0 g. Furthermore, the weather in early spring is less likely to provide a ready supply of flying insects for food.

By mating in the late summer and early fall, and storing sperm through the winter, each female bat ensures that if something should happen to all of the males over the winter, she can still have an offspring in the next season. Little Brown Bats are a convenient North American example of this behavior, but the same pattern persists for all temperate Plain-nosed and Horseshoe Bats studied to date. Are females and males subject to different rates of mortality? The question remains unanswered, but many females disappear between summer and winter roosts, suggesting that some use hibernation sites that differ from those occupied by males.

THE MATING GAME

During mating, male bats mount females from the rear, typically using wings and thumbs to restrain the females. At this time the male may also clutch the female by the scruff of her neck. In Little Brown Bats, mating may last anywhere from 5 to 20 minutes, and among other bats there is similar variation. The penises of male bats are often very long, particularly in species with well-developed interfemoral membranes. For mating to succeed, the penis must be long enough to reach past the interfemoral membrane to the vagina.

The interests and strategies of male and female bats are not necessarily the same because of the requirements of pregnancy and milk production. This situation is part of the reality of being a mammal. It is not surprising to learn that sperm is the male bats' main contribution to reproduction. Females invest much more, carrying the developing embryo and then feeding the baby milk which, as noted on page 63, is energetically expensive to produce. This difference in investment in reproduction means that while a female can bear only one litter at a time, by mating with many females a male can achieve a much higher production of young.

Biologists use the nature of the relationships between male and female to classify mating systems. Three basic types of mating systems occur in bats. The first involves one male and many females and is called polygyny. In this system, the group of females is called a harem. When males and females mate with more than one partner and there is no bond between mating pairs, the sit-

This pair of Little Brown Bats is mating in an abandoned mine in southeastern Ontario. The male has mounted the female from the rear and holds her with his forearms and wrists while biting the back of her neck. This mating occurred in September, after both male and female had mated with other partners. The female will store sperm in her uterus until the following spring.

uation is called promiscuous. There is circumstantial evidence that in some species of bats, long-term relationships are maintained between individual males and females; hence, a monogamous system. To date, the support for this view comes largely from situations in which pairs of bats roost or fly together.

In polygynous bats such as Greater White-lined Bats from the New World tropics, groups of females roost in areas protected by individual males. These bats often roost between the buttresses on tree trunks. The males use aerial displays, scent marking and vocalizations to mark their territories. The females within a harem exert some influence over its composition as some individuals are permitted to join and others are driven off. A male Lesser White-lined Bat also defends the areas where the females of his harem go to feed. In both species, however, females move among harems, spending time with first one male, and then with another.

Harems are the basic reproductive unit in Short-tailed Fruit Bats. Here too, females move among harems. This contrasts sharply with the situation in Greater Spear-nosed Bats, where the females in a harem are a cohesive social unit that may last for years. For these four species, observations of bats with individual tags have revealed the details about behavior and movement.

Since harem males can realize a high reproductive output, it is not surprising that males compete intensively for possession of harems. In Short-

Some male Schneider's Roundleaf Bats establish territories at the entrances to caves and other roosts. These bats are common in many parts of India.

tailed Fruit Bats, rival males engage in boxing matches, striking at other males with their wrists and thumbs. Similar interactions between males have been observed in camps of Gray-headed Flying Foxes and Gigantic Flying Foxes during the mating season. There, males compete for the best roosting sites which attract the most females. Males mate with the females in the area they control.

In Commerson's Leaf-nosed Bats and Greater Spear-nosed Bats, the same caves that house the harems also harbor huge numbers of bachelor males. These individuals, although sexually mature, have not established themselves as harem males. In Greater Spear-nosed Bats, harem ownership is decided by interactions between males. The females remain together as a social unit regardless of which male lives with them.

The large investment that females make in their young should encourage them to mate with the "best" available male. The behavior of many harem-forming bats seems to bear out this prediction, although the movement of females among harems raises interesting questions about just how females select their mates. It remains to be seen whether females pick males for themselves or for the resources they control.

Promiscuous mating systems are logical extensions of situations in which males contribute only sperm to reproduction. At night sexually mature male Hammerhead Bats form long lines and advertise their availability and vigor by continuous honking calls. Female Hammerhead Bats fly up and down the lines of males, selecting one, with whom they mate. The association between male and female lasts as long as the coupling and we presume that the females make their decisions based on their view of male quality. The females tend to agree about which male is best, for in the populations studied to date, a small number of males does virtually all of the mating.

The mating system of Hammerhead Bats is called a "lek." Four features describe leks. The first is strong differences in appearance between males and females, technically known as sexual dimorphism. The second is the lack of male involvement in rearing young. The third is that the male is the only resource at the site where he is displaying. Lack of interaction between individual males and females beyond copulation is the fourth feature. In India, male Schneider's Old World Leaf-nosed Bats defend territories at the entrances of caves, but the females do not roost there. Also in India, Wroughton's Pipistrelle males roost separately from females, tenaciously returning to their preferred sites. The details of these bats' mating systems are not known, but the males' behavior suggests a lek.

Sperm storage complicates the mating systems of Plain-nosed and Horseshoe bats. During the August mating season, male and female Little Brown Bats copulate repeatedly with different partners. Some mating continues into the winter, when males will try to mate with torpid bats. As often as not, they end up on the backs of other males. Mating in Little Brown Bats is truly promiscuous because of the numbers of partners involved. The multiple matings and matings with torpid bats mean that neither males nor females can protect any time they spent in choosing the "right mate." Homosexual matings in Little Brown Bats appear to be cases of mistaken identity.

In other Plain-nosed and Horseshoe Bats the reproductive tracts of the females are blocked after mating. The blocks or plugs may be formed from coagulated seminal fluid or by-products of the female's vagina or cervix. Some researchers have proposed that in bats, vaginal plugs are "chastity belts"

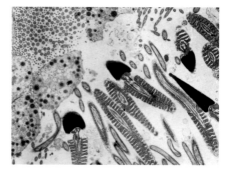

This transmission electron micrograph shows sperm stored in the uterus of a Little Brown Bat. Stored sperm may live here from September until April, when the female ovulates, the sperm activates and fertilization takes place. The scale is one micormeter long. Taken from a paper published by P. A. Racey and colleagues (1987).

preventing mating by other males. Others presume that the plugs help to keep sperm inside the female. There is little experimental support for this proposal.

Our current knowledge about the mating systems of bats is just the tip of the iceberg. Recent breakthroughs in molecular genetics, specifically in the area of DNA fingerprinting, should permit future researchers to prove unequivocally which males sire which offspring. Some DNA analyses have revealed that the young born in nursery colonies of Little Brown Bats at Chautauqua, New York, are more closely related to one another than are the mothers. These findings suggest that some males do more successful matings than others—a reality not suggested by the behavioral studies. Other genetic analyses have demonstrated that by moving between harems, females of other species mix up the genetic contributions of males, so males may have in their harems young that are not their own.

THE YOUNG

Baby bats are enormous at birth. Newborn Little Brown Bats weigh 25–30% of their mother's weight. A pair of newborn Wroughton's Pipistrelle twins weigh about 25% of their mother. Producing such large babies makes the birth process difficult. In female bats the ligaments that hold together the two halves of the pelvic girdle, including the hip bones, show a remarkable capacity to relax, making possible the birth of large young.

This young Little Brown Bat is about eight days old. Note that compared to the young on page 62, this baby has fur. Its feet and thumbs are large and conspicuous, like those on page 62. Although its forearms are longer than the other's, they are still at least 10 mm shorter than those of an adult.

A portrait of a young Little Brown Bat shows the enlarged glands on either side of the muzzle. These glands may give the youngster a distinctive scent and make it easier for its mother to recognize it.

Baby bats are born bottom-first, which is known as a breech presentation in humans. This arrangement minimizes the chances of the baby getting its wings tangled in the birth canal. Although newborn baby bats are large, their wings are tiny compared to those of an adult. The thumbs and hind feet, however, are virtually adult-sized at birth so that the newborn can cling to its mother or to a roost.

Young bats grow very quickly. Little Brown Bats can fly about 18 days after birth and during this time their wing bones have reached virtually adult size. However, their first flights are clumsy and many die during the season when young bats are first trying their wings (see page 109). By age three weeks, Little Brown Bats have shed their milk teeth and have added insects to their diets. For Big Brown Bats, the time from birth to first flight is closer to four weeks. Young Common Vampire Bats continue to nurse until they are six to nine months old, representing the longest period of dependency known for bats.

In Little Brown Bats, there is little evidence that mothers provide any assistance to their young as they learn to fly. In Yellow-winged Bats, however, young spend considerable time hanging from their mothers' shoulders suspended by their hind feet. In this position they vigorously flap their wings and in this way, female Yellow-winged Bats appear to help their young learn how to fly.

Mother bats are devoted to their young. One indication of this is a mother bat's uncanny ability to find and recognize her own baby. The precision of this relationship ensures that female bats do not give milk to other bats' babies. The challenge differs between species. Red and Hoary Bats, and other species that roost alone, need only remember where they left their babies. Since the females roost alone with their young there is little chance of mistaken identity.

Bats that form nursery colonies take different approaches to the business of caring for their young. Some species, such as Egyptian Slit-faced Bats, Indian False Vampire Bats or Schneider's Roundleaf Bat, remove their young from the day roost and deposit them somewhere else while they are foraging. In these species, mothers must remember just where the baby was left. Other species, such as Little Brown Bats, Big Brown Bats, Jamaican Fruit Bats, or Mouse-eared Bats, leave their young behind in the day roost when they are hunting. In this situation, the babies left in the nursery tend to cluster together, so a mother must find her own baby in a crowd of others. The size of the crowd depends upon the size of the colony. As we shall see, a variety of communication signals facilitates reunions between mothers and young.

The mother bats that face the biggest problem in retrieving their young are those that deposit their babies in crèches, or day nurseries. We know most about Mexican Free-tailed Bats, but some Bent-winged Bats and flying foxes show similar behavior. After birth, female Mexican Free-tailed Bats leave their babies in crèches and visit them once or twice a day for nursing. In big cave colonies these crèches are huge, with up to 3,000 babies per square meter of ceiling. Each crèche may contain hundreds of thousands of baby Mexican Free-tailed Bats.

This situation led some researchers to suggest that female Mexican Free-tailed Bats behaved like a milk herd. Each female landed on the crèche and gave milk to the first baby that approached her. This explanation seemed attractive because of the sheer magnitude of the task facing a female looking for her young. When the cost of milk production is taken into account, however, a female bat should feed only her own baby. Genetic studies show that

This close-up view of the crêche shows an adult female Mexican Free-tailed Bat surrounded by a sea of pink babies. Photograph by Gary F. McCracken.

while nursing, mother Mexican Free-tailed Bats care for young that could be their own 85% of the time.

In Pallid Bats and some other species, a few adults may remain at the nursery colony with the young while the other adults go out to forage. This behavior has been compared to "baby sitting." The full details remain unknown and it is not clear just what action baby-sitters take to protect the young left in their charge.

Whatever the bats, Mexican Free-tailed Bats or Little Brown Bats, the babies view milk differently than do the mothers. Many studies have shown

Shown here is part of a huge crêche of baby Mexican Free-tailed Bats. There is one adult bat among the pink-colored babies. Photograph by Gary F. McCracken.

that baby bats will try to take milk from any female that comes their way. Female bats will repulse strange young that try to take milk, sometimes quite violently.

COMMUNICATION

Bats use different channels for communication, but the main ones are sound and smell. In some species, high contrast patterns on fur or white wings (see pages 55 and 56) probably provide valuable visual information. These three channels, sight, sound and smell, are not mutually exclusive; each may deliver the same message in a slightly different way.

The honking of a line of male Hammerhead Bats as they display to females is conspicuous, and, to us, monotonous. Other related species of Old World Fruit Bats use more bell-like calls which, while not so harsh, seem just as monotonous to the human observer. Other bat communication vocalizations are ultrasonic and beyond our range of perception unless we are using a bat detector (Box 8) to listen in on the action.

Pallid Bats use vocalizations known as directive calls in several settings. These bats depend upon these calls to bring the group together as they select a roost site just before dawn. The same calls are also used in communication between mothers and young.

In Plain-nosed Bats, mothers and babies use special calls to communicate with one another. The babies produce tonal isolation calls which last about 20 ms, gradually ascending in pitch from about 10 to 20 kHz. As the bats get older, the pitch of their isolation calls increases. The females, for their part, produce double note calls. Very young Little Brown Bats call almost continuously when their mothers leave them in the day roost. Older young do not call until they hear their mother return. The young respond to the double note calls and perhaps to their mothers' echolocation calls.

In Mexican Free-tailed Bats a similar array of calls mediate interactions between mother and young. Watching reunions at a crèche in a crowded cave shows that the returning female uses her general memory to pick the area where she left her baby. She then lands, calling to her baby, and the two move toward one another, the female fending off the attempts of other young to steal milk. Before she gives her baby milk, she smells it carefully, evidently using its odor to confirm her impression from memory and calls. Experiments in the laboratory with washed and unwashed babies confirm that odor is important in final recognition.

The distinctive odor of a young Mexican Free-tailed Bat could come from several sources. It could be produced by the young or come from the mother's saliva as she licks and grooms her baby. It also might originate in the mother's milk. In some other bats, such as Evening Bats from North America, mothers mark their babies with exudate from specialized scent glands on either sides of their muzzles (pararhinal glands; see page 100). Young Little Brown Bats have prominent pararhinal glands, but their significance has not been studied.

Glands play an important role in communication between bats. Males in many species of Free-tailed Bats and Sheath-tailed Bats have scent glands under their chins (gular glands). They use the secretions of these glands to mark their roosting places and the females occupying them. Greater White-lined Bats have small holding sacs on the wing membranes in front of their

A male Black-bearded Tomb Bat seen in profile shows no evidence of the beard that gives the species its name.

forearms. They use them to mark the roost areas and females by shaking the wings. This marking behavior is called "salting."

In Schneider's Roundleaf Bat, adult males have frontal glands behind their nose-leafs. Males with larger testicles have larger frontal glands, and these are the individuals occupying territories at the entrance to maternity roosts. In this species, like many other bats, urine and feces are also used for marking. In some bats, glands are conspicuous because they support tufts of hairs which sometimes are specialized for communication (see Box 13).

It should come as no surprise that the signals a bat uses for echolocation may simultaneously function in communication. One of the more spectacular examples involves mother-young interactions in Greater Horseshoe Bats in Japan. There a female and her baby begin to call separately and, as the mother moves closer, eventually call in synchrony as mother is reunited with baby.

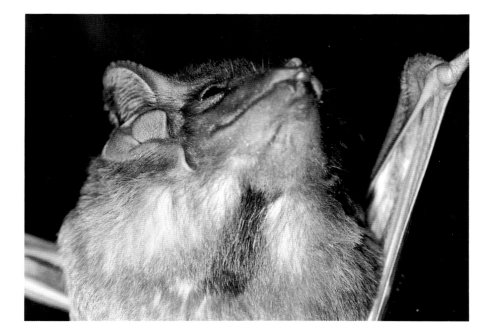

Viewed from below, the beard-like patch of dark fur growing from a gland on the throat of a male Black-bearded Tomb Bat is conspicuous. Females lack the beard.

BOX 13

BAT HAIRS

Hairs are a distinctive feature of mammals and they grow in profusion on the body skin of all but two of the 900 or so living species of bats. Hairs are important to bats because they provide insulation and protect the skin. Some patterns in the fur may contribute to a camouflage effect, while more striking ones probably serve in communication (see Chapter 4).

Like other mammals, bats spend considerable time each day grooming themselves. To do this, bats use their toenails, their tongues and often their teeth. Anyone who has watched a roosting bat for any time must have been impressed by the amount of energy bats invest in grooming (forgetting, for the moment, hibernating bats). Healthy bats have clean fur, and grooming also helps them to keep populations of ectoparasites under control.

Like some other mammals, some have hairs that appear to be specialized for visual and chemical communication. Bands or tufts of hairs of different color give a striped or spotted appearance, particularly in some epauletted bats, some sheath-tailed bats and Spotted Bats. Patterns of high contrast are probably important in visual communication. Hairs used in chemical communication grow out of or close to glands on bats' skin. These glands produce chemicals for communication, and, in a few bats, hairs growing from glands are specialized to hold and disperse the glandular products. Such hairs are called "osmetrichia" and they work like paint brushes.

Having used her toenails to comb out her fur, the Hoary Bat uses her tongue and teeth to groom her wing membranes.

The accompanying figure compares the appearance of the crests in male and female Long-crested Free-tailed Bats. In males, the crests are large and conspicuous. In females they are small and hardly developed. Also

On feeding grounds echolocation calls also can serve a communication role. If recordings of Spotted Bat echolocation calls are played through a speaker, the bats' reactions are quite instructive. The playback experiments have demonstrated that Spotted Bats listen to one another's echolocation calls to space themselves in suitable habitat. In Little Brown Bats, the effect is more general. These bats fly toward the echolocation calls of other Little Brown Bats, and the calls of other species such as Big Brown Bats. Little Brown Bats appear to eavesdrop on other bats to find good places to roost and feed.

Playback experiments with Red Bats have revealed that individuals listen to the feeding buzzes of other Red Bats, using them to identify vulnerable targets. Red Bats fly toward feeding buzzes of other Red Bats. To the human observer, the response appears to be like a chase, with one bat flying after another. But the chases do not seem to be aggressive since afterward (less than 5 minutes), both chaser and chasee are still feeding in the same area. Furthermore, the second bat in the procession is much more often successful than the first one when it comes to catching the insect (usually a moth) that the first bat is shown are the detailed structures of body hairs and crest hairs of a male Long-crested Free-tailed Bat. Note the differences in hair size and scale structure. Crest hairs are larger than body hairs and their scales have smoother edges. Angola Free-tailed Bats have smaller crests than Long-crested Free-tailed Bats. But, there too, the crest hairs differ from the body hairs by being larger in diameter and having scales with smoother edges.

In Cave Nectar Bats, Old World Fruit Bats from Southeast Asia, sexually mature males have conspicuous neck ruffs. Hairs growing from the glands on the neck differ in structure from body hairs. The ruff hairs are larger in diameter and have a profusion of scales compared to body hairs.

The fur of bats also has other impacts. Experiments in a wind tunnel have revealed that longer fur generates more drag for a flying bat than shorter fur. Known as "parasite drag," the cost of moving a flying bat's body through the air is lowest in naked bats.

There is more to bat hairs than meets the eye.

Compared here are the crests of a male (left) and female Long-crested Free-tailed Bat. These 10-g bats occur in the savanna woodland over much of Africa. The difference in crests between males and females suggests that they serve a function in courtship.

Scanning electron micrographs show details of differences between hairs growing from glands and those on the bodies of three species of bats. Compared here are body hairs (a, c, e) and gland hairs (b, d, f) of a male Long-crested Free-tailed Bat (a, b), a male Angola Free-tailed Bat (c, d) and a male Cave Nectar Bat (e, f).

chasing. In Pipistrelles in northern Scotland, individuals chase one another when food is scarce. Here, chases represent the efforts of one bat to protect its feeding space. In Red Bats, the numbers of chases are not determined by the numbers of insects, only by the numbers of bats. In short, chases in feeding bats do not always mean the same thing.

When two Greater Bulldog Bats are on a collision course, one of the bats will alter its echolocation call and "honk" at the other. The honking allows the bats to avoid a collision. The bats honk by lowering the pitch of the terminal part of their echolocation calls. Calls like honks are known from other bats that forage in groups.

• • •

Are bats the most social of mammals? Some clearly are, and the best example is Common Vampire Bats, as we shall see in Chapter 10. Most bats, however, are solitary or gregarious and not particularly "social." The variety in their social arrangements reflects the overall diversity of the group.

BAT POPULATIONS

Production, Predators and Parasites

The belief that bats are just flying mice is completely misleading, especially when it comes to reproduction. We have seen that female bats typically bear one or two young at a time and the combined weight of the litter is one quarter to one third of the mother's mass. For example, like most other mouse-eared bats, a female Daubenton's Bat bears a single young each year. The mother, who weighs about 8 g, bears a 2.5-gram young. Compare this with a female house mouse weighing about 20 grams. She may have up to 10 litters a year, each with four to six or even more young. The combined weight of the newborn baby mice is approximately 25% of their mother. Though house mice and many bats are similar in appearance, the house mouse can produce many more young.

In reproductive output, bats are more like large mammals than small ones. For example, compare an average adult female Little Brown Bat (weight 8 g) with an average adult female human (55,000 g). Both can bear a single young in any 12-month period. Unlike the Little Brown Bat, the human female may occasionally have multiple births (twins, triplets, etc.). Relatively speaking, newborn Little Brown Bats are bigger than newborn humans, 25% versus less than 10% of the mother's weight after birth. Baby Little Brown Bats grow faster, reaching full adult size in about three weeks. The human does this in about 15 years. Many humans live more than 70 years. In the wild the record for Little Brown Bats is over 30 years. Theoretically, human females can have young for about 20 years. Female Little Brown Bats usually have a baby every year from age two until they die. This means that an average human female could possibly have 20 young in her lifetime. A female Little Brown Bat would have to reach age 22 to achieve this output, a realistic age for many of these bats.

Bats vary in their reproductive output, and this is evident when different kinds of bats are examined. To put the bats in perspective, consider that three years is a ripe old age for a White-footed Mouse in a northern New York State woodland. In the same area, many Little Brown Bats live more than 20 years. During its three-year lifetime, a female White-footed Mouse might have 80 young. In 20 years the female Little Brown Bat would have 18. In the same area, a female Big Brown Bat that had twins every year and lived for 15 years would produce 26 young. In west-

How Many Bats Live Here?

In 1988, the Bird, Tree and Garden Club of Chautauqua, New York began a study of the Little Brown Bats that summered on the grounds of the Chautauqua Institution. Members of the club were concerned that the bats' numbers were dwindling. But subjective impressions about bat populations can be misleading, so the club set out to answer three questions: First, how many buildings did the bats use? Second, were female bats roosting in the buildings having young? Third, how many bats lived in buildings at Chautauqua during the summer?

By watching buildings at dusk as bats emerged, they discovered that bats lived in about 60 of the 725 buildings on the institution grounds. Examination of more than 4,000 females captured in a Tuttle trap as they left their roosts showed that virtually all (about 90%) of them had a baby every summer.

A capture-recapture technique was used to estimate the size of the population. This depended upon the relative numbers of banded and unbanded bats in any sample caught at any colony. Each bat captured during the three-year study received a numbered aluminum band. Careful records about when and where which bats were captured and recaptured provided the numbers needed to estimate the population size. A subsample of nine of the 60 colonies was trapped at least six times over three summers. The results from these colonies were adjusted to reflect the total number and size of bat colonies in buildings at Chautauqua. The data suggested that about 10,000 Little Brown Bats roosted in the buildings at Chautauqua. The records for individual colonies showed no evidence that the numbers of bats at any colony declined over the three-year period. This was good news.

Recaptures of banded bats showed, however, that Little Brown Bats persistently and consistently roosted in the same buildings year after year. So, the populations in individual colonies may be stable, but loss of colonies would mean an overall decline in the population. Big Brown Bats are quite different, readily switching to alternate roosts when their preferred ones are sealed. Not all species of bats respond the same way to loss of roosts.

The Chautauqua example shows how population studies of bats use different techniques to obtain different answers. When there are vast numbers of bats in single roosts, the approach used at Chautauqua would not work. There, or when the bats must not be disturbed, photographic techniques or thermal imaging may be better for measuring bat populations.

ern North America and in the West Indies, Big Brown Bats usually bear just one young each year, so there a female would have just 13 young over a life span of 15 years.

Some tropical bats achieve higher rates of reproduction by having young more often. In South Africa, for example, female Little Free-tailed Bats have one young in each litter, and may produce three or even five litters a year. In India, some female Wroughton's Pipistrelles have twins three times a year. Short-tailed Fruit Bats in Costa Rica bear a single young twice a year.

On average, virtually all of the bats for which there is information live a long time. Female bats produce few young compared to other mammals of similar size. Other animals that live a long time and have relatively low reproductive outputs tend to have lower mortality. If mortality is low, even slow-reproducing animals, like most bats, could increase in number. To learn more about mortality, we need to know what kills bats.

ACCIDENTS AND PROBLEMS OF THE YOUNG

Perhaps flight puts bats at risk; every year many people find bats that miscalculated in the air and paid for it with their lives. Dead bats are often found impaled on barbed wire and armed plants such as burdocks. Whenever I have looked closely at dead bats in these circumstances, their fur color and finger joints (see page 24) have identified them as young. The scientific literature is full of anecdotal reports of bats that died impaled on fences and plants. These kinds of accidents befall both echolocating and non-echolocating bats. There are no figures indicating the rate of these accidents or the chances of an entangled bat freeing itself and surviving the experience. When several bats are found impaled on the same plant or the same small section of fence, scientists surmise that the calls of a trapped individual may have drawn others to their deaths.

Young bats, like young animals of any kind, face higher risks than adults, including many older bats that presumably learned by their mistakes. The numbers of telephone inquiries about bats in the north temperate parts of the world suggest that stray bats are most common in June, July and August. These calls nearly always come when people encounter bats roosting in conspicuous and accessible places, such as in plain view on the side of a building. Investigation usually reveals that the bats in question were young born that year. It is easy to suspect that these animals set out from their home roost and just ran out of steam. Their failure to return home could come from dehydration or failure to catch enough food to fuel the return flight.

But young bats have other problems too. Those born in temperate climates face an additional challenge: surviving their first winter. Where bats hibernate, the young must enter hibernation with a good supply of body fat, for they only have this body fat to fuel them over the winter. The low body weights of Little Brown Bats caught swarming at hibernation sites in Ontario in August show the problem. The same must be true of virtually all temperate bats, and failure to survive their first winter is a major cause of

This young Gray-headed Flying Fox died impaled on a barbed-wire fence.

mortality in hibernating bats. In England, about 70% of Greater Horseshoe Bats born each July are dead within a year.

Young bats must learn to fly. Most insectivorous bats also must learn to echolocate to find their prey. Their flight must be coordinated enough to capture flying insects located by echolocation. For a bat, becoming independent is probably a real challenge, particularly when it must prepare to pay the costs of hibernation or migration. As we shall see, bats foraging for insects in agricultural areas often ingest loads of insecticides—that is, they ingest the chemicals sprayed on their insect food. The problems of pesticides stored in body fat are particularly severe for female bats and young.

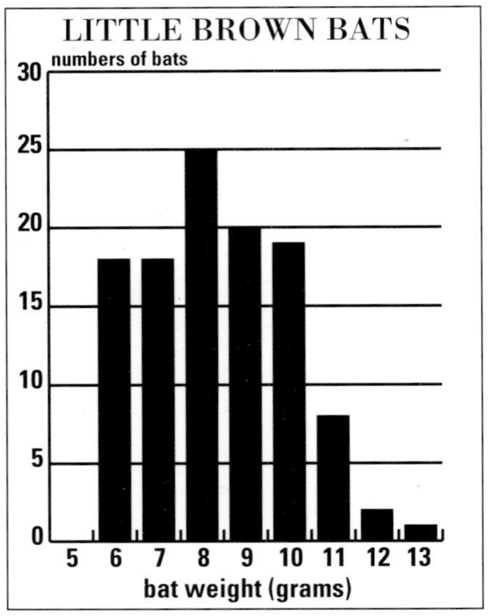
LITTLE BROWN BATS
numbers of bats
30
25
20
15
10
5
0
5 6 7 8 9 10 11 12 13
bat weight (grams)

On August 25, 1988, 36 of 111 Little Brown Bats caught swarming at a cave in southeastern Ontario weighed less than 8 g. These animals, which had been born in June, must quickly put on weight or they are unlikely to survive their first winter.

Predators of Bats

Since most bats are quite small, they are bite-sized for many different kinds of predators. Bats are fair game for many mammals such as cats, weasels, dogs, raccoons, skunks, mongooses; for birds such as owls, hawks, falcons, jays and shrikes; for reptiles such as snakes; and even for some large frogs. There also are records of large spiders eating small bats captured in their webs. What's worse, some bats eat other bats.

A bat's anatomy means that most of the meat is on the body where the largest muscles are found. Bat wings contain little muscle, so when most predators eat a bat, they bite off and discard the wings. Bat legs have little meat on them because the legs are mainly used for hanging from a perch. The drumsticks of virtually all bats are a diet meal for almost any predator.

You are most likely to see other animals hunting bats in places where clouds of them emerge from a roost. Since most bats are small, they are marginal food items for larger predators because of the small return they offer. However, the benefit to the predator increases when many bats can be caught in a short time. This can be the scene at the entrance to a roost used by many bats.

You can expect to find a good array of predators around a large colony of bats, particularly if the colony has to emerge through a small opening. In Cuba, some boas live just inside caves that harbor many bats. These snakes make a living by picking bats out of the clouds that fly by twice a day. In Jamaica, feral house cats show similar behavior. At Carlsbad Caverns in New Mexico and other large bat colonies throughout the world, birds such as hawks and owls commonly gather at dusk. In Kruger National Park in South Africa, large colonies of Little Free-tailed and Angola Free-tailed Bats attract up to 10 species of hawks at emergence time.

Most of these predators, even the hawks and owls, probably catch relatively few bats. If you are one of the bats emerging from the roost, your chances of being taken are probably small, particularly if you are part of a large crowd that emerges together. In Puerto Rico, bats leaving a cave roost changed their pattern of emergence in response to persistent attacks by Merlins, a type of medium-sized falcon. Before the birds appeared on the scene, the Parnell's Mustached Bats and some other species emerged as a column, coming out of the cave and flying up over the vegetation. After several encounters with Merlins, the bats still emerged as a group, but the column stayed low, flying down a wash closer to the ground and vegetation.

The birds that stand out as predators of bats are Bat Hawks. These hawks have an unlikely pattern of distribution that includes Africa and the East Indies. They are probably the only birds specialized to feed on bats. Analysis of the contents of pellets cast by Bat Hawks has been used to study their diet. In Zimbabwe, a pair of Bat Hawks fed mainly on bats but also took some swifts, swallows and insects. The same picture of the birds' diet emerged when observers counted the prey items brought to young Bat Hawks at their nests. Bat Hawks in Africa and the East Indies make bats a main part of their menu. Long-crested Free-tailed Bats were first discovered when one was found in the crop of a Bat Hawk that was shot in Zaire.

In the New World tropics, Bat Falcons are mentioned as another bird that sometimes specializes on bats. But when Bat Falcons are feeding their young, they bring them many birds and very few bats. Bat Falcons are widespread in the Neotropics but their diet does not reflect their name.

Bat Hawks leave their perches and begin to hunt just at dusk. They fly high, swooping down on their victims. Flying bats are snatched in the talons and then swallowed whole. This permits the bat hawk to proceed directly to the pursuit of its next victim. In 20 minutes, a bat hawk hunting over the shores of Lake Kariba in Zambia took six bats, probably Angola Free-tailed Bats. This rate of harvest meant that the 650-g bird caught about 120 g of bats an hour, emphasizing the importance of both hunting where there are many bats, and rapid food processing.

Among hawks, the Bat Hawk has a beak with a particularly wide gape, making it easy to swallow its prey whole. Not having to tear up each victim contributes to fast feeding. The wings are digested and the fur is later cast as waste pellets. In Zimbabwe, bat hawks eat mainly Plain-nosed Bats, Free-tailed Bats and Old World Leaf-nosed Bats, species that often hunt in the open. They are not known to take larger (greater than 75-g) bats such as Old World Fruit Bats or Commerson's Leaf-nosed Bats.

The behavior of Peregrine Falcons and Wahlberg's Eagles attacking bats highlights a Bat Hawk's specializations. Both of these raptors also pursue flying bats

Small predators like this Slender Mongoose from Africa often eat bats, particularly in settings where large numbers of bats are concentrated in one area.

Owls, like this Ferruginous Pygmy-owl from Central America, may occasionally take bats, but they rarely make bats a regular part of their diet.

The wings are all that remains of this Egyptian Slit-faced Bat that was taken out of a Tuttle trap set near Harare in Zimbabwe.

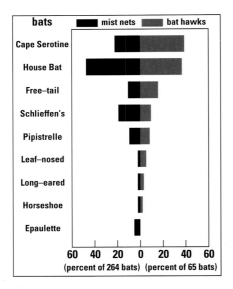

bats	mist nets	bat hawks

Cape Serotine
House Bat
Free–tail
Schlieffen's
Pipistrelle
Leaf–nosed
Long–eared
Horseshoe
Epaulette

60 40 20 0 20 40 60
(percent of 264 bats) (percent of 65 bats)

Compared here are the bats caught in mist nets set in woodland in Zimbabwe with those caught by a pair of Bat Hawks feeding in the same area. The bats listed include the Cape Serotine, the Lesser Yellow House Bat (abbreviated as House Bat), two species of Free-tailed Bats (Free-tail), Schlieffen's Bats (Schlieffen's), Banana Bats (Pipistrelle), Sundevall's Leaf-nosed Bats (Leaf-nosed), Laephotis wintoni *(Long-eared), several species of Horseshoe Bats, and several species of epauletted fruit bats. Modified from data presented in a paper published by Fenton and colleagues (1977).*

and grab them in their talons. But, having caught a bat, Peregrine Falcons take it to a perch for processing and eating. Only then does the Peregrine or Wahlberg's Eagle embark on its next chase. Although Peregrine Falcons can fly and dive faster than Bat Hawks, their eating behavior makes them much less deadly from the bat's perspective. Differences in processing time mean that in a given time period a Peregrine Falcon or Wahlberg's Eagle will eat many fewer bats than a Bat Hawk. The numbers tell the story. While a Bat Hawk may take 10 seconds or less to consume each prey item (often a bat), a Wahlberg's Eagle or a Peregrine Falcon takes at least 23 seconds for each bat.

Specialized predators can be very dangerous to bats. Squirrel monkeys live in the New World tropics and some individuals have learned to exploit tent-making bats as prey. As we have seen, tent-making bats roost in small groups under leaves with long stems. The leaves vibrate if a predator tries to climb the stem. Some squirrel monkeys, however, scout the leaves from below. Having found a group of tent-making bats, an experienced squirrel monkey launches its attack from above, grabbing some bats and knocking others to the ground. The tent screens the attacker from the bats and the strategy avoids the bats' usual alarm system, the long leaf stems.

Perhaps the most intriguing predators of bats are bats themselves. There are species of bat-eating bats in three families: False Vampire Bats, Slit-faced Bats and New World Leaf-nosed Bats. In Australia, the Ghost Bat often preys on other species of bats, as do Indian False Vampire Bats and Heart-nosed Bats, the former from India and Southeast Asia, the latter from East Africa. Both species are False Vampires. Large Slit-faced Bats, another African species, prey on bats, as do Linnaeus' False Vampire Bats and Woolly False Vampire Bats of the Neotropics.

Wherever bat-eating bats occur, the victims are always smaller species. In captivity, bat-eating Large Slit-faced bats use flight sounds and vocalizations to detect their targets. Other bats are grabbed in the predator's mouth and killed with a powerful bite to the face. The prey is usually eaten from the head down, and the wings, flight membranes, legs and tail are usually dropped uneaten. When the prey is another species of Slit-faced Bats, Large Slit-faced Bats also bite off and drop the large ears. Bat-eating bats treat other prey the same way, killing with a powerful bite to the face and eating them from the head down. As we have seen, these bats usually eat a variety of other small vertebrates such as rodents, frogs, fish and birds.

Bat-eating bats are not cannibals because their victims are other species. As many bat biologists have discovered, sometimes to their dismay, putting a large bat in a bag or cage with a smaller one can be the end of the smaller bat. In a confined space, a large, hungry bat often will catch and eat the smaller one. Records of this kind are common in the literature. They usually involve larger insectivorous species such as Hoary Bats, Noctules or Big Brown Bats. There is no other evidence that these temperate bats are real bat-eaters. However, if they are hungry and are given the opportunity, they exploit it.

Thus, bats are an easy snack for many predators under some circumstances, but there is little evidence that many predators specialize on them. Bat Hawks are a notable exception, making bats a major part of their diet both in Africa and in the East Indies. Their behavior and morphology is specialized for dealing with bats. In the tradition of "it takes a thief to catch a thief," bat-eating bats can also be deadly predators of bats. For the time being, however, we do not know just how important bats are in the diets of bat-eating bats. As we shall see in Chapter 12, today many humans are the most dangerous and implacable enemy threatening bats.

A portrait of a Bat Hawk photographed by Anthony Harris in southern Africa. Note the striking eye and very large gape which permits the bird to swallow its prey whole.

PARASITES

Like other animals, bats are home to an array of parasites. Some of them, the endoparasites, live within bats' bodies, while others, the ectoparasites, live on the outside. Most bat parasites are specialized to the extent that they will not survive outside of or away from bats, so they pose little threat to animals other than bats.

The list of bat endoparasites, although long, is still incomplete as biologists continue to catalog them. The list includes a variety of one-celled organisms that live in bats' blood. Some, the plasmodia, resemble the organisms that cause malaria in humans. Mosquitoes and other biting flies probably move these plasmodia from bat to bat. We do not know their effect on their bat hosts. Bat blood also harbors several species of trypanosomes, similar in general form to the animals that cause sleeping sickness in humans. Bedbugs are known to move trypanosomes between bats, but we do not know how bats are affected by trypanosomes.

The bodies of bats, like those of other mammals, including humans, are home to many parasitic species of worms and worm-like animals. Tapeworms usually occur in the intestines, and so do hookworms. Roundworms, the nematodes, may live along the intestine, in the body cavity, the lungs, the bladder or the blood. Flatworms known as flukes may live in the liver or gallbladder. Animal-eating bats tend to have a richer array of endoparasites than species feeding on fruit and nectar and pollen.

The life cycles of parasitic worms are often complex and divided into different stages. "Definitive" hosts are the animals housing the adult tapeworm, while "intermediate" hosts harbor larval stages. Unraveling the life cycles of these and other parasites is a challenge for parasitologists. The live cycles of tapeworms, for example, usually involve intermediate hosts that live in water. Copepods, small shrimp-like arthropods, are often victimized. For example, one tapeworm whose definitive host may be a human, bear or otter, spends time in two intermediate hosts, a copepod and a fish. To date, the life cycles of tapeworms and other parasites living in bats remain relatively unknown. Tape-

All that remains after a Darling's Horseshoe Bat was caught and eaten by a Large Slit-faced Bat.

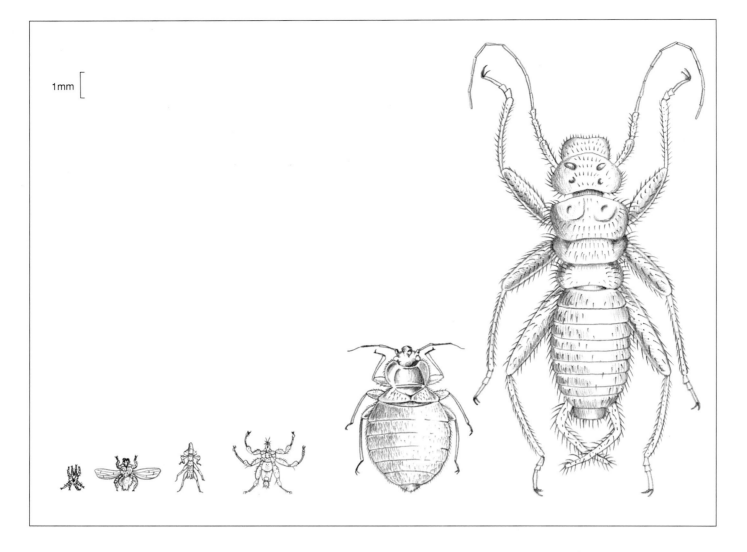

A selection of arthropods that live with bats either as parasites or covivants. Shown here and drawn to the same scale are, from left to right, a wing mite, a streblid fly, a flea, a nycteribiid fly, a bedbug (all parasites) and an earwig (covivant). The scale is 1 mm long. Drawing by Max Licht.

worms for whom bats are definitive hosts probably use aquatic insects as intermediate hosts.

Like most ectoparasites, the animals living on the outsides of bats are arthropods such as mites, ticks and insects. The list of insects that are parasitic on bats includes flies, fleas and bedbugs. Ectoparasites use piercing mouthparts to penetrate the bats' skin and then gorge on blood and body fluids. Ectoparasites are specialized for feeding, for moving around on their hosts and for withstanding grooming.

Looking closely at a bat's wing, you may notice mites on the membranes. Under a magnifying glass, these small dots resemble typewritten periods with eight legs. Some of the mites living on bat wings use their mouthparts to cut through the skin and rupture small blood vessels. These mites often appear in the digestive tracts of bats, making it clear that living on a bat can be dangerous.

While some mites firmly attach themselves to bats' ears or wing membranes, other species live in bats' gums. The ears and tragi of some North American Plainnosed Bats often are studded with groups of small, orange-colored mites called trombiculids (also known as chiggers). These colorful ectoparasites occasionally live on the wing membranes. Firm attachment seems to be their defense against the grooming action of their bat hosts.

The fleas of bats are grouped together in one family because they rarely occur on other animals. Bat fleas lack wings and live in the bat's fur. Like the mites, fleas often appear in bats' digestive tracts or droppings. Some fall victim to the bats' careful grooming. Bat fleas, like other fleas, have bodies flattened from side to side, making it easy to move between the bats' hairs. In many parts of the world, fleas are flattened, orange-colored wingless insects that emerge when you gently blow into a bat's fur.

Several species of bedbugs live on bats and feed on their blood. Although these bedbugs resemble the ones that feed on humans, our blood is usually beneath the taste of bat bedbugs. Bat bedbugs are much larger than fleas and, unlike the fleas, rarely are found on bats outside their roosts. Bedbugs live in the roosts, feeding when the bats return and then sneaking back into the woodwork.

Streblidae and Nycteribiidae are two families of flies that live only as parasites of bats. Most streblids have wings, live in the bat's fur and feed on its blood. The nycteribiids are spider-like in appearance and lack wings, but they also live in the bat's fur and feed on blood. Fleas and bedbugs lay eggs, but female streblid and nycteribiid flies keep their fertilized eggs within their bodies and give birth to live larvae.

One nycteribiid fly parasitizes the two species of Bamboo Bats that roost in the hollows within bamboo stems. A newly-hatched larvae of this fly attaches itself to the roof of the bamboo shelter, immediately becoming a pupa. It must remain pupate, or in the resting stage, for at least 25 days, when the adult fly is ready to emerge from the pupa. However, emergence is triggered by bat activity within the bamboo stem. Increased carbon dioxide levels and vibrations will cause the adult fly to emerge from the pupa. Either condition is associated with the bats' return. The carbon dioxide comes from the bats' breathing, the vibrations from their movements in the roost. These nycteribiid flies can extend their pupal resting period for up to 50 days as they await the bats' return. Pupae do not have to feed so the absence of bats imposes no hardship on them.

Streblid flies also are specialized for life with bats. Some species stay with their bat hosts even through hibernation. One species from western North America often lives in the fur of Western Big-eared Bats. Most of these streblids spend the winter on female bats. During the winter in Kansas, these bat flies are relatively quiet and do not breed. Two streblids are sitting just by the elbow of the hibernating Western Big-eared Bat shown in the photo on page 56.

Two bedbugs sucking blood from behind the ear of a Big Brown Bat.

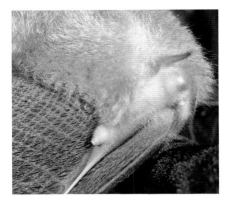

The male Schneider's Roundleaf Bat has a large hippoboscid fly lodged under the skin on its upper thigh.

Other flies, members of the family Hippoboscidae, almost live as ectoparasites of bats and other mammals. After mating, female hippoboscid flies make a small hole in the bat's skin. They then shed their wings and most of their legs and enter the hole head first. There the fly's body enlarges and eventually produces a single larva. Several species of hippoboscid flies are parasitic on bats, usually in tropical and subtropical areas. They can be easy to spot, embedded near the body in the skin of the wings.

COVIVANTS

At least two other kinds of insects live with bats but are not parasites because they do not eat bat blood or body fluids. One species is unique to New Zealand and lives with the Short-tailed Bats there. The New Zealand Bat Fly belongs to the family Mystacinobiidae. Mystacinidae, the scientific name for the family which includes the Short-tailed Bat of New Zealand, is the root for the name of the fly. New Zealand Bat Flies lack wings and live in the roosts used by bats hiding in the nooks and crannies there. These flies lay eggs instead of giving birth to larvae, and both the flies and the larvae feed on the yeasts and fungi that grow in the bats' guano. Although they do not feed on bat blood, their claws, like those of nycteribiids and streblids, are specialized for moving on and through bat fur.

In Southeast Asia, one species of earwig had been reported to be a parasite of Naked Bats. Earwigs, familiar to many gardeners, are not usually parasites. They lack piercing mouthparts for breaking the skin and getting blood, so it was no surprise when careful study revealed that the earwigs living with Naked Bats were not really parasites. These earwigs feed on fragments of skin and body secretions, but also may feed on bat guano when the bats are absent from the roost for extended periods of time. The earwigs are large relative to the Naked Bats. An earwig sitting on a Naked Bat is as conspicuous as a dinner-plate-sized object would be on a human.

PARASITES, DISEASES AND SURVIVAL

Bats seem to suffer no particular ill effects from the various parasites that live on them or in them. Biologists rarely encounter bats that are obviously sick, although as we shall see, rabies disables and kills bats. Bats living in hot, crowded nursery colonies have been thought to suffer higher levels of parasite infestation than bats living alone or in smaller, cooler groups. This has been used as one explanation for high rates of mortality among young, but it has not been fully tested. Furthermore, what is true of one species of bat may not be true of another. It is upsetting to find a baby Big Brown Bat festooned with four or five bedbugs, all happily sucking away on the baby's blood. But the discovery does not mean that the bat's life is threatened.

Like other animals, bats probably succumb to various diseases. It is, however, unlikely that sick bats would readily come to the attention of biologists. For the time being, it is impossible to assess the impact of disease and parasites on the life expectancies of bats. Internal or external parasites of bats are obviously well specialized for their way of life. Part of a parasite's specialization package is minimizing its debilitating effects on its host.

AND NOW SOME BATS

THE OLD WORLD FRUIT BATS, THE PTEROPODIDAE

As their name implies, the Old World Fruit Bats occur in the tropics of Africa, India, Southeast Asia, the East Indies and Australia. Dog- or fox-like faces are common in the 150 species comprising this group of bats. The species studied to date eat either fruit and leaves or nectar and pollen.

Hammerhead Bat

Hammerhead Bats are large fruit-eaters of the African rain forest. Males are larger than females and distinctly different in a number of features, epitomized by their distinctive skulls, which set them apart from any other bats from Africa or elsewhere. Although female Hammerhead Bats superficially resemble some other African fruit bats, their teeth are quite different. Hammerhead Bats have bilobed second premolars and molars, which are unique among bats. While males have forearms that are 120–140 mm long, those of females measure 118–128 mm; males are heavier than females, 228–450 g versus 218–377 g. Compared to females, males have larger muzzles and voice boxes, differences associated with the mating behavior of these bats.

Hammerhead Bats live in relatively low-lying rain forest (below 1,800 m elevation), where they roost 20–30 m above the ground under the canopies of trees. The bats' day roosts are usually beneath thick layers of vegetation, and, by day, Hammerhead Bats tend to hang quietly from exposed branches. Although several Hammerhead Bats may roost together in one tree, the only individuals in actual physical contact are females and their dependent young.

Hammerhead Bats eat leaves and the juice and pulp of fruits such as mangoes, bananas, guavas and soursops. These bats, however, rarely feed on cultivated fruits because figs comprise the bulk of their diet. Female Hammerhead Bats use a trap-lining foraging strategy, meaning they fly along reg-

Compared here are the skulls of a male (top) and female Hammerhead Bat. Note that the male's skull is larger, particularly along the rostrum.

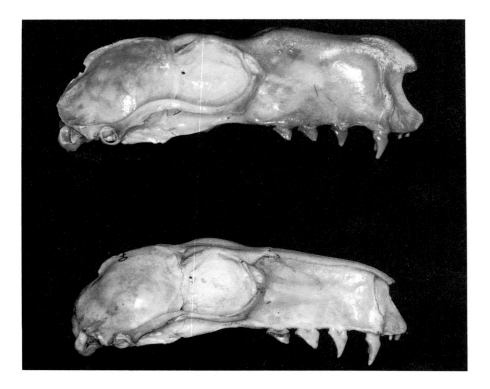

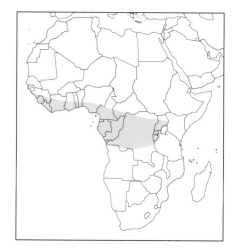

The shaded area shows the range of Hammerhead Bats.

ular routes, collecting fruits along the way. This strategy provides females with a constant food supply of moderate quality. The males, meanwhile, search for and exploit rich patches of food such as fruiting fig trees. They may fly 10 km from their day roost to a feeding site where they can gorge on abundant figs. In one evening a Hammerhead Bat may handle three times its body weight in fruit, about three pounds of fruit for a large male. This behavior makes the bats important to the plants whose fruit they consume because of the vast quantities of seeds the bats disperse in the rain forest.

The distinctive differences in the face and chest between males and females relates directly to courtship behavior. Enlarged muzzles, inflatable sacs on their shoulders and huge voice boxes are all associated with the calls males use to attract females. Males typically call in groups known as "leks" and their honking displays attract females that are ready to breed. Radio-tagged females fly up and down the line of displaying males. Each time a female closely approaches a male, he increases the rate at which he calls, producing a "staccato buzz" that makes it easy for a human observer to hear which males get the most visits. Radio-tagged males roost at the same specific sites within leks night after night, so the performance of an individual male can be studied over time. Passing females may mate with a preferred male, usually one near the center of the line. Mating females produce a distinctive "groaning" sound, making the copulations conspicuous. Most females tend to select the same males as mates. Other males, although they appear to call as vigorously as the chosen males, attract little attention from females and, if the groaning is a true indication of copulation, do not mate. The female Hammerhead Bats' choice of mates appear to be respected by other males, for the females are left alone after they leave the lek and return to their feeding or day roosts. Male Hammerhead Bats contribute nothing to the care or raising of their offspring.

Breeding in Hammerhead Bats occurs during the dry season, which happens in different months at different locations across the bat's range. Typically there are two breeding seasons each year, with females coming into heat (estrus) just after the birth of a young. A single young is born per pregnancy.

There is a record of bats said to be Hammerhead Bats scavenging scraps of meat and attacking chickens, but the evidence is questionable. More detailed studies of the ecology and behavior of Hammerhead Bats produced on further evidence of this "carnivorous" behavior.

The sounds of male Hammerhead Bats are familiar to many people who have spent time in the African rain forest. Although their calls are monotonous to the human ear, they are powerful attractants for receptive female Hammerhead Bats. These fruit bats are specialized relatives of the Epauletted Fruit Bats that are more widespread in Africa.

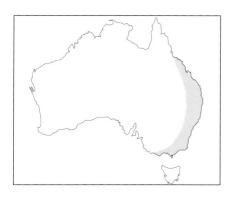

The shaded area shows the range of Gray-headed Flying Foxes.

Gray-headed Flying Fox

These large fruit-eating bats (weight 800 grams) occur in eastern Australia, where they are considered pests when they eat fruit grown as cash crops. The day roosts of Gray-headed Flying Foxes are known as "camps." Camps usually are located in trees, but sometimes the bats roost on cliff faces. Camps of Gray-headed Flying Foxes are conspicuous because the bats are noisy, squawking at one another and flapping loudly as they change positions.

In summer camps (September to April or June) mating occurs and the young are born and raised. In winter camps, the sexes are segregated and most of the residents are young in their first year. In summer camps in February, adult males begin to stake out territories around roosting females. Some males select roosting areas used by individual females and their young. Other males defend small groups of females and their young. In Queensland, the intensity of male-male fights over territories and the females therein peaks in late February.

Males mark their territory boundaries with exudate from the glands on their shoulders. Territorial males become more and more aggressive until mating is over. Females sometimes respond to approaching males by flapping their wings and calling, behavior that usually keeps the male at a distance. A passive female, however, is approached more closely as the male attempts to sniff her shoulders or to lick her genitals. Over time, the association between a male and the female or females in his territory becomes more peaceful. The bats often roost close together and may groom one another. Males defending territories containing several females may intervene to stop fights between the females.

Most copulations occur in late March, and fertilization follows immediately. Males trying to initiate mating approach females with their ears directed back and down. This "frightened expression" is the antithesis of an aggressive expression. Before actual mating, males and females groom one another and to mate, males mount females from the rear. The females that have mated and are now pregnant leave the territories and gather together in different parts of the summer camps. This heralds the breakup of the summer camps and the dispersal of the Gray-headed Flying Foxes to their winter roost sites.

The young conceived in late March are born in the next summer camps in late September and early October, about six months later. Each female bears a single young and takes very good care of it. Female Gray-headed Flying Foxes selectively nurse their own babies. By the time the young is three weeks old, its mother leaves it in the camp when she departs to forage, retrieving it on her return. Baby bats are usually deposited in well-foliated trees at the edges of the camp. Returning females call to their young which, in turn, respond by calling. A female Gray-headed Flying Fox appears to use

The "frightened face" of a male Gray-headed Flying Fox.

her baby's calls to generally locate it. Final reunion comes after the mother recognizes her baby's scent.

By age three months, the young bats begin to make short flights. From there they progress to flights away from camp and eventually to foraging flights. By late January packs of juveniles, young born that year, form in the summer camps. These usually are groups of two or three young associated with an adult male.

Gray-headed Flying Foxes, like other fruit-eating bats, handle large quantities of food every night and feed on a variety of fruits and leaves. These habits do not contribute to the bats' popularity among fruit farmers. Furthermore, their camps often are noisy and conspicuous. The two factors can be hazardous to the bats. In summer, males of lower social stature do not obtain territories and must roost around the edges of the camp. These are the individuals that sound the alarm when danger approaches. The combination of social status and roosting location makes these males the sentries.

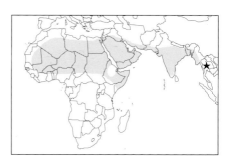

The shaded area denotes the geographic range of Lesser Rat-tailed Bats. The star marks the location from which Hog-nosed Bats have been reported.

RAT-TAILED BATS, THE RHINOPOMATIDAE

The three species of Rat-tailed Bats occur from Northwest Africa east to Burma and southern India. As their name implies, the long slender tail is mouse-like, and protrudes well beyond the end of the interfemoral membrane. Tails longer than their forearms make these bats unique among the living Microchiroptera. A distinctive band of skin joins their ears across the tops of the

A portrait of a Lesser Rat-tailed Bat showing the distinctive band of skin connecting the two ears and the rudimentary nose-leaf.

foreheads and there are small leaf-like projections at the ends of the nose. The nostrils are slit-like and closed by valves.

Lesser Rat-tailed Bat

Lesser Rat-tailed Bats have the same range as the other species in this family. They are medium-sized with forearms 52–60 mm long and can be distinguished from the other two species of Rat-tailed Bats by their size. One species is larger (forearm 57–75 mm), the other smaller (forearm 45–52 mm).

In some places, Lesser Rat-tailed Bats bear a single young each year, but the time of birth varies geographically. Around Madurai in India, Lesser Rat-tailed Bat colonies produce young during the two rainy seasons. Whether individual females bear young in alternate rainy seasons or have two young each year remains unknown. Females nurse their young from a pair of pectoral mammary glands, but they also have a pair of pelvic teats without mammary glands. In Lesser Rat-tailed Bats and some other species, the young cling to the pelvic teats when they are not nursing.

Lesser Rat-tailed Bats eat a variety of insects, from flies to beetles. The bats occur mainly in arid and semi-arid areas and show great seasonal variation in fat deposits. These deposits act as energy reserves during times when insects are scarce or unavailable. Lesser Rat-tailed Bats roost in natural and artificial hollows. Colonies have been found in caves and tunnels as well as in mosques, temples and other buildings. Within their colonies, Lesser Rat-tailed Bats tend to roost out of physical contact with one another.

This face-on view of a Lesser Rat-tailed Bat shows the distinctive valve-like nostrils, the nose-leaf and the mustache-like fringe of hairs on the bat's upper lip.

The echolocation calls of Lesser Rat-tailed Bats are narrow in bandwidth with a number of harmonics or overtones. Bats searching for targets emit calls that are up to 30 ms long with most of their energy between 34 and 45 kHz. The hearing of Lesser Rat-tailed Bats is most sensitive to sounds in this frequency range. Narrowband calls are typical of aerial-feeding species, bats hunting for prey in open areas where echoes reflect from few objects other than targets or other bats.

When several Lesser Rat-tailed Bats forage together, each individual changes the frequency dominating its echolocation calls. This behavior minimizes overlap between the calls of different bats. Shifts in call frequencies could minimize interference by jamming. The shifts also could represent exchanges of communication signals between foraging bats. These two explanations are not mutually exclusive.

In several features of anatomy and their chromosomes, Rat-tailed Bats are considered unspecialized or "primitive." This does not seem to have impeded their success, for the bats are numerous and widely distributed.

HOG-NOSED BATS, THE CRASEONYCTERIDAE

Hog-nosed Bat

There is just one species in this family that was first described scientifically in 1974. Also known as Kitti's Hog-nosed Bat, Hog-nosed Bats are tiny. Adults weigh just 2 g, making them the smallest of mammals. Their forearms are 22–25 mm long. These Hog-nosed Bats have only been found in some limestone caves in west-central Thailand. Since there has been relatively little work on the bats of caves in some parts of Southeast Asia, Hog-nosed Bats may eventually be found over a larger area. But since explorer-naturalists usually look for bats in caves, our current knowledge may reflect real distribution of these tiny bats.

Apart from their small size, Hog-nosed Bats have several features that make them easy to recognize. The most conspicuous is a distinct plate-like structure on the nose. Large ears, a tragus projecting from the ear with a conspicuous swelling halfway along its length, and unique premaxillae combine to make Hog-nosed Bats distinctive. They lack an external tail and calcar and their wings are relatively broad.

These tiny bats are insectivorous and produce echolocation calls of high intensity. The calls begin with 2-ms-long narrowband components and end in broader band frequency modulated sweep that lasts about 1 ms. People have watched Hog-nosed Bats foraging by day producing echolocation calls when the bats might have used vision to find their prey.

Hog-nosed Bats appear to roost only in caves, usually in the remote passages of smaller caves. Roosting bats are alert and difficult to approach because they readily take off. Clearing of forest around their cave roosts may threaten their survival.

One of the most interesting things about Hog-nosed Bats is their blend of characteristics. In some features they resemble the Rat-tailed Bats, including the features of their noses, the leading edges of their wings and their lack of calcars. But they lack an external tail, and they also differ in the details of their ears and tragi as well as in the structure of some bones. In other structures Hog-nosed Bats are similar to Sheath-tailed Bats, but again the resemblances are matched by conspicuous differences. At one time Rat-tailed Bats were placed in the same superfamily as the Sheath-tailed Bats and Hog-nosed Bats (Emballonuroidea). The more current view places the Rat-tailed Bats and the Hog-nosed Bats in their own superfamily (Rhinopomatoidea) as illustrated in the family tree of bats (shown on page 10).

False Vampire Bats, the Megadermatidae

The five species of False Vampire Bats occur in Africa, India, Southeast Asia, the East Indies and Australia. A distinctive bifurcate tragus and no upper incisors make False Vampire Bats easy to recognize. Flexibility in foraging behavior and large size means that these bats are voracious predators that eat a wide variety of prey. These bats have broad wings and are agile, maneuverable fliers.

Ghost Bat

Ghost Bats are among the largest of the microchiropterans with wing spans approaching 0.6 m (forearms 103–105 mm; body mass 120–130 g). Their pale fur gives them a ghost-like appearance. Ghost Bats live across the northern part of Australia in habitats ranging from rain forest to dry savanna. About 10,000 years ago (the Pleistocene epoch) these bats were more widely distributed in Australia than they are today. Elsewhere in the world, other bats with white fur are also known as "ghost" bats, for example, the Honduran Ghost Bat and the Northern Ghost Bat.

Ghost Bats, like other megadermatids, cannot tolerate lowered body temperatures. Laboratory observations suggest that these bats maintain their bodies between 35°C and 39°C over ambient temperatures ranging from 0°C to 35°C. When roost temperatures are higher or lower than 30°C to 35°C, the bats increase their metabolic rates to keep warm or stay cool. Fluctuations in the distribution of Ghost Bats in Australia may reflect changes in climate, with the bats moving to the warmer north during cooler periods and farther south during warmer ones.

The day roosts of Ghost Bats are in hollows, almost always caves or old mines. At night, however, these bats may roost in a wide range of situations, from the lower branches of trees and shrubs to sites in and around buildings. Some night roosts also serve as hunting perches, others as feeding perches. Feeding perches are conspicuous because of the prey remains the bats drop beneath them. Perches on the branches of trees or bushes may be conspicuous because of the claw marks left by the hanging bats.

Ghost Bats eat insects and other arthropods as well as vertebrates such as bats, birds, mice and lizards. At one site in the Northern Territory, Ghost Bats had eaten at least 29 species of birds, including doves, owlet-nightjars, honeyeaters, finches and woodswallows. In some cases in the laboratory and in the field, Ghost Bats have captured, killed and partly eaten prey that is 80% of their own weight. Evidence of the diets of these bats comes mainly from the remains of prey that accumulate beneath their feeding roosts.

Like other False Vampire Bats, Ghost Bats produce low-intensity echolocation calls that are short (less than 1 millisecond long) and broadband. These bats also have extremely sensitive hearing and well-developed senses of vision. Their large eyes and ears reflect their abilities. The suite of Ghost Bats sensory features means that they can locate prey by echolocation, by listening for sounds coming from targets or by vision. Variation in hunting techniques may reflect this sensory flexibility and explain some of the variety of foods taken by these bats.

Slit-faced Bats, the Nycteridae

As their name implies, Slit-faced Bats have a conspicuous slit running up and down the middle of their faces. The 13 or so species occur mainly in Africa, but

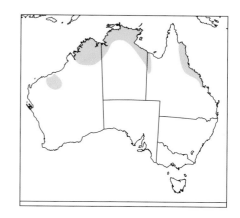

The shaded area indicates the current range of Ghost Bats.

two species live in Indonesia, ranging from southern Burma to Malaya, Sumatra, Java and perhaps beyond. Slit-faced Bats have broad wings and their tails end in a distinctive "t" shaped cartilage. These bats have long, fine fur that is grey, brown or reddish in color.

Large Slit-faced Bat

With forearms 57–66 mm long, Large Slit-faced Bats are bigger than all other species of Slit-faced bats. They occur over much of Africa in areas of rain forest and savanna woodland, ranging as far south as the Zambezi River.

Like most bats, Slit-faced Bats cannot tolerate lowered body temperatures. Exposed to air temperatures below 30°C, the bats raise their rates of metabolism and burn energy to keep warm. They can do this as long as their energy supplies last, but when the supply runs out they die. This feature means that Slit-faced Bats are more numerous nearer the equator and that fewer species occur in the cooler parts of Africa. It also means that the bats must feed every night to survive and roost in warm places. Slit-faced bats rarely last a night in a holding cage or bat trap unless they have had plenty of food.

Like other nycterids, Large Slit-faced Bats spend their days roosting in hollows such as the open spaces in buildings, standing or fallen trees, and in caverns. Along the Zambezi River in Zimbabwe, Large Slit-faced Bats roost in hollow acacia trees (*Acacia albida*), disused military bunkers and the attics of buildings.

Large Slit-faced Bats also use night roosts in hollows or foliage of trees or in buildings. Along the Zambezi River, radio-tagged individuals consistently came to the same night roosts both as places to rest between bouts of foraging and as sites for eating. These bats typically remove the wings and legs from their insect victims and drop them, making it easy to recognize night roosts used as feeding perches.

Large Slit-faced Bats eat larger arthropods such as beetles, mantids, katydids, crickets and sun spiders. Along the Zambezi River they also take many frogs at some times of the year and bats at other times. Large Slit-faced Bats also eat fish and small birds such as sunbirds and finches. This species may survive as far south as the Zambezi because they use this broad range of prey. If this is correct, the populations nearer the equator may feed more on arthropods, as do other species of Slit-faced Bats.

Female Large Slit-faced Bats have one baby each year. South of the equator the baby is born in October or November near the beginning of the rainy season. Newborn Slit-faced Bats are naked and weigh 25–30% of their mother's mass. Mother Large Slit-faced Bats leave their young behind in day roosts when they emerge to hunt. Mothers return several times during the night to eat prey they have captured and to nurse their babies.

The eyes of Slit-faced Bats are relatively small. Their echolocation calls are very low in intensity, only detectable at less than a meter even by a sensitive bat detector. The calls are short (less than 1 ms) with multiple harmonics and have most energy between 60 and 100 kHz. The bats open the slits in their faces when they produce vocalizations.

Captive Large Slit-faced Bats locate prey items by listening to sounds they produce. In these situations the bats can be tricked into attacking the wrong target such as a piece of stick moving beside a frog. When searching for food, Large Slit-faced Bats produce echolocation calls but do not appear to use them to collect information about their targets. These bats pre-

A Large Slit-faced Bat showing the distinctive slit running down the center of the bat's face

sumably use echolocation to assess the background while depending upon sounds of movement to find prey.

Radio-tracking studies also show that Large Slit-faced Bats use two hunting strategies. Sometimes they sit on perches waiting for passing prey. Flying or walking insects and other prey are attacked from perches by flights lasting from 30 seconds to 2 minutes. At other times the bats fly for from 5 minutes to over 6 minutes, 1–2 m above the ground. The perch hunting strategy costs the bats less energy but covers less ground. Hunting from continuous flight costs more energy but gives the bats access to a wider area and range of targets. On any night Large Slit-faced Bats use both strategies, but when prey are very scarce they fly continuously much more than they wait at perches.

Virtually nothing is known of the social organization of Large Slit-faced Bats or of other nycterids. Some collections of specimens suggest roosting aggregations of one adult male with several females and young. This is the expected arrangement if a harem is the basic unit of social organization.

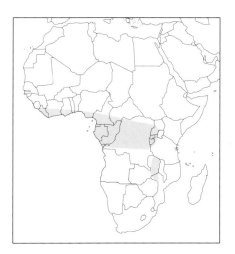

The shaded area shows the distribution of Large Slit-faced Bats.

Horseshoe Bats, the Rhinolophidae

The 69 species of Horseshoe Bats occur throughout the Old World, from tropical to temperate regions. Like Plain-nosed Bats, Horseshoe Bats can tolerate lowered body temperatures, a feature that gives them access to temperate regions. Horseshoe Bats have unique nose-leafs that distinguish them from all other bats (see photo on page 43).These are high duty cycle echolocators specialized for detecting the flutter of flying insects.

Hildebrandt's Horseshoe Bat

Hildebrandt's Horseshoe Bat is one of the largest species in the family, with forearms that are 62–67 mm long; their adult body mass varies between 25 and 35 g. These bats occur in eastern Africa, from Ethiopia and Somalia in the north to South Africa in the south, and from the east coast to about the middle of the continent.

Hildebrandt's Horseshoe Bats have a distinctive hairy nose-leaf, a feature they have in common with one other African species, Ruppell's Horseshoe Bat. Like other Horseshoe Bats, this species has broad wings and is capable of slow maneuverable flight. Hildebrandt's Horseshoe Bats use hollows as day roosts, places like caves, mines, warthog or aardvark holes, hollow trees and the attics of buildings. In some caves and large baobab trees, large numbers of Hildebrandt's Horseshoe Bats have been found roosting; smaller hollows usually harbor fewer individuals. Within their roosts, individuals are not in physical contact with one another, with the exception of females and their dependent young.

Along the Luvuvhu River in Kruger National Park, radio-tagged Hildebrandt's Horseshoe Bats forage mainly in riparian (riverside) woodland, usually hunting between the canopy and the ground cover. Although foraging bats make excursions into drier adjacent woodland, most of their hunting time is spent in the forest along the river.

The hunting Hildebrandt's Horseshoe Bats use two strategies. In some cases they sit on a perch and make short flights to intercept passing prey, but as often they fly continuously in search of targets. Foraging bats spend about

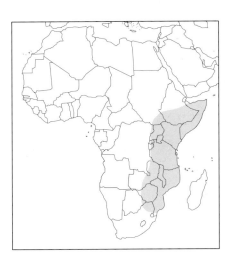

The distribution of Hildebrandt's Horseshoe Bat is shown by the shaded area.

two hours a night actively hunting, although they may remain away from their day roosts through the whole night. Under these conditions, periods of activity, whether longer flights or short ones from a perch, are separated by long bouts of roosting. These bats eat insects, and examination of their feces indicates that moths and beetles are often the principal food.

The echolocation calls of Hildebrandt's Horseshoe Bats are typical of Horseshoe Bats in general, being dominated by a long narrowband component of the signal. In this species, the frequency of the narrowband signal is 45–50 kHz, making them among the lowest frequencies used by Horseshoe Bats.

Female Hildebrandt's Horseshoe Bats bear a single young each year, usually at the beginning of the rainy season. South of the equator, births most commonly occur from October to December, while north of the equator they are six months earlier.

BULLDOG BATS, THE NOCTILIONIDAE

The two species of Bulldog Bats occur widely in the New World tropics. They can be recognized by their large, swollen lips which are reminiscent of those of bulldogs..

Greater Bulldog Bat

Greater Bulldog Bats occur in parts of South and Central America and on many islands in the Caribbean. The bats are identifiable by their large swollen lips. Long legs and huge hind feet with strong, gaff-like claws are the most distinctive of Greater Bulldog Bats—forearms are 81–88 mm long, and adults weigh 60–70 g and have wingspans of about half a meter. Their size distinguishes them from Lesser Bulldog Bats (forearm less than 70 mm, mass 20–40 g), which lack the enlarged hind feet and claws.

In Greater Bulldog Bats the fur is short and water-repellent. The fur on the backs of these bats varies from pale to dark orange, brown to grayish brown; their bellies are whitish or bright orange. Variations in fur color arise from bleaching. There is no consistent sexual or geographic pattern of color variation in Greater Bulldog Bats.

Greater Bulldog Bats are most common in tropical lowlands where at night they hunt over water. These bats forage over small streams, ponds, large rivers, lakes and even saltwater. Using echolocation, these bats detect the small ripples on the water's surface that indicate a fish swimming near the surface. Experiments in the laboratory have revealed that Greater Bulldog Bats use echolocation to track targets on water, adjusting their flight paths to intercept potential prey. The bats can track targets moving at different speeds, and dip at a target whose position they have predicted from its earlier course.

When foraging over water, Greater Bulldog Bats occasionally dip at the surface with their enlarged hind feet. The dips coincide with feeding buzzes, suggesting that the animals are actively attacking a moving target. Earlier researchers proposed that Greater Bulldog Bats caught their prey by random trolling. This view is contradicted by two factors. First, that directed dips coincide with feeding buzzes. Second, that the bats track prey and make interception courses with moving targets.

Although Greater Bulldog Bats may eat a lot of fish, they also take arthropods, including flying insects and fiddler crabs. In Greater Bulldog Bats, cheek

A roosting Greater Bulldog Bat showing the enormous hind feet.

pouches are extensions of one of the cheek muscles that play two roles. First they permit foraging bats to quickly harvest abundant prey and process it later. The cheek pouches may also make it easy for parents to bring solid food to their offspring.

Greater Bulldog Bats roost in hollows in caves or trees. They are colonial and live in two kinds of aggregations. Some colonies consist only of males, while others include males and females, adults and young. Groups with young usually have one adult male with several adult females and their babies. This is a harem organization, so the aggregations of males are bachelor groups composed of individuals with very low reproductive activity. Each colony appears to have a distinctive odor.

Most female Greater Bulldog Bats bear a single young each year. Some, however, may have two, one in May or June, the other in October. In the northern hemisphere, breeding usually begins in November and the young are born in May and June.

The distribution of the Greater Bulldog Bat, which occurs in South and Central America and on many of the islands in the West Indies.

SHORT-TAILED BATS, THE MYSTACINIDAE

This family has but one species, represented by two populations in New Zealand, one on the North Island, the other on the South Island.

Short-tailed Bat

Adult Short-tailed Bats weigh 12–15 g and have forearms 40–43 mm long. The North Island population is smaller and has bigger limbs than the South Island population. By the late 1970s the South Island form still occurred on just a few islands and islets around Stewart Island. Short-tailed Bats and Long-tailed Bats are the only other mammals native to New Zealand, although there is a record of a storm-blown Red Fruit Bat having arrived from Australia.

Short-tailed Bats are remarkably agile on the ground and on the branches of trees and bushes, largely because of their robust legs and hind feet as well as the way they fold their wings. When folded, the wings of Short-tailed Bats are quite out of the way because the first joint of the third digit folds inward beneath the wing. Short-tailed Bats retain the ability to fly, but we do not know how much they use flight.

At one site on the South Island, Short-tailed Bats roost in fallen kauri trees. The bats chew out cavities and tunnels to use as roosts, some of which are 10 cm high, 8 cm wide and 50 cm deep. Signs of heavy wear suggest that Short-tailed Bats use their upper incisor teeth for burrowing. These are the only bats known to make burrows. Like many other bats, Short-tailed Bats often roost together in large clusters.

Short-tailed Bats seem to have the most eclectic diets of any bats. They eat flying insects and other arthropods, as well as fruit, nectar and pollen, tree-fern spores and carrion. The diet suggests flexible hunting and feeding behavior. Short-tailed Bats leave distinctive marks on the fruit they visit. Their preferred fruits include succulent bracts of kiekie, berries and hinau fruits. The bats visit several kinds of flowers to take nectar and pollen, particularly in summer and autumn. An extensible and flexible tongue may make Short-tailed Bats effective consumers of nectar and pollen.

On the South Island, Short-tailed Bats bear a single young each year in the middle of summer (December). Newborn Short-tailed Bats weigh about 19% of their mother's mass, are naked and have their eyes open. Mating has been observed in May, suggesting a period of extra delay between mating and parturition, or childbirth. This delay could involve a postponement of fertilization or arrested development of the embryo. The few records available from the North Island population suggest a different timing of reproduction there. On the South Island, the nursery colonies of Short-tailed Bats are located in the excavated chambers in which the bats roost.

Short-tailed Bats may go through some form of hibernation during prolonged inclement periods, but the details remain unknown. There is a great deal to learn about these bats. For example, beyond a few relatively recent deposits, there are no fossil Short-tailed Bats, making it difficult to judge their relationships to other bats. Short-tailed Bats are obviously microchiropterans. Traditionally they have been considered to be somewhat intermediate between the Free-tailed Bats and the Plain-nosed Bats. Their geographical isolation and a unique blend of characteristics makes it difficult to identify their closest relatives.

Short-tailed Fruit Bats have robust hind limbs and feet which superficially resemble those of Free-tailed Bats and Vampire Bats and reflect agility on the ground. Their hairs most closely resemble those of Bulldog Bats, Slit-faced Bats, Funnel-eared Bats and some New World Leaf-nosed Bats. Studies of some proteins had suggested that Short-tailed Bats were most closely related to New World Leaf-nosed Bats. The most current view of their relationship to other bats, however, is reflected in the family tree of bats presented earlier (page 10).

MUSTACHED BATS, THE MORMOOPIDAE

There are eight species of Mustached Bats which occur in the northern part of South America, Central America and much of the West Indies. Mustached Bats have distinctive tufts of stiff hairs flanking their upper lips which give a mustached appearance. Two other species, known as Ghost-faced Bats, have elaborate leaf-like structures around their mouths and their eyes are located almost in their ears. Two other species of Mustached Bats are naked-backed, so-called because their wing membranes meet in the middle of their backs (see Box 12).

Parnell's Mustached Bat

Parnell's Mustached Bats occur in the northern part of South America, Central America and much of the West Indies. Their forearms are 50 to 60 mm long and adults weigh 12–18 g. Their size, faces and the way their wings join their bodies make it easy to distinguish Parnell's Mustached Bats from other species in the family.

In color, Parnell's Mustached Bats vary from a brilliant fulvous or orange to dark brown or blackish. When these bats molt, the new fur is usually dark in color, becoming paler with age or progressing to the brighter condition. In other species of bats, seasonal variation in color may reflect the roosting environment. It is not clear if this situation applies to Parnell's Mustached Bats.

This species typically roosts in hollows, usually in caves and mines. Within caves and mines they usually roost in large chambers where the humidity is high. Parnell's Mustached Bats seem to fly continuously from the time they leave their roosts until their return. They are insectivorous and they forage in areas of thick vegetation and below the canopies of trees, often being caught in mist nests set just above the ground. The bats leave their cave roosts and fly

This portrait of a Sooty Mustached Bat shows the leaf-chin that is typical of mormoopid bats. This 10-g bat is widespread in the New World, and this photograph was taken in Jamaica.

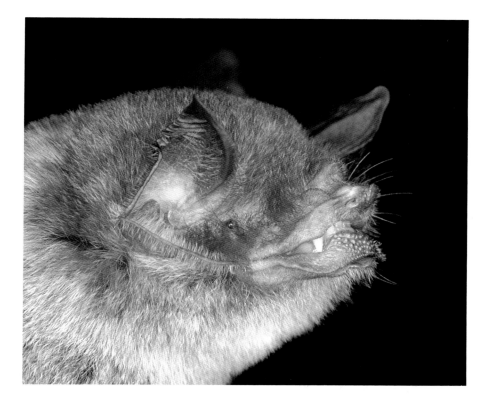

to their feeding areas at about 17.5 km/h. Parnell's Mustached Bats eat insects such as beetles and moths. In captivity they prefer some species of moths over others. In general, these bats avoid bad-tasting insects such as tiger moths or stink bugs.

Parnell's Mustached Bats are the only New World high duty cycle echolocators, separating pulse and echo in time. Their echolocation behavior has received a great deal of attention. Like other high duty cycle echolocators, their echolocation calls are dominated by narrowband components and their auditory system is finely tuned to the prevailing frequencies. This combination of characters permits Parnell's Mustached Bats to distinguish fluttering from non-fluttering targets, and may explain their success at hunting in environments where they are bombarded by echoes from background vegetation.

In spite of the similarity between the echolocation behavior of Parnell's Mustached Bats and the Horseshoe and Old World Leaf-nosed Bats, the details of the specializations for flutter detection are strikingly different. The similarity of Parnell's Mustached Bats and the Old World flutter detectors is an example of a convergent solution to the problem of detecting fluttering targets against a cluttered background.

NEW WORLD LEAF-NOSED BATS, THE PHYLLOSTOMIDAE

The variety of food taken by New World Leaf-nosed Bats makes them the most diverse group of bats, which is reflected by the array of skull shapes. The 123 species in the family are arrayed in seven subfamilies, generally according to diet; the names of subfamilies end in -inae. Most species in the Phyllostominae feed mainly on animals. For species weighing less than 20 g, this means arthropods. Some larger species also eat frogs, lizards, birds and bats, while

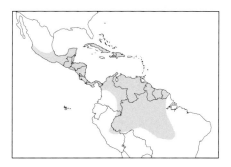

The shaded area shows the distribution of Parnell's Mustached Bats, which also occur on many of the islands in the West Indies.

others, such as Spear-nosed Bats (genus *Phyllostomus*) eat mainly fruit and probably leaves.

Species in the Glossophag*inae*, the Lonchophyll*inae* and the Phyllonyct-er*inae* feed mainly on nectar and pollen. The Caroll*iinae*, the Stenoderm*inae* and the Brachyphyll*inae* feed mainly on fruit and leaves, but some also feed on nectar and pollen. Some of these bats, notably the Carolliinae, frequently mix insects with fruit. Their blood-feeding makes the three species in the sub-family Desmodont*inae* the most specialized of the New World Leaf-nosed Bats.

California Leaf-nosed Bat

This is one of the few species of New World Leaf-nosed Bats occurring in the United States. As the name implies, California Leaf-nosed Bats live in the southern part of California and adjacent Arizona; there is one record of the species from Big Bend National Park in Texas. Most of its range is in Mexico and some other parts of Central America. A closely related species, Water-house's Leaf-nosed Bat, is known from several islands in the West Indies.

These delicate bats have a prominent nose-leaf, large ears (see page 46) and broad wings. They are small to medium-sized with forearms 45–58 mm long; adults weigh 10–15 g. California Leaf-nosed Bats eat mainly insects such as crickets, moths, beetles and a variety of terrestrial arthropods. The bats always take their catch to a roost where they eat it, dropping items such as legs and wings to the ground below.

California Leaf-nosed Bats may use echolocation to find targets, even items such as crickets walking on the ground or foliage. Their echolocation calls are low-intensity, short and broadband, typical of bats that commonly search for prey on surfaces. These bats, however, also listen for sounds coming from prey to find their targets. California Leaf-nosed Bats also have excellent vision, which they often use for finding insect prey. Laboratory work reveals that California Leaf-nosed Bats see very well in the light cast by bright starlight. When using vision to find their prey, California Leaf-nosed Bats stop producing echolocation calls.

These bats typically roost in hollows and are commonly found in caves or mines and occasionally in buildings. The bats may roost in quite well-lighted areas close to the entrances of caves or mines. Colonies may number in the hundreds of individuals, but smaller groups also have been reported.

A study of the energy consumption by captive California Leaf-nosed Bats showed the critical importance of appropriate roosts from their survival in the northern parts of their range. In California and Arizona, these bats live in a geothermal zone where mines and caves are relatively warm. Geothermally heated roosts allow the bats to winter in these cooler regions because the heat from the ground keeps them warm. In heated roosts, California Leaf-nosed Bats do not have to expend energy to stay warm.

Heated roosts and versatile feeding behavior explain the occurrence of California Leaf-nosed Bats in some parts of the United States. Even on relatively cool winter nights, some insects and other arthropods are active on the ground when none are flying. By using non-volant prey the bats are assured of a food supply, and their roosts permit them to save energy.

California Leaf-nosed Bats mate in August and September and in the following spring each female bears a single young. The long period between mating and birth is accomplished by delayed development. In California Leaf-nosed Bats, fertilization follows mating, but the development of the

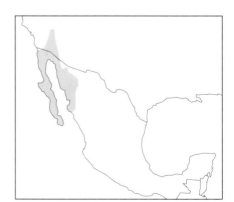

The distribution of California Leaf-nosed Bats.

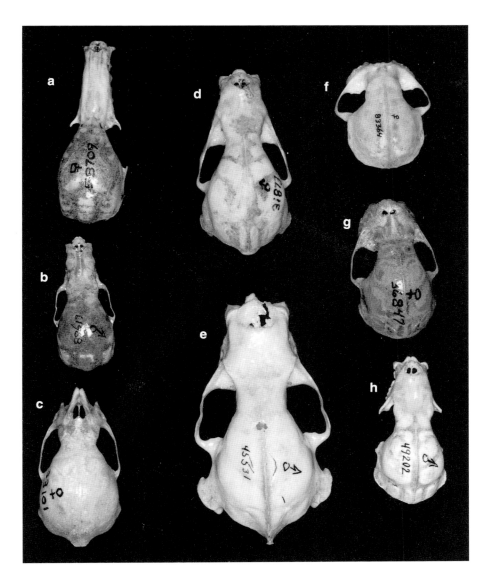

The skulls shown here illustrate the tremendous variety of New World Leaf-nosed Bats. Included are Mexican Long-tongued Bats (a), Pallas' Long-tongued Bat (b) and Common Vampire Bats (c), three species whose diet is mainly liquid; a Fringe-lipped Bat (d) that eats frogs, lizards and insects; and a Greater Spear-nosed Bat (e) that feeds mainly on fruit, but may also take animals. Wrinkle-faced Bats (f), Brown Fruit Bats (g) and Short-tailed Fruit Bats (h) are fruit-eaters. The skulls of the Mexican Long-tongued Bat (a) and Fringe-lipped Bats (d) are 3.0 cm long.

embryo is arrested over the winter. Functionally, the timing of mating and birth resembles that of Plain-nosed or Horseshoe bats, but the mechanism is different.

Linnaeus' False Vampire Bat

Linnaeus' False Vampire Bat is the largest species of bat in the New World, with a forearm 105 to 115 mm long, a wingspan of 0.6 m and a body mass of 150–180 g. The broad wings allow the bat to lift heavy prey and their flight is maneuverable. This species occurs from central South America north into the southern part of Central America, and on the island of Trinidad.

Linnaeus' False Vampire Bats roost in hollows, usually hollow trees. Roosting groups are small and typically include one adult male with several adult females and their young. A single young is born each year, but the timing of births varies depending upon the seasons where the bats live.

These bats eat both arthropods and vertebrates. The vertebrate prey includes bats, rodents, birds and some lizards. One group of Linnaeus' False Vampire Bats in Costa Rica brought their food back to their day roost, where they ate most of it and dropped inedible pieces on the ground. Analysis of the discarded prey remains revealed that these bats had eaten 18 species of birds

The distribution of Linnaeus' False Vampire Bats.

ranging in size from 20 to 150 grams. Some of the birds were almost as big as the bats themselves!

Most of the bird prey were foliage-roosting species of the dry forest in which the roost was located. How had the bats found the birds they had eaten? Groove-billed Anis have a strong body odor and were frequent victims of the bats. These circumstances suggest that the bats used their sense of smell to locate Groove-billed Anis on their nests. A concurrent study showed that some predator frequently took male Groove-billed Anis from their nests at night. The information from the bat and bird studies pointed to Linnaeus' False Vampire Bats as the predator, and to a sense of smell as the means they used to find the Groove-billed Anis on their nests.

Linnaeus' False Vampire Bats are capable echolocators, producing low-intensity calls that are short (less than 1 ms) and broadband. In the laboratory, the bats have little trouble detecting and avoiding obstacles in situations where they use echolocation. Echolocation also permitted the bats to distinguish between two similar targets. Linnaeus' False Vampire Bats also have relatively large eyes. It is clear that when hunting, these bats can use a combination of cues, including sound, sight and smell.

Short-tailed Fruit Bat

Short-tailed Fruit Bats occur widely through Central and South America and are among the best studied of bats. They are found from southern Veracruz in Mexico in the north to Paraguay in the south, and from Colombia in the west to Brazil in the east. Short-tailed Fruit Bats also occur in Trinidad and Tobago and in Grenada in the Caribbean. These bats are one of four species in the genus *Carollia*, one of the most abundant groups of bats where they occur. Size is one way to distinguish Short-tailed Fruit Bats from other *Carollia*, but other important differences include the appearance of the fur and the details of the skull and teeth. Adult Short-tailed Fruit bats weigh 16–20 g, and their forearms are 40–45 mm long. Although these bats usually are dark brown or gray in color, some are bright orange.

In Costa Rica, and in other parts of their range, female Short-tailed Fruit Bats breed twice each year. One of the birth periods occurs in the dry season, the other in the middle of the wet season. The actual timing of births within the Short-tailed Fruit Bats population at any location is not highly synchronous, so that in Costa Rica, most adult females are lactating in April and May and in August and September, but some are lactating as early as late March or as late as mid-October. During pregnancy, the body weight of a female increases by one third, and the newborns weigh about 5 g, 28% of the female's postpartum mass.

Female Short-tailed Fruit Bats produce large quantities of milk for the first month after their young is born, and some milk production continues for an additional two to four weeks. Females typically leave their young behind when they depart to forage, but unlike some other bats, the babies are not deposited in crèches. Baby Short-tailed Fruit Bats may be left in the day roost or in some other location while their mothers are out foraging. The babies grow quite quickly, their forearms increasing from about 24.4 mm at birth to adult size (forearm 41-45 mm) by age six weeks. Between age 18 and 24 days, Short-tailed Fruit Bats change from being clumsy fliers to adept ones, but it takes another few weeks before their flight patterns are adult-like in terms of speed and control of flight.

The day roosts of Short-tailed Fruit Bats are located in hollows which may be situated in caves, buildings, culverts or trees. Within these roosts there are three classes of bats: adult females, territorial (harem) males and bachelors.

The distribution of Short-tailed Fruit Bats.

The adult females form tight clusters that average two to three individuals but may include up to 18. Each group of reproductive females is attended by one adult male, the harem or territorial individual. The bachelor groups include subadult females and subadult and adult males.

A *Short-tailed Fruit Bat roosting in a Colombian cave.*

Both in captive colonies and in the wild, males compete vigorously for the position of territorial or harem male. The clusters of breeding adult females often roost at specific places within a hollow, suggesting that by defending a site, males can control access to females. Females do move between groups and sometimes in captivity a female has mated with the male in one group, then moved and had her baby in another group.

The harem system of social organization means that Short-tailed Fruit Bats are polygynous (one male with a group of females). In these systems, relatively few males are sexually active because only the territorial male has a hope of attracting females and mating. In one study in Costa Rica, only 12–17% of the adult males in a roost mated with females; adult males in bachelor groups are not known to mate. Males that successfully hold harem positions tend to be the oldest and heaviest individuals with the largest testicles. To draw this conclusion, biologists examined the amount of wear on the bats' teeth to determine their ages

Unlike bachelor males, the territorial or harem individuals will not tolerate other adult males close by. Confrontations between males can escalate from displays to "boxing." During a low-intensity encounter, males stick out their tongues, flick their wings and emit harsh-sounding vocalizations. These interactions usually occur when individuals are several centimeters apart. Boxing is the next level of escalation. Boxing males approach one another and make alternate swipes at one another with their forearms, thumbs and folded wings. Most boxing displays last less than one minute and are common between males in adjacent harems.

Short-tailed Fruit Bats eat the fruit from more than 50 species of plants and the nectar and pollen from at least 11 species. They also eat insects. Most of the plants that Short-tailed Fruit Bats visit for feeding are shrubs of the ground story in the forests where they occur. In Costa Rica, these bats vary their diets considerably over the year, reflecting changes in food availability related to seasonal differences in rainfall. Adult males and females do not have exactly the same diets, reflecting differences in the cost of reproduction.

Although Short-tailed Fruit Bats consume a wide range of fruits, they choose fruits that have pulp relatively rich in protein and low in fiber. Early in the evening the bats eat high-protein fruits, later switching to energy-rich fruits. They usually eat insects early in the morning. When foraging, these bats quickly find available fruit in the areas they visit. At one site in Costa Rica most Short-tailed Fruit Bats forage within 1.5 km of their day roosts. Individual bats predictably use the same foraging areas night after night, adjusting their selection of food according to the season.

Some behavior of Short-tailed Fruit Bats seems designed to minimize their exposure to nocturnal predators. These bats avoid flying in bright moonlight, especially in the dry season, and they make extensive use of feeding perches. A foraging bat selects a fruit and takes it away to eat elsewhere. Avoiding flying in bright moonlight probably makes the bats less conspicuous to predators. Feeding perches and dispersed food resources permit Short-tailed Fruit Bats to avoid predators lying in wait at large, predictable, rich patches of fruit.

We do not know who these predators are. We can guess that Linnaeus' False Vampire Bat and Woolly False Vampire Bats are likely candidates, along with several species of owls and mammals such as opossums, ringtails and small cats. Biologists rarely see Short-tailed Fruit Bats attacked by predators or find evidence that predators often eat these bats. This leaves two possible explanations: Short-tailed Fruit Bats are very good at avoiding and evading predators, or the predators are very good at catching these bats outside the notice of biologists.

PLAIN-NOSED BATS, THE VESPERTILIONIDAE

Almost anywhere you go in the world where there are bats, some will be Plain-nosed Bats. With 283 species, this is the largest family of bats, and insects are their staple diet. Variable thermostats permit Plain-nosed Bats to hibernate and to enter daily torpor. These features make them the chief bats of temperate areas. In the Old World, Horseshoe Bats also have such thermostats and live in the temperate zones.

Vespertilionids are called "plain-nosed" because most species lack conspicuous leaf-like ornaments. Some species, however, such as the Australian Northern Bat have modest nasal ornaments and others like the Greater Tube-nosed Bat, have tubular nostrils.

Little Brown Bat

Over much of the United States and Canada, Little Brown Bats are abundant. They occur from Alaska, the Yukon and the Northwest Territories in the north to the southern United States and some parts of the highlands in Mexico. In spring, female Little Brown Bats form nursery colonies in the attics of buildings, usually older structures within 1 km of water. The bats leave these sites at the end of the summer and migrate to hibernation sites.

As the name implies, Little Brown Bats are small and brown in color. The bats' color varies over their range and the fur on their backs may be light or dark brown. The fur on their bellies is lighter in color, often whitish. The wing span is about 20 cm and their forearms are 35–40 mm long. Adults fluctuate in weight over the year from 7 or 8 g when they leave hibernation to 10–14 g at the end of the summer before hibernation.

Little Brown Bats eat insects and use a combination of migration and hibernation to survive the winter. But there is a mystery here. In summer the Little Brown Bats commonly encountered by biologists are females and their young. In hibernation sites in many parts of North America, the winter bats are mainly males. In the 1950s and 1960s in eastern North America, thousands of Little Brown Bats were banded, either in summer nursery colonies or winter hibernation sites. Relatively few of the tagged bats from summer were found in winter, and vice versa.

Where do Little Brown Bats go between summer and winter? A simple explanation is that the summer bats use hibernation sites that remain undiscovered by people. The obvious places are parts of known hibernation sites that are accessible to the bats and not to biologists. Heavy fall traffic of Little Brown Bats at caves where few are actually found hibernating suggests this explanation in some cases. An alternative is that females hibernate in cracks and fissures in cliff faces. These openings sometimes extend well back into the rock, and climbers occasionally report hearing bats squawking from inside crevices during autumn climbs.

Virtually all of the known Little Brown Bat hibernation sites are underground, either in caves or in mines. I have heard of Little Brown Bats hibernating in an old well and adjoining earthen basement in an old house in Prince Edward Island (eastern Canada). There also are stories of woodcutters

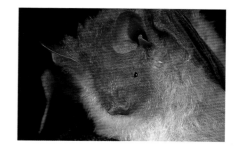

The appearance of its nostrils and its size explain the common name of this Greater Tube-nosed Bat from China.

Some Plain-nosed Bats, such as this Australian Northern Long-eared Bat, have a small leaflike structure on their nose.

finding hibernating bats in hollow trees in the Adirondack mountains of the American northeast. Perhaps biologists have been looking in the wrong places.

Hibernating Little Brown Bats select sites with above freezing temperatures and high humidity. Rising or falling temperatures stimulate them to arouse from hibernation. Banded Little Brown Bats often move from one part of a cave to another over the course of a winter. We suspect that these movements adjust the bats' positions according to changing conditions. There are some records of banded Little Brown Bats moving 160 km between different caves and mines in mid-winter.

Little Brown Bats leave their hibernation sites about the time when nighttime temperatures regularly exceed 10°C, the threshold for increased activity of flying insects. In the southern parts of their range, the bats may leave hibernation in February, while in northern Ontario, their departure dates may be late in April. Upon departure from hibernation sites, females fly to nursery colonies where they gather to have their young. This increase in activity corresponds to the time when females ovulate and their eggs are fertilized by sperm stored over winter in the uterus

The gestation period is about 60 days and the single baby is born bottom first. Newborn Little Brown Bats weigh about 2.5 grams, 25–30% of their mother's mass; they have no fur and their eyes are closed. Contrary to a common belief, after birth, mother Little Brown Bats do not carry their young with them when they go out to forage. Mothers leave their babies in nursery colonies at these times. Mothers returning to the nursery after feeding and recognize their babies by their calls and, at closer range, their odor. Mothers are

A portrait of a Little Brown Bat.

quick to recognize and nurse their own young but may aggressively reject other babies that try to nurse

Baby Little Brown Bats grow rapidly, and by age three weeks are beginning to fly. At age three weeks, the babies' forearms are as long as their mothers' and their permanent teeth have completely erupted. Now, the young begin to eat insects, for a time combining milk and insects in their diet. We do not know if a young catches its own first insects or if they are provided by its mother.

When females are busy with young, the male Little Brown Bats are rarely encountered by biologists. Although some males live around nursery colonies, they do not assist in caring for the young.

The shaded area identifies the distribution of Little Brown Bats.

In southern Ontario in August (later in locations farther south), Little Brown Bats begin to visit the caves and mines that later serve as hibernation sites. These visits are called "swarming behavior." The bats arrive at the sites about an hour after dark and, from then until about an hour before dawn, hundreds may fly through the underground passages. About half of the swarming population is young born that year, while adult males comprise about 60% of the adult population. Swarming seems to familiarize young with potential hibernation sites.

By the middle of August, bats in the swarming population begin to mate. Using light tags, biologists have found that males may mate with several females in succession and that females also visit and mate with several males. Mating activity is limited to adult males and females. In southern parts of their range, Little Brown Bats may become sexually mature in their first year, but farther north they reach this stage during their second year.

During the swarming and mating season, adult males sit at locations on the wall or ceiling and produce echolocation calls. Females fly around, often passing by several males before landing and joining one. Groups of bats form around calling males and each group contains one adult male, some young of that year and some adult females. Apart from some nose-to-nose contact between the male and female, there is no evidence of courtship behavior or foreplay. The male mounts the female from the rear, grasping the back of her neck and holding her with his wrists and thumbs. The act of copulation may last from 3 minutes to more than 20 minutes. Within 20 minutes of mating, sperm reaches the female's uterus, where it will remain until the following spring.

Biologists banding Little Brown Bats in winter often noticed that animals waking up after banding began to copulate. These observations suggested that most mating took place in winter. But studies during the swarming season in southern Ontario revealed that many more copulations occur in the last two weeks in August than during the winter, indicating that the late summer and early autumn is the main mating period for Little Brown Bats.

Two other lines of evidence support this view. The first is that males cease to produce sperm at the end of the summer, after which their supplies of sperm are limited. Since sperm is the key to male's mating success, he should not waste it. The second is the observation that mating couples in winter are in many cases homosexual, something that has not been seen in the summer and early fall. Over 35% of the mating couples of Little Brown Bats seen in winter were pairs of males. During winter, active males try to copulate with torpid bats, while in the late summer and early autumn, both participants are active. An active bat probably gives off more information than a cold one, so homosexual winter matings are probably the result of mistaken identity.

Their abundance and wide distribution have made Little Brown Bats the prime study animal for much research, and so we know a great deal about their biology, from anatomy and physiology to behavior and ecology. This bank of knowledge only highlights the many things remaining to be discovered about these bats.

Big Brown Bat

Big Brown Bats occur throughout much of North America and the northern part of South America, as well as many islands in the West Indies. These bats are small to medium-sized, and adults weigh 14 to 25 g; their forearms are 39–54 mm long. The wings of Big Brown Bats are relatively broad and their ears are short and thick. The ears and wing membranes are blackish in color, and the fur color on the back varies geographically from pinkish tan to a rich chocolate color; the fur on the belly is paler than the fur on the back.

In eastern North America, female Big Brown Bats typically bear twins each year, while in more western locations and in the West Indies, a single young is born. From studies in Kansas, we know that female Big Brown Bats usually release five to seven eggs per ovulation, all of which may be fertilized. The litter size of one or two suggests some form of uterine control over the number of young that develop to term. Newborn Big Brown Bats are naked and almost immobile, but their eyes and ears open within a few hours of birth. In New England, the newborns weigh about 3.3 g each, together representing 20% of the mother's postpartum mass. Females produce milk for 32–40 days in New England, and the young first begin flying at age 18 to 35 days.

Big Brown Bats fly continuously while foraging and eat flying insects. These bats typically begin hunting about 18 minutes after sundown, and radio-tracking studies show that they spend about 90 minutes a night foraging. Big Brown Bats hunt in a variety of habitats, sometimes searching for insects over woodlands, fields or bodies of water. They also hunt in parklands in cities throughout their range.

Big Brown Bats consume 50 to 100% of their body mass in insects every night, and the menu includes a variety of prey. Sometimes Big Brown Bats feed mainly on beetles, but at other times they eat insects such as caddis flies, moths, flies and mayflies. Foraging Big Brown Bats have been observed catching 5 to 20 insects a minute. Their actual rates of prey capture are affected by the insect density where they are hunting.

In eastern Ontario, female Big Brown Bats often form nursery colonies in buildings. The colonies may be in attic spaces, in the boxed part of the eaves, in parts of the eaves or in the walls. The numbers of bats in a colony varies geographically. In eastern Ontario, nursery colonies average 40 females, while in buildings in Indiana, hundreds of bats roost together. In the Okanagan Valley of British Columbia, Big Brown Bats roost in hollow Ponderosa Pine trees with up to 200 individuals in one tree. Variations in roosting habits are paralleled by differences in foraging behavior.

In eastern Ontario, radio tracking has indicated that Big Brown Bats leave their roosts and fly off in a different direction each night. The bats usually fly about 5 km away from the colony and then turn and fly back when they have finished eating. The total foraging time is 60–90 minutes. In the Okanagan Valley, radio-tagged Big Brown Bats forage nightly over the same section of the Okanagan River, exploiting the high concentrations of insects emerging there. In Ontario the bats predictably return to the same building roosts night after night, while in British Columbia, Big Brown Bats switch roost trees every night. In short, Ontario Big Brown Bats use different foraging areas but the same roosts every night; in British Columbia the reverse is true.

Big Brown Bats have a variable thermostat. In winter, these bats hibernate for varying periods depending upon where they live and the lengths of the winters there. In summer, the bats lower their body temperatures to save energy (heating costs) on cooler days (see page 90). While males, non-reproductive

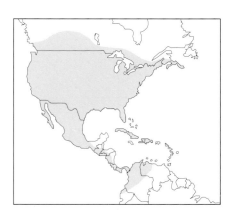

The distribution of Big Brown Bats.

females and pregnant females frequently enter torpor during inclement summer weather, lactating bats rarely do so. The cost of entering torpor for pregnant individuals is prolonged pregnancy. The advantage of entering torpor is conserving energy on nights when prey is scarce. Lactating females benefit from remaining active because they produce more milk than torpid ones. The increased milk supply means faster growth for the babies of active females.

Some banded Big Brown Bats live 19 years in the wild, and ages of over 10 years are common. Most of our knowledge about their longevity comes from individuals banded during hibernation. Although Big Brown Bats often hibernate underground, they also hibernate in buildings. Some of the building records come from earthen basements or the spaces over cisterns, places with cave-like environments. Other records are of Big Brown Bats hibernating in attics or in walls. Big Brown Bats hibernate in attics in areas with milder winters. In southern Ontario where winters are more severe, Big Brown Bats seem to hibernate in the walls of buildings.

Big Brown Bats sometimes hibernate where the air temperature falls below freezing; we do not know if the bats' body temperatures also are subfreezing. In caves and mines, hibernating Big Brown Bats typically occur in cooler, drier locations compared to other species such as Little Brown Bats or Northern Long-eared Bats.

The echolocation behavior of Big Brown Bats has been intensively studied because these animals are common, are widely distributed and adapt well to captivity. Echolocating Big Brown Bats first detect a 19-mm-diameter sphere when it is 5 m away. A 4.8-mm-diameter sphere is first detected at 3 m. Echolocation also allows Big Brown Bats to collect information about the details of a target's surface. For example, trained bats can use echolocation to distinguish between holes that differ in depth by less than 1 mm.

In eastern North America, hunting Big Brown Bats use echolocation calls that are intense and broadband sweeping from about 65 to 27 kHz in 5–8

Hibernating Big Brown Bats in an abandoned mine in southeastern Ontario. The banded bats in the photograph were at least 15 years old when the picture was taken.

ms. In the Okanagan Valley, this species produces longer calls of narrower bandwith. In eastern North America, Big Brown Bats will fly toward 1-cm-diameter stones thrown into the air, but they rarely contact them. In the Okanagan Valley, Big Brown Bats often strike airborne stones. The differences in behavior reflect the design of the echolocation calls and thus the information available to the bat.

In spite of their distribution and abundance, and our knowledge about them, we have no information about the mating behavior of Big Brown Bats. Genetic studies indicated that the twins born to a female Big Brown Bat had been sired by two different males, indicating that at least some females mate with more than one male. Big Brown Bats are common house bats throughout much of their range, often bringing them into direct contact with people. Furthermore, Big Brown Bats are large enough to deliver painful bites that can draw blood. Since Big Brown Bats bite in self-defense, they are frequently the main bats implicated in the possible transmission of rabies virus from bats to other animals, including people.

Spotted Bat

Three 15-mm-diameter white spots on a background of jet black fur (see photo on page 56) give Spotted Bats their common name. The distinctive pattern on the bat's back, coupled with their enormous (45–50-mm-long) pink ears, make them among the most distinctive of mammals. Spotted Bats occur from northern Mexico through the western United States to southern Canada in the Okanagan Valley of British Columbia. Although widespread in certain areas, they are relatively uncommon in most locations and most specimens have been taken in mist nets set over water holes.

Spotted Bats are small to medium sized, with forearms 48 to 51 mm long, and adult body masses of 16–20 grams. In their wing dimensions and shape, Spotted Bats exactly resemble Big Brown Bats, although their enormous ears make them distinct in profile from Big Brown Bats. Only some related species of big-eared bats (genus *Plecotus*) have ears that are proportionally as large as those of Spotted Bats.

The first Spotted Bats known to science was described in 1892, but by 1958 only 16 specimens had been reported. In the 1960s when biologists began more extensive sampling with mist nets, the numbers of specimens increased, and it became obvious that in some places these bats were quite common. Captures in mist nets suggested that Spotted Bats were late fliers. Other measures of their activity, such as monitoring echolocation calls and the movements of radio-tagged animals, showed that Spotted Bats fly all night.

The echolocation calls of Spotted Bats make them distinctive in most of the areas where they occur. Indeed, their echolocation calls are the most conspicuous features of these spectacular mammals, since they are entirely audible to most humans, contradicting the general impression that all bat echolocation is ultrasonic (beyond the range of human hearing). Experienced naturalists often are familiar with the sound of Spotted Bat echolocation calls but presume them to be the sounds of an insect.

Spotted Bat echolocation calls last about 5 milliseconds and during this time sweep from about 15 kHz to 9 kHz. Like other echolocating bats that hunt airborne targets, Spotted Bats produce feeding buzzes during attacks on prey. Like the other echolocation calls of Spotted Bats, those in the feeding buzz are quite audible to humans.

In the Okanagan Valley (British Columbia), Spotted Bats often hunt over areas of open meadow, or swamp, or in stands of Ponderosa Pine. A hunting

The huge pinkish ears make Spotted Bats very distinctive, but it is their black fur with white spots that gives them their name (see page 56).

Spotted Bat usually flies 5–10 m above the ground, but when pursuing an insect such as a moth, the bat may dive to within a meter of the ground. These dives are always accompanied by feeding buzzes. Foraging Spotted Bats do not focus their activity in areas of high insect density. In the Okanagan Valley, these bats spend little time hunting among the insects attracted to lights, and unlike many other species there, they do not forage in the swarms of insects emerging from the Okanagan River. There is little information about the diet of Spotted Bats beyond the fact that they eat insects. The bats eat many moths as well as beetles and caddis flies.

Radio-tracking studies have shown that hunting Spotted Bats fly all night, leaving their day roosts at dusk and returning just before dawn. The actual foraging time fluctuates according to the length of the night, which changes over the summer. Hunting Spotted Bats usually cover 10–20 km every night. Radio-tagged bats return nightly to the same general foraging area, and there is considerable overlap in the foraging areas of different bats.

Spotted Bats roost by day in the nooks and crannies of cliff faces. Radio-tagged bats return at the end of each night to the same cliff faces. This predictability means that by counting bats as they emerge, biologists can accurately estimate the size of Spotted Bats populations. The cliff faces in which the bats roost are relatively inaccessible to humans and many other predators.

Female Spotted Bats bear a single young in May or June, depending upon the latitude. Like other newborn bats, Baby Spotted Bats are naked and have their ears and eyes closed. The radio-tracking evidence suggests that unlike some other bats, female Spotted Bats do not return during the night to nurse their young.

In British Columbia and in some other areas, Spotted Bats disappear from their summer ranges during winter. It is not clear if this disappearance is the result of the bats' seeking local hibernation sites, or migrating to completely different surroundings.

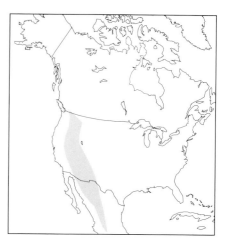

The shaded area identifies the range of Spotted Bats.

PALLID BATS, THE ANTROZOIDAE

This family includes two species (Pallid Bats and Van Gelder's Bats) that formerly were included among the Plain-nosed Bats. Both species occur in the New World, their combined range extending from Central America through western North America as far north as southern British Columbia (Canada).

Pallid Bat

Pallid Bats are light-colored, large-eared, broad-winged and occur from Mexico north to British Columbia. Most of their range is in the United States, but there are some records from Western Cuba. The bats, with forearms ranging in length from 45 to 60 mm, weigh 13–25 g and have a distinctive ridge on their noses. Although their eyes are relatively large, the visual acuity of Pallid Bats is not as good as that of California Leaf-nosed Bats.

Pallid Bats often live in semi-arid to arid regions. Their ability to produce quite concentrated urine allows them to conserve water and live in deserts. These bats can go for long periods without drinking, getting the water they need from their prey. Roosting posture also affects water conservation. A Pallid Bat with its wings tightly folded loses half as much water as one with its wings spread.

Female Pallid Bats bear young once a year, at different times in spring depending upon the geographic location. These bats usually have twins, but some produce single young. Like other Plain-nosed Bats, female Pallid Bats store sperm in the uterus, so that mating and parturition are separated by several months even though the gestation period is only about nine weeks. During mating, male Pallid Bats mount females from the back, grasping the female with their forearms and thumbs. Unlike some other bats, males do not appear to bite the females' necks during copulation.

Newborn Pallid Bats are naked and have their eyes and ears closed, but they can crawl on horizontal surfaces and cling to their mothers. By age six to seven weeks the forearms have grown from 17 mm at birth to adult size. Young Pallid Bats begin to fly between age four and five weeks, but in the wild their flight is not adult-like until about age six weeks.

The echolocation system of Pallid Bats develops at about the same pace as the bats' flying ability. At the time when the bats first begin to fly, they show an adult pattern of directional hearing sensitivity and can rapidly process information. When they first begin to fly, Pallid Bats produce echolocation calls that are slightly lower in frequency than those of adults. By age six weeks, the calls of adults and young are indistinguishable.

Pallid Bats roost in hollows and crevices. Their roosts may be in and around buildings, rock faces or hollow trees. Rock crevices are common roost sites, selected according to prevailing weather conditions. By changing their positions along a horizontal rock crevice, the bats choose the temperature that suits them, moving closer to the entrance on cool days, and farther away from it on

A handful of Pallid Bats appears to be mainly ears, forearms and pale fur.

hot days. Like many Plain-nosed Bats, Pallid Bats have a variable thermostat and can enter torpor. This energy-saving strategy permits the bats to conserve energy they might have used to keep warm. Pallid Bats eat mainly insects but take a variety of other prey. These bats eat crickets and beetles, mantids, moths, cicadas, scorpions and centipedes. There is even one record of a Pallid Bat taking a pocket mouse. Studies of prey handling indicates that although they will attack large prey such as sphinx moths, they do not handle them efficiently. Pallid Bats also visit flowers to obtain nectar and pollen and the insects that visit the flowers.

Although Pallid Bats are capable echolocators, producing feeding buzzes as they attack airborne targets, they often stop echolocating. When Pallid Bats are listening for sounds coming from prey or using their eyes to locate targets, they stop producing echolocation calls. Pallid Bats attend to the sounds of wing beats or the scuffling sounds associated with movement when hunting prey on surfaces.

Under a variety of circumstances, Pallid Bats emit piercing, bell-like vocalizations known as "directive calls." Unlike their ultrasonic echolocation calls, directive calls are entirely audible to most humans. In one setting, directive calls facilitate reunions between mothers and young, but they also serve more general communication functions. Just before dawn when several Pallid Bats are flying together, apparently looking for a suitable roost site, they produce directive calls. This behavior, known as "rallying," draws the members of the group to the same crevice roost. Directive calls are good indicators of the presence of Pallid Bats.

Pallid Bats, once considered to be Plain-nosed Bats, now are placed in their own family. Note the difference between this Pallid Bat and most plain-nosed bats illustrated in this book.

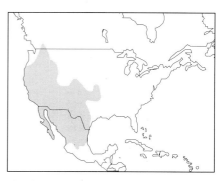

The distribution of Pallid Bats.

Free-tailed Bats, the Molossidae

The 82 species of Free-tailed Bats are found mainly in the tropics, although some range into the temperate zones on both sides of the equator. Africa and South America have the most species of Free-tailed Bats; but there are some species in India, Southeast Asia and Australia. The thick tails of these bats extend beyond the end of the interfemoral membrane (see page 27). Like most Plain-nosed Bats, Free-tailed Bats lack nasal ornaments. Two species of Free-tailed Bats, the Naked Bats of Southeast Asia, are virtually without fur or hair. While some species of Free-tailed Bats have wrinkled upper lips, a distinctive trait, others have smooth upper lips.

Mexican Free-tailed Bats

Mexican Free-tailed Bats have the distinction of attaining higher population densities than any other mammals, including humans. Some caves in the American southwest house more than 5 million individuals, and colonies numbering hundreds of individuals are common in structures such as hollow trees, buildings, crevices on the outsides of buildings and the expansion joints in bridges. The population size in any colony may directly reflect the amount of available space.

Colonies of hundreds of thousands of Mexican Free-tailed Bats have provided biologists with a number of unique opportunities. One of the most interesting is the impact that one of these bats (12–15 g, forearm 38–45 mm) can have on a jet-powered aircraft. At Randolph Air Force Base in Texas, twin-engined trainer aircraft have been damaged when Mexican Free-tailed Bats have been drawn into the air intakes on the engines. One 12-g bat can destroy the engine; one bat in each engine can destroy the aircraft. These collisions led to an interesting study.

The clouds of bats emerging from Bracken Cave at the end of the base runway were clearly visible on radar, permitting technicians to note the schedules of the bats' comings and goings. The radar information showed that after they left the cave, many Mexican Free-tailed Bats flew up to an altitude of about 10,000 feet, before dispersing toward feeding grounds. At their dawn return, individual bats went as high as 15,000 feet before diving into the cave. By scheduling the flights of aircraft around the flights of the bats, the U.S. Air Force resolved the problem

Free-tailed Bats, like this Red Mastiff Bat from Mexico, lack leaflike or other ornaments on their noses. The stiff hairs beneath the nostrils of this bat have collected some lint, giving the impression that the bat has a small white mustache. When seen in profile, the bat is obviously a species of Free-tailed Bats with smooth upper lips. In this species the ears arise from different points on the bat's forehead.

of expensive and dangerous collisions between bats and the aircraft. For more about high flying bats, see page 187.

Size, color pattern and wrinkled lips make Little Free-Tailed Bats easy to recognize.

Mexican Free-tailed Bats are widespread, occurring across the southern United States, through Central America and the West Indies, and south along the Andes into southern South America. Among Free-tailed Bats in the New World, Mexican Free-tailed Bats are the only species with deeply wrinkled upper lips. In other parts of the world, especially Africa, there are many more species of Free-tailed Bats with deeply wrinkled upper lips.

The large populations of roosting Mexican Free-tailed Bats have important consequences for the animals. An important one is the high concentrations of ammonia associated with the droppings and urine of the bats. Another consequence of high population levels in roosts is local depletion of food resources. Evidence from a variety of sources suggests that Mexican Free-tailed Bats fly up to 50 km a night to find food. These bats are insectivorous, often preying on moths. Radio tracking studies show that Mexican Free-tailed Bats fly all night, some only returning to the cave roost well after dawn.

Their long, narrow wings make long-distance flights relatively economical for the bats. The wings, however, are just one reflection of a combination of other features, including skeletal and physiological mechanisms all contributing to efficient flight.

Living in huge colonies also makes Mexican Free-tailed Bats conspicuous. It is little wonder that a host of predators waits for the bats at the entrances to their roosts. A number of species of birds harvest Mexican Free-tailed Bats at the entrances to their roosts. The list is long and includes everything from owls and road-runners to kites and other raptors. Less mobile predators such as snakes, raccoons, opossums, skunks and coatis also exploit the opportunity. Inside the cave roosts, a

A portrait of the Mexican Free-tailed Bat. Note the wrinkled upper lips and the ears arising from separate points on the bat's forehead.

The Egyptian Free-tailed Bat is a Free-tailed Bat with deeply wrinkled upper lips. In this species, a band of skin joins the ears across the forehead.

The distribution of Mexican Free-tailed Bats.

whole community of invertebrates exploits the by-products of the bats, mainly their guano, but also bats that fall from their roosts.

Mexican Free-tailed Bats bear a single young each year, but the timing of births varies considerably, as expected from a species ranging so far north and south of the equator. In Texas, young are born in late June and early July. Female bats deposit their young in crêches, visiting them once or twice a day for nursing. In crêches, the density of babies can exceed 3,000 per square meter, and some early evidence suggested that female Mexican Free-tailed Bats could not possibly find their own young in this setting.

More recent studies using genetic markers have established that 85% of the time Mexican Free-tailed Bats nursed young that could be their own. The females accomplish this selectivity by relying on spatial memory, each seeking to recognize the voice of her baby and its smell. Although baby Mexican Free-tailed Bats will try to obtain milk from any passing female, the females are the selective part of the combination.

As noted elsewhere (page 61), extensive banding studies showed that some populations of Mexican Free-tailed Bats migrate from the American southwest to cave sites ranging from 800 to 1,800 km away in Mexico. Other populations are not migratory, remaining in the United States through the winter. In these populations there is evidence of hibernation.

In a species as widespread as Mexican Free-tailed Bats, biologists have expected to find populations that are isolated from others. Isolated and distinct populations are sometimes called "subspecies," and in 1989 at least nine subspecies of Mexican Free-tailed Bats were recognized by some researchers. Genetic analyses, however, have not supported the proposal that populations in the United States are genetically isolated from one another.

VAMPIRE BATS

Vampire bats feed only on blood, a fact that sets the human imagination racing. The three species are medium-sized, with adult wingspans of 320 to 350 mm and weights of about 30 to 40 grams. While they are larger than most of the bats of the temperate zones of the world, vampire bats are much smaller than Gigantic Flying Foxes, which weigh in at 1,500 g. Horror movie depictions of vampire bats often use flying foxes as models because larger bats are easier to photograph. This contributes to the public perception of vampire bats as large, terrifying animals. But animals that feed on blood, whether they are insects, leeches or bats, tend to be small because blood is a precious commodity and hard to obtain in large amounts.

Vampire bats are members of the New World Leaf-nosed Bats, the Phyllostomidae. All three species of living vampire bats occur in South and Central America. Fossils of three other species reveal that several thousand years ago vampire bats were more widespread. They are known from Cuba and from as far north as West Virginia and northern California, places where they no longer occur. With the exception of captive animals, vampire bats have never been found outside of the New World.

People are often surprised to learn that vampire bats are not found in central Europe. It seems common to suppose that human myths about vampires and stories about Dracula somehow involve vampire bats. The truth is that vampire bats got their names from human myths about vampires. In many human cultures, vampires are people who return from the dead to feed on the blood of living people. After the bats were discovered by European explorers, they were given the name vampire, denoting blood-feeding. The blood-feeding bats were well known to many of the human inhabitants of South and Central America well before their discovery by Europeans. Bram Stoker, intrigued by the publicity surrounding bats that fed on blood, included bats in his book, *Dracula.*

Naturalists returned from South and Central America with many fascinating plants and animals. Among the collections were many bats, which were

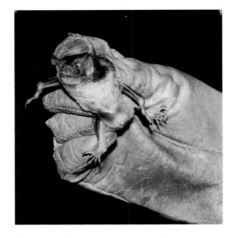

My gloved hand gives an excellent impression of the relative size of this female Common Vampire Bat.

described and given scientific names. Today in South and Central America bats in several genera have names reflecting an earlier preoccupation with vampires. There are bats in genera called *Vampyrum*, *Vampyressa*, *Vampyrodes* and *Vampyrops*. Linnaeus' False Vampire Bat (*Vampyrum spectrum*) is a versatile predator that takes a variety of prey. True, whether it eats a bat, mouse or bird it gets some blood, but *Vampyrum spectrum* is neither a vampire nor a blood-feeder. The others, *Vampyressa*, *Vampyrodes* and *Vampyrops*, are fruit-eating bats that occasionally may take an insect. Together these three genera house about 11 species but none of them is a blood-feeder.

Vampire bats are among the most fascinating of mammals, although we know relatively little about the details of their lives. Common Vampire Bats, as their name implies, are the most widespread of vampires. They adapt well to captivity and often are exhibited in zoos. These bats may be among the best studied in the world. Hairy-legged Vampire Bats and White-winged Vampire Bats are less common and are less often caught by biologists. While Common Vampire Bats may feed on the blood of mammals or birds, the White-winged Vampire Bat and the Hairy-legged Vampire Bat are thought to prefer bird blood.

ORIGINS

Biologists have argued for years about whether vampire bats should be housed in their own family (the Desmodontidae) or included among the New World Leaf-nosed Bats (the Phyllostomidae). People on both sides of this argument agree that the New World Leaf-nosed Bats are the vampire bats' closest relatives. Vampire bats are highly specialized for feeding on blood. This situation raises several questions: How did blood-feeding arise in bats? Why is it restricted to the New World tropics? When did it appear?

Three theories account for the origin of vampire bats. The first proposes that vampire bats originated from fruit-eating bats. This theory suggests that large, strong upper incisor teeth would make fruit bats well suited to switching to blood. This theory does not explain why blood-feeding did not also appear among the Old World Fruit Bats, the Pteropodidae.

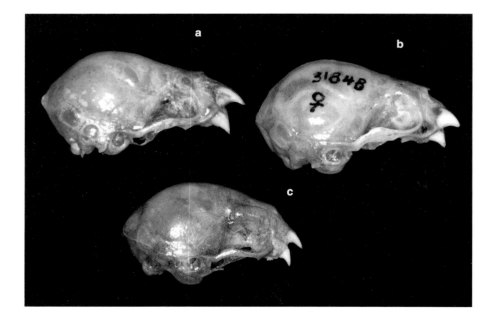

Shown here are the skulls of the three species of vampire bats, the Common Vampire Bat (a), the Hairy-legged Vampire Bat (b) and the White-winged Vampire Bat (c). The Common Vampire Bat's skull is about 2.5 cm (1 inch) long.

The second theory suggests that the ancestors of vampire bats acquired a taste for blood by feeding on ticks and other blood-feeding ectoparasites of large mammals. Today in Africa, birds known as Ox-peckers make their living by feeding on ticks. It appears to be a viable life-style. But as the Ox-peckers show, both ticks and blood-feeding ectoparasites and large mammals occur in Africa. Again we are left with the question, why did blood-feeding bats not appear in the Old World tropics?

The third theory proposes that the ancestors of vampire bats began to feed on insects and insect larvae they found in wounds on large animals. This theory notes that insectivorous bats often feed where there are many insects and some of them adjust their hunting style according to the situation. Throughout the tropics, flies known as screwworms lay their eggs in wounds and their larvae develop into large masses. This theory identifies strong, sharp upper incisor teeth as the key to why blood-feeding only appeared in New World bats. Many New World Leaf-nosed Bats have large, strong upper incisors. These teeth are lacking from those Old World bats with flexible foraging behavior, namely the Slit-faced Bats and the False Vampire Bats.

None of these theories about the origin of vampire bats has been proved. Evidence from proteins suggests that vampire bats have been around for 6 to 8 million years. These are the dates when the Hairy-legged Vampire Bats separated from the evolutionary line that produced the White-winged Vampire Bats and the Common Vampire Bats.

The shaded area shows the distribution of three species of vampire bats. Stars indicate locations from which fossil vampire bats have been recovered.

BLOOD AS FOOD

Even though living off of blood is a challenge, it is the metier of many species of animals from different evolutionary backgrounds. In many ways blood is an ideal food. Within the bodies of animals with backbones, the vertebrates, blood is the central ingredient of the circulatory system. It flows in vessels, dispensing food and oxygen through the body and collecting wastes for removal. Blood consists of water-like plasma, chemicals, red blood cells and white blood cells. The blood cells represent the nutritious part of blood. Keeping blood in vessels, arteries, veins or capillaries ensures that it flows more efficiently. The systems that protect blood illustrate its importance to animals. A variety of mechanisms, such as clotting and constriction of veins, keep an animal from bleeding to death through a small wound. Blood is constantly manufactured in the body, so it is a renewable resource and a complete food.

In mammals and birds, which are thought to be the usual prey of vampire bats, blood amounts to 6–10% of the animal's weight. This means that a 100-kilogram person (220 pounds) would have no more than 10 kilograms of blood, or a 1,000-kilogram moose would have 100 kilograms of blood. A 450-gram (1-pound) rat would have no more than 45 g of blood, and the vampire bats themselves have only 4 g of blood.

Each vampire bat, whatever the species, needs about two tablespoonsful of blood every day. This represents about 60% of the bat's body weight, or 20 g of blood. The bats extract this blood through a wound they make with their front (upper incisor) teeth. The wounds are approximately 5 mm deep and 5 mm in diameter and the bites do not cut arteries or veins. If you made a wound this size on your body, it would produce about one drop of blood or less than a gram. It appears that vampire bats are "one stop shoppers," feeding on one victim each night. Getting 20 g of blood from a wound that normally produces just one drop is a specialized business.

When you remember how much blood is available in different sized mammals and birds, it is obvious that one stop shopping for vampire bats will only work with large prey. The availability of large prey and the difficulty of obtaining large amounts of blood probably explains why vampire bats are no bigger than 40 g. Fossil species that probably weighed about 60 g may have had more large mammals and birds to tap.

Let's follow the process as a Common Vampire Bat sets out for a night's foraging.

THE HUNT

Common Vampire Bats usually roost in hollows, so they may be found in caves, hollow trees and buildings. The bat leaves its roost just after dusk, setting out to find a meal. The relatively long and narrow wings—providing a high aspect ratio and high wing loading—make it possible for the Common Vampire Bat to fly rapidly and consume relatively little energy in doing so.

Radio-tracking studies suggest that a foraging Common Vampire Bat returns to a general area where it has found prey before. Having reached its for-

A portrait of a Common Vampire Bat shows the detail of the face and nose-leaf. The bat's heat detecting system is located on the nose-leaf. Also evident are the tips of the upper incisors, the teeth used to make the feeding wound.

aging area, the bat must find and select a victim. The fine details of its search and selection behavior remain unknown. However, the inferior colliculus, part of the bat's brain that processes sound, is specialized for detecting the regular breathing sounds of a sleeping animal such as a cow. The bat lands on the ground near its intended victim and approaches on foot. Among bats, Common Vampires are the most agile on the ground, hopping about like ballet dancers.

There is a heat (infrared) sensor on the nose-leaf of Common Vampire Bats, permitting them to locate an area where the blood flows close to the skin. If there is fur on the skin, the Common Vampire Bats uses its canine and cheek teeth like a barber's shears to clip away the hairs. The bat's razor-sharp upper incisor teeth are then used to make a quick cut, leaving the 5-mm wound described above. The upper incisors lack enamel, making it easier to keep them razor sharp.

The bat then begins to use its tongue in the wound as well as its saliva. The action of the tongue keeps blood flowing, while grooves on the underside of the tongue draw blood toward the bat's mouth. Meanwhile, the saliva has at least three active ingredients that promote bleeding. One is an anticoagulant that counters the clotting defenses. A second keeps red blood cells from sticking together and a third inhibits the constriction of veins near the wound. It may take the bat about 20 minutes to fill its tank; then it is time to take off and return to its roost.

The tank is the bat's stomach, and its lining rapidly absorbs the blood plasma. In turn, the circulatory system shunts the plasma to the kidneys. From there it passes to the bladder and out of the bat. Within 2 minutes of beginning to feed, a Common Vampire Bat begins to urinate. The urine is very dilute—no wonder, it is the plasma from that blood meal. The plasma is heavy but contains no nutritive value, so the bat benefits from leaving it behind.

Shedding the plasma makes taking off from the ground easier. But the bat still has added almost 60% of its body weight in blood. To take off from the ground the bat must generate lots of lift. Common Vampire Bats have very long thumbs. As the bat prepares to take off it crouches close to the ground and then, by contracting its chest muscles, flings itself skyward. The thumbs provide extra leverage for takeoff. Usually within two hours of setting out, the Common Vampire Bat returns to its roost and settles down to spend the rest of the night digesting its blood meal.

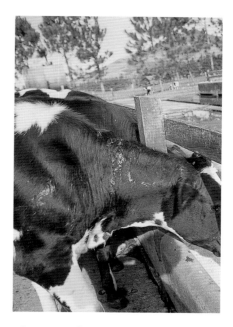

The source of a trail of blood on this cow's neck locates the feeding wound made by a Common Vampire Bat. Photograph by Cathy B. Merriman.

RISKS AND SOCIAL SUPPORT

Studies of Common Vampire Bats in Costa Rica indicate that it is risky to depend upon blood as the only source of food. Each adult Common Vampire Bat has a 7% chance of not feeding on any night. This means that about once every 25 nights the bat will miss its meal and go hungry. Common Vampire Bats cannot survive two nights without a meal, so fasting is dangerous. For young bats, the risk of not finding food is higher, 33%. So, twice a week each young Common Vampire Bat will probably miss a meal.

Other blood-feeding animals such as ticks, insects and leeches do not face the same problem as vampire bats because they can go for weeks, months or even years without a meal. Vampire bats, however, are warm-blooded, and the cost of staying warm means that fasting is soon fatal. The costs of keeping warm account for the absence of vampire bats from cooler parts of North, Central and South America.

Common Vampire Bats live together in structured societies that provide a network of social support. Like other bats, Common Vampires are long-lived, and banding studies suggest that some survive almost 20 years in the wild. Banding studies also reveal that individuals remain in their roosting groups for at least three years and probably for their entire lives. Colonies of Common Vampire Bats usually include one adult male with several females and their young. The bats may not all roost together at any one time, for they move between several roosts within the home range of the colony. Females that roost together often forage in the same general area, and several bats may line up, feeding in succession at a wound.

When Common Vampire Bats return to the roost, they often meet face-to-face and groom one another. A bat that fails to feed uses this face-to-face contact to beg blood from a roostmate. The successful bat may then regurgitate some blood to the unsuccessful one. The cost to the donor is relatively small, particularly since before the month is out it will need a donation itself. The benefit to the receiver is high, for it is survival.

Genetic analyses have revealed that colonies of Common Vampire Bats are mixtures of relatives and nonrelatives. This means that the social support provided by the colony transcends the business of helping relatives. Cooperation may be one of the central keys to the success of Common Vampire Bats. We would expect that Common Vampire Bats that are not part of the colony would not get blood from the members of the group. Giving blood appears to depend upon the prospect of a donation in return.

Blood-feeding is a risky business, particularly for a warm-blooded animal. Among bats, the vampires are exceptional because they spend so much time caring for their young. Young Common Vampires nurse for up to nine months, three months longer than flying foxes, which are many times their size, and at least six months longer than most other bats. Female Common Vampire Bats show no seasonal pattern of reproduction. But even though they may have young at any time of the year, the long period of nursing means that each female produces just one young a year.

THE OTHER VAMPIRES

Unlike other living vampire bats, Common Vampires have very long thumbs which are crucial to its ability to take off after feeding. Video footage of Hairy-legged Vampire Bats feeding on chickens reveals how the bats climb up small branches to their prey, often feeding at a bite made in the bird's cloacal region. In this approach to feeding, the distinctive curved calcar of these bats improves their grip on small branches. Furthermore, these vampires can drop from their feeding perches and take flight without having to worry about launching themselves from the ground. Not surprisingly the force exerted by Common Vampire Bats taking off from the ground greatly exceeds that generated by Hairy-legged Vampire Bats, again relating to differences in foraging behavior. Clearly there is more than one way for a vampire bat to feed on its prey.

Whether you consider their anatomical or physiological specializations or their amazing social structure, the vampires are among the most exciting of bats.

BATS AND PUBLIC HEALTH

Most bats spend their entire lives without ever coming in direct contact with people, and vice versa. However, the exceptions are sometimes traumatic, and usually occur in and around buildings. Whether bats roost in cracks and crevices or hollows, buildings offer excellent opportunities for roosting. Many, but by no means all, species of bats quickly take advantage of the housing opportunities provided by human activities.

Since almost everyone who has heard anything about bats also knows about the blood-feeding vampires, people often fear bats. Like most phobias, a fear of bats need not have any rational basis, but reason is not usually the important point. Chapter 14 explores some images of bats: this chapter looks at why many people are afraid of bats and do not like them.

Are there reasons to fear bats? People quickly associate bats with rabies or with histoplasmosis, a fungus disease of the lungs. Do rabies and histoplasmosis make bats dangerous?

Are there other diseases that could involve bats and humans?

RABIES

Rabies is a disease caused by the bullet-shaped Rhabdovirus, which affects the nervous system. It is a disease of mammals and there are few records of individual mammals that recovered after showing clinical symptoms of rabies. Think of rabies as a disease that is uniformly fatal to humans and all other mammals.

Animals afflicted with rabies become progressively sicker, usually dying within two or three days of the onset of symptoms. Some animals with rabies go berserk, attacking anything and everything in their path. Others suffer from progressing paralysis that usually begins with the hind legs and moves forward in the body. A rabid animal may go through both stages, the "furious" one when they go berserk and the "dumb" one when they are immobilized and die. In either manifestation, the throat muscles often are paralyzed so the victim cannot swallow its saliva. This makes the animal drool and appear to foam at the mouth. Spasms in the throat muscles are aggravated by attempts to drink water, explaining "hydrophobia," another name for rabies.

A few years ago it would have been true to say that rabies in bats occurs mainly in the New World and in North America, Central America and South America. Although these areas account for the highest numbers, rabid bats have been reported from Europe and Thailand, and a virus with similar effects is known from some African bats.

Although it is tempting to think that the animal with furious rabies is more dangerous than the one with dumb rabies, first impressions may be wrong. Almost everyone recognizes the danger posed by a bat (or other mammal) that makes an unprovoked attack. Someone bitten under these circumstances is likely to seek immediate medical advice.

A bat with dumb rabies, however, such as the one lying helplessly on the ground, often arouses our humane instincts. The person going to help the stricken animal may be bitten, but pay little attention to the bite. Ignoring the bite seems sensible because bat bites are usually relatively small and the bite was provoked. The Good Samaritan may think nothing more about it. This is the situation surrounding the first human death reported from bat rabies in the United States (in 1958). The lady who helped a Silver-haired Bat she saw flopping on the ground beside her house was bitten, contracted rabies from the bite and died. Animals with furious rabies may not be more dangerous to people than those with dumb rabies.

Biting is the usual way for rabies to spread from one animal to another and bats are no exception. The virus often concentrates in the saliva and when a bite breaks the skin, the virus may be spread from an infected animal to an uninfected one. The blood-feeding vampire bats are ideally suited to spread rabies: every year in Central and South America, Common Vampire Bats play an important role in spreading rabies to cattle. The economic consequences of this are important because cattle mean employment and they are often a source of foreign currency.

But there may be three other routes for transmission of rabies. First, in the laboratory, animals can be exposed to rabies virus by eating infected tissue. The importance of this in the wild and to bats remains unknown. Second, it is possible that rabies could be spread by the bites of ectoparasites, but no strong evidence supports this view. Third, a possibility exists of rabies being spread by the "aerosol route." This means by inhaling airborne virus. In the 1950s two people went into Frio Cave in Texas. Neither was bitten by any resident bats, but both died of rabies. The cave then harbored about 13 million Mexican Free-tailed Bats; the high temperature and humidity seemed to offer the opportunity for airborne rabies virus. Presumably, the rabies is passed in the bats' urine, becomes airborne and enters other animals through the lining of their lungs. Aerosol transmission remains very unlikely even in Frio and nearby caves that harbor huge colonies of Mexican Free-tailed Bats. Aerosol transmission is not a possibility in most bat colonies because the conditions are not suitable. There are no suggestions of it from buildings. The possibility of airborne transmission of rabies virus make Mexican Free-tailed Bat caves a good place to avoid.

Whatever the route of infection, rabies is a frightening disease. Everyone should avoid aggressive animals and people without appropriate protection and training should not handle sick, dying or dead animals (see box 15).

BOX 15

SOME DOS AND DON'TS ABOUT BATS

1. Remember that bats of all sizes will bite in self-defense but most never attack people. By not handling bats, everyone can reduce their chances of being bitten by one. The risk of contracting rabies is an excellent reason to avoid being bitten by any bats. Bats, like all other mammals, are susceptible to this disease, which usually is spread from one animal to another by biting. Rabies is uniformly fatal.

2. If you must handle a bat, take precautions to minimize the chances of its biting you. By wrapping the bat in a thick towel, or by wearing heavy gloves, you can make it virtually impossible for a bat to bite you.

3. Do not keep bats as pets. Enjoy them by going for a walk in the evening and watching them as they hunt insects. Get a bat detector and eavesdrop on their echolocation calls.

4. If you are bitten by a bat, see a physician immediately. If the bat is available, it can be killed and tested for rabies. When there is any doubt, the physician will probably recommend post-exposure rabies shots. Today most people receive a human diploid vaccine that involves a series of three relatively painless shots in the arm.

5. If you are working in an area with bat droppings, wear a mask or respirator that will remove particles 2 microns or larger in diameter. Should you develop flu-like, respiratory or other symptoms after working in an area with bat droppings, mention the situation to your physician. A skin test will indicate if you have been exposed to histoplasmosis.

6. Avoid disturbing bats in their roosts. Roosting bats, particularly those with young, or those that are hibernating, are very sensitive. Disturbing these animals can lead to their deaths.

7. Avoiding disturbing and handling hibernating bats maximizes their chances of survival.

8. If you are regularly obliged to handle bats, obtain pre-exposure rabies vaccinations. Analysis of a blood sample can indicate your level of protection. Expressed as an anti-rabies titer, values of 1/64 indicate a level of protection accepted by many public health authorities. Even with pre-exposure immunization and good titer readings, booster shots are necessary after any exposure to a rabid animal.

Since 1978 it has been possible to identify different variants of rabies, reflecting the animal source of the virus. This is achieved by analysis of the major internal protein of the rabies virus and the viral RNA gene sequences. In the United States and Canada rabies variants are associated with foxes, skunks and raccoons. Several rabies variants have been associated with bats: in the American Southwest with Mexican Free-tailed Bats, in southeastern and Mid-Atlantic States with Red Bats and with Big Brown Bats in the American northeast. Different variants of strains raise interesting questions about the role of bats in the epidemiology of rabies.

How do bats contract rabies in the first place? How do bats spread rabies to other animals? Biting is an obvious answer to either question, but let's consider some details. Aggressive behavior between bats often involves biting, so it is easy to see how a bat infected with rabies might bite a roost-mate and spread the virus. In southern Arizona in 1978, within 20 minutes a Hoary Bat was seen attacking three other bats, a Mexican Free-tailed Bat, a Silver-haired Bat and a Big Brown Bat. Each attack bore the victim to the ground and left it with bleeding wounds. The Hoary Bat was evidently rabid. Bites by bats on other bats may occur in roosts or in feeding areas. The bitten bats may be members of the same or different species.

A Hoary Bat or a Big Brown Bat, or perhaps any bat bigger than 15 g, can bite hard enough to break a person's skin. One of these bats afflicted with rabies could easily bite just before it was killed and eaten by a fox, coyote, jackal, skunk or raccoon. Such bites could move rabies from bats to other animals such as terrestrial carnivores. For example, a Red Fox in Newfoundland was found to be infected with a bat strain of rabies virus. However, there is no evidence of bat rabies causing an outbreak of the disease in other animals.

Vampire Bats feeding on other mammals is an obvious way for rabies to enter the bat population. It is difficult, however, to imagine a bat catching rabies from a fox, skunk or raccoon. Any of these animals is so much bigger than the bats they might encounter, that the bat is unlikely to survive the attack. In the same way, people rarely worry about getting rabies from a Grizzly Bear, an African Lion or a Tiger because the bites themselves are often life-threatening. An adult Red Fox weighs about 5,500 g, 367 times the weight of an adult Big Brown Bat. Since Grizzly Bears, at 350 kg, are 3.5 times heavier than a 100-kg person, humans may have a better chance of surviving a bear attack than a Big Brown Bat does a fox attack.

Like all other mammals, bats are susceptible to rabies. But bats are not asymptomatic carriers of rabies virus. In other words, a bat with active rabies virus is a rabid bat that will probably be immobilized within two days and dead within four or five days. An asymptomatic carrier could have active rabies virus, show no symptoms, and carry on.

The situation is complicated though, because bats, like other mammals, can harbor dormant rabies virus. On several occasions, healthy Big Brown Bats have been captured in the field in summer or winter. In my laboratory, these animals have been trained to participate in behavioral experiments and have performed for several months. Then, three to nine months later, a few (less than 5%) of these 150+ bats contracted rabies and died. It seems obvious these bats had the dormant virus when they arrived and something later activated it.

Rabies colors human perspective of bats. From 1946 to 1965, bats were the source of 5 of 236 human cases of rabies; in other words 2.6% compared to dogs—51.7%. From 1980 to 1997 there were 36 cases of human rabies in the United States and many of these were diagnosed only just before death or in the postmortem stage because rabies had not been suspected. Although 12 of these cases involved dogs, 21 involved bats, 15 of them with the rabies variant associated with Silver-haired Bats and Eastern Pipistrelles.

This is an alarming set of statistics about bats—specifically Silver-haired Bats and Eastern Pipistrelles—and rabies. But it also is somewhat of a mystery when you consider some other numbers. From 1956 to 1992, just 3% (796) of the 25,000 bats submitted for testing in the United States were Silver-haired Bats. Only 41 of them (5%) were positive for rabies. From 1988 to 1992 in New York State, 312 of 6,810 bats tested positive for rabies (4.6%). Just 25 of the 6,810 bats submitted for testing were Silver-haired Bats and only 2 of them were positive for rabies.

To further complicate the picture, Silver-haired Bats are rarely found in buildings. In my experience, they are smaller than Big Brown Bats and do not bite as hard. Silver-haired Bats form nursery colonies in hollows or under loose pieces of bark (see page 184). During fall migrations Silver-haired Bats sometimes may be found roosting on the outside walls of buildings.

The topic of rabies challenges bat biologists to give the public accurate, non-alarmist information. It is true that one's chances of being bitten by a rabid bat are very low. But this is only statistical figuring. If you are the one who has been bitten, you probably do not care what the chances were of this happening.

HISTOPLASMOSIS

Histoplasmosis is a fungus disease of the lungs. The spores that spread the disease often occur in the droppings of chickens and pigeons, and of bats. The fungus that causes histoplasmosis usually lives in soil. It is widespread in the warmer parts of North America, Central America and South America, as well as from Africa to southern Europe and southeast Asia.

A dry cough and other flulike symptoms are the usual signs of histoplasmosis in people. The disease also can cause a high fever, may affect vision and can be life-threatening for some people. Histoplasmosis is presumably the cause of "mine fever," which occurs in some people who mine bat guano in Mexico. It also may explain afflictions such as the "curse of the mummy's tomb," because tombs in Egypt and elsewhere frequently house large colonies of bats and contain large accumulations of bat droppings.

Histoplasmosis is usually associated with bat guano in warmer parts of the world. Caves where bats hibernate will not harbor histoplasmosis from bats because hibernating bats do not eat, and produce no guano. In New England (eastern United States) a survey of guano accumulations in several colonies of Big Brown Bats and Little Brown Bats produced no evidence of histoplasmosis. In the same area, and in Canada, histoplasmosis occurs in people who appear to have contracted it from the droppings of pigeons and/or chickens.

Histoplasmosis is an occupational hazard of chicken farmers, pigeon fanciers, bat biologists and cave explorers. It does not pose the immediate threat that rabies does, but it can be debilitating and should not be taken lightly. People can minimize their chances of exposure to histoplasmosis by wearing a mask or respirator when they are cleaning up after their birds or working in bat roosts. The mask or respirator should remove particles as small as two microns in diameter.

This pile of droppings represents several years' accumulation in a nursery colony of Little Brown Bats located in the attic of a farmhouse in southeastern Ontario. Each year at least 2,000 bats had contributed to this accumulation.

In the same colony, pissicles, composed of urine and feces, grow from the beams supporting the roof.

On the veranda floor, a scattering of bat droppings has accumulated beneath the entrance and exit hole used by about 300 Little Brown Bats. Dry bat droppings crumble at a touch, reflecting the fact that they contain insect remains. By comparison, rodent droppings do not crumble because they contain mainly plant fiber.

A stained area on the wood and a small smattering of bat droppings identify the hole the bats used to get into and out of the hotel. By sealing this hole with caulking, the hotelier evicted the bats.

BATS: HAZARD OR NUISANCE?

Both rabies and histoplasmosis mean that bats are involved in matters of public health. The actual chance of contracting either disease from bats varies from place to place and bat to bat. Neither rabies nor histoplasmosis makes bats dangerous per se. For example, in the United States and Canada between 1955 and 1985 eight people are known to have died from rabies caught from bats. Many more die every year from bee stings and dog bites. In some cities more people die every day at the hands of other people. The statistics indicate that public health risks do not justify bat phobias.

However, many people object to sharing their homes and offices with bats. Bat droppings, by-product of bats' voracious appetites, are one good reason that bats are unwelcome. The bat that eats its body weight in insects every night deposits 5–10% of this as droppings in its roost every day. Most people do not want accumulations of urine and droppings in their homes, whether they come from people, pets, bats or elephants. The noise made by bats is another reason why some people do not welcome them. It is a good thing for us that most of what house bats have to say is beyond our range of hearing.

Thus people's main objections to house bats are odors and sounds, but a study near Ottawa, Canada showed that in 80% of the houses harboring Big Brown Bats, the human residents did not know they were there. These are good grounds for complaint, but they represent a nuisance rather than something life-threatening.

BAT CONTROL

There are two different problems when it comes to removing bats from buildings. The first is presented by the bat that happens to enter a room and flies about. Stray bats are most common in mid-summer when young bats are learning to fly and find their way around. The best way to deal with an intruding bat is to open a window or door, remove the screen, turn off the light and let it fly out.

Another method is to wait for the bat to land and then catch it by throwing a bath towel over it. Wrap the bat up in the towel and then shake out the towel outside. This solution can cause minimal trauma for the people and for

Opposite page: The front of a stately hotel in western New York State illustrates how to locate the routes Little Brown Bats use to enter a building. The two smaller pictures on page 160 were taken on the second balcony just to the left of the window flanked by two columns.

The arrows identify openings to houses used by Big Brown Bats. The numbers show the relative incidences of different bat access routes. Drawing by Max Licht, information from Brigham and Fenton (1987).

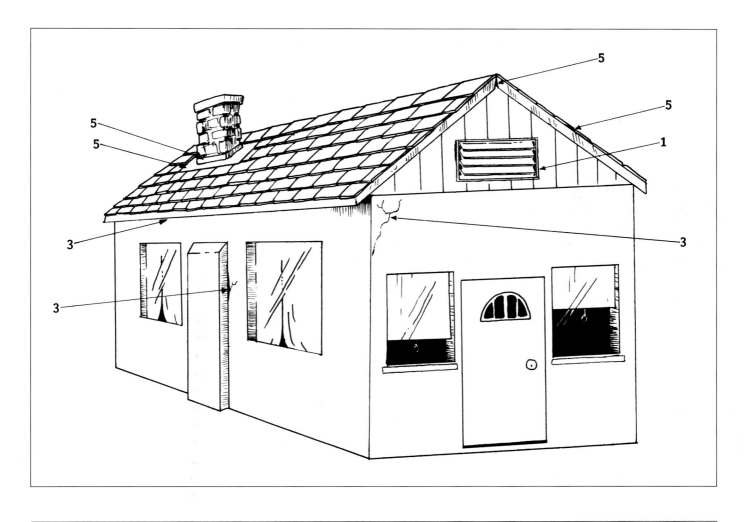

BOX 16

HOUSE BATS IN WINTER

Winter is a time when many species of bats leave their summer roosts and migrate either to hibernation sites or to warmer climes (see Chapter 4). In temperate areas, however, some species of bats stay in buildings and hibernate through the winter. Two examples are Pipistrelles from Europe and Big Brown Bats from North America.

Bats hibernating in buildings are less of a nuisance to people than bats which make their nursery colonies there. A hibernating bat does not eat, so it produces no droppings. Furthermore, hibernating bats are quiet, giving human occupants of the building no cause for complaint about noise. Hibernating bats roost in places where the temperatures do not drop below freezing. In buildings they may be found in the attics in areas where winters are not too severe. Where winters are more challenging, Big Brown Bats hibernate in the walls of buildings, rarely in the attics.

From time to time hibernating bats wake up and become active. At this time the bats are usually dehydrated and fly about looking for water to drink. When they are hibernating in a building, this behavior can bring them into contact with people. In houses with unfinished basements, bats hibernating in the walls or in the attic can move down between the walls into the basement. People washing clothes in basements sometimes find bats trapped in the sink or washing machine, where they went to get a drink of water. When the door to the basement is left open, bats can fly from the basement up into the living quarters. When the door is closed, bats may land on the floor and walk under the door. These bats are often found in the kitchen or bathroom sink or in the toilet, places where the bat had gone in search of water.

These patterns of behavior make the control of winter house bats different from the summer scene. Since the bats spend most of their time in torpor, there is no convenient way to locate the points where they entered the building. Although Big Brown Bats are often found in the walls during building renovations, we have no clear idea of the precise sites they occupy.

By keeping the door to the basement closed and ensuring that it fits snugly (by attaching weatherstripping to the bottom of the door), people can minimize the chances of bats moving from the basement into their living quarters. Sealing up the openings that lead from the walls into the basement (sometimes by finishing the basement) will prevent the bats from entering this part of the building.

As usual, by avoiding handling bats they encounter in their houses in winter, people can minimize their chances of being bitten.

the bat. Furthermore, the bat will try to bite in self-defense but will not be able to get through the towel. Always avoid being bitten by the bat (Box 15).

The second problem is presented by a colony of bats residing in a building. Before even contemplating the eviction of resident bats, remember that in countries such as Great Britain, bats, including the ones in your attic, are protected by law. In Great Britain, the Wildlife and Countryside Act 1981 provides that the Nature Conservancy Council (NCC) (19/20 Belgrave Square, London SW1X 8PY, United Kingdom) must be notified about plans to deal with problem bats. There is no guarantee that they will agree to the bats' eviction. Indeed, if Greater Horseshoe Bats are involved, you can bet that they will be welcomed and protected by the NCC. (In Chapter 12 questions of bat conservation will be addressed, including those raised by situations involving bat control.)

There are no quick ways to exclude house bats. Chemical repellents such as moth balls, or pesticides such as DDT, are not effective against bats. Fumigants that kill bats directly are likely to be equally fatal to humans. Electronic devices, such as ultrasonic repellers, have been tested with bats and have no effect. Exclusion is the only effective way to control house bats.

Where do bats usually roost in buildings? Buildings are usually a shell within a shell and bats tend to roost between the two shells. This puts them in the attic or between the walls. With the exception of New Zealand's Short-tailed Bats, bats' teeth and claws are not suited to making holes in building materials (wood, stone or brick). Therefore, bats enter buildings through existing openings, usually where the roof joins the walls or where the chimney protrudes through the roof. To seal bats out of a building just close the openings they use for access. Openings important for building ventilation should be blocked with screening. Others can be sealed with caulking, lathe, molding or foam insulation.

Buildings should be bat-proofed when the bats are not at home. If the colony uses the building only in the summer, a winter bat-proofing operation will not seal bats inside. If the bats use the building throughout the year, seal the holes after they have left for the night. Never exclude bats when there are non-volant young in the colony, because this would seal the mothers outside and the young inside.

Suspending bird netting in front of the openings used by the bats is one relatively easy way to exclude them. The netting, which should hang about one meter below the opening, allows bats to leave and prevents them from returning. Emerging bats drop past the netting and fly away, but returning bats find their ways blocked. There are commercially available one-way valves that can be inserted into the openings bats use for coming into and leaving buildings. Netting and the valves permit exclusion operations when the bats are in residence.

In houses where the bats come and go through one obvious opening, it can be quite simple to evict them. An unscreened louver or a broken piece of facer board can easily be repaired. Some cracks are easily sealed with caulking or foam insulation. But then there are buildings, usually older ones, with literally hundreds of access routes for bats. In my experience, most bats living in log buildings or those made of squared timbers are quite safe because large-scale renovations would be necessary to evict them.

Fortunately for the homeowner and unfortunately for the bats, it may be easy to find the bats' access routes. In summer the bats leave every night to forage, so watching them emerge simplifies finding the openings they use. Even better, openings used by many bats are conspicuous because of the accumulations of bat droppings beneath them. Bats that winter in buildings present a different set of control problems (see Box 16).

As we shall see in the next chapter, bat control operations may or may not be compatible with bat conservation.

BATS AND OTHER DISEASES

The agent that causes a disease in one species, its normal host, may not produce fatal or even disabling symptoms or consequences there. But, when the same disease-causing agent infects another species, the effect may be much less benign. The term "emerging viruses" describes what happens when a virus that causes one disease in one species moves to another species in which it has fatal consequences. Some diseases caused by emerging viruses have ghastly effects, the Ebola virus being a prime example.

In Africa, bats have been accused of being the possible normal hosts for viruses like Ebola which can have such well documented and horrible effects on people. Bats' association with Ebola virus, however, remains unclear in spite of repeated efforts to describe a direct connection. Sometimes cave-dwelling bats are the possible sources of Ebola, other times it might be foliage-roosting fruit-eaters.

BAT CONSERVATION

Two immediate problems jeopardize the future of bats, namely habitat destruction and human attitudes toward bats. These issues are related to one another because the human view of the world in general contributes directly to habitat destruction. Behind the scenes, but still an important part of both problems, is the size of the human population. As the number of people increases, more and more pressure is placed on natural resources, in turn contributing to increased habitat destruction. Although the threats to the survival of bats are essentially the same as those affecting other organisms, bats also are uniquely vulnerable.

HABITAT DESTRUCTION

For any organism to survive it needs the basic essentials of life. For bats, these include secure roosting sites, an adequate supply of food and a reproductive rate that balances mortality. Phenomena that destroy tracts of habitat directly jeopardize bats by removing roosting and feeding areas. Without either of these resources, bats, like other organisms, are doomed. When enough of a species' population disappears, then the species itself will probably become extinct.

Many phenomena destroy habitats. In the first half of 1991, volcanic eruptions in the Philippine Islands and powerful cyclones in Bangladesh caused extensive habitat destruction in those two countries. Early in 2000, rains upstream along the Limpopo and Save Rivers produced devastating floods in parts of Mozambique. Volcanoes and severe weather have often devastated vast areas. Floods and forest fires, whether the results of human activities or natural phenomena, can destroy large areas of habitat. On more local scales, avalanches and beaver dams are other examples of phenomena that destroy habitats.

Technology has given humans the ability to destroy habitats on a vast scale. One of the most familiar methods is clear-cut logging, a forestry practice that

This Peters' White-lined Bat, a 15-g species, was caught in a mist net set in an old field. This species was not caught in areas with undisturbed forest. Note the faint white line running down the middle of the bat's back.

This Schmidt's Large-eared Bat is busy snacking on a preying mantis. The bat is a member of the subfamily Phyllostominae, and was only caught in mist nets set in forested areas. This 6-g species feeds mainly on insects and lives in Central America.

is as widespread as the chain saws and heavy equipment used to achieve it. But other, more subtle factors are involved, too. Increasing human populations often generate more extensive urban sprawl. This destroys habitats, including woodlands, and its effect is compounded by agricultural practices. In many parts of the world, growing human populations need more firewood, in turn leading to further destruction of forest and woodlands.

Whatever its cause, habitat destruction directly affects bats. Flight makes bats mobile, permitting many of them to exploit roosting and feeding resources over large areas. Consider some aspects of foraging as revealed by radio tracking individual bats. A Big Brown Bat usually covers about 10 km of ground every night as it forages. For a Spotted Bat, Noctule, Hoary Bat or Mouse-eared Bat this figure is closer to 20 km. Midas' Free-tailed Bats and other large Free-tailed Bats may cover much larger areas, as do Mexican Free-tailed Bats. While Big Brown Bats, Spotted Bats, Noctules, Hoary Bats and Midas' Free-tailed Bats use a variety of habitats, Mouse-eared Bats forage only in forest. So, any destruction of forest could affect Mouse-eared Bats more than it would the other species.

Bats tend to be more sensitive about their roosting than about their foraging sites. Cave roosts can be vital to the survival of large numbers of Mexican Free-tailed Bats in the southern United States. But other populations of these bats roost in buildings, expansion joints in bridges and other locations. Caves are not necessary for the survival of Mexican Free-tailed Bats, although most of their population may depend upon the cave roosts. Noctules usually roost in hollow trees, sometimes in cliff faces. These bats do not achieve the high populations typical of Mexican Free-tailed Bats, and their tree roosts are vulnerable to deforestation. Hoary Bats and Red Bats also roost in forests, but among the foliage of trees or vines. There appear to be more roosts available to foliage-roosting bats than there are to species roosting in caves or hollow trees.

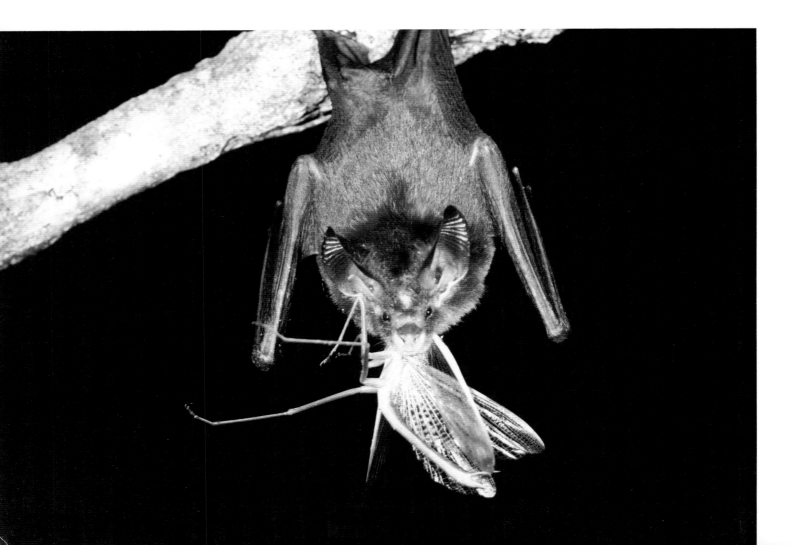

In January 1991, captures in mist nets were used to survey bats in some habitats in the province of Quintana Roo in Mexico. While some bats were caught almost everywhere, others disappeared as soon as the forests were felled. Captures of Jamaican Fruit Bats and Parnell's Mustached Bats suggested that they were oblivious to habitat destruction. Wrinkle-faced Bats, Peters' White-lined Bats, Pallas' Long-tongued Bats and Common Vampire Bats were encountered more frequently in areas of extensive wood-cutting than they were in less disturbed forest. Six species of bats in the Phyllostominae, a subfamily of the New World Leaf-nosed Bats, disappeared with the trees. Woolly False Vampire Bats, Tome's Long-Eared Bats, Little Big-eared Bats, Yellow-throated Bats, Davis' Round-eared Bats and Cozumel Spear-nosed Bats were caught only in forested areas. These patterns could reflect the availability of food and/or roosts.

Habitat destruction affects different bats in different ways. Species that depend upon special roost conditions, perhaps restricted to some caves, will disappear with their roosts. The Hog-nosed Bats may exemplify this situation, for they are known from an extremely limited area in Thailand. Marinkelle's Sword-nosed Bat may be another example. This spectacular species has been found in just one cave in eastern Colombia (South America) near the town of Mitu.

For species of temperate regions, hibernation sites may be the critical factor. Caves figure prominently as hibernacula, and they are vulnerable in several ways. Quarrying activity, combined with groundwater pollution and urban sprawl can render some caves unsuitable for bats. Quarrying activity may destroy the caves outright, while pollution may contaminate them. Urban sprawl

A Davis' Round-eared Bat, another Phyllostominae, is insectivorous and lives in forested areas. These bats weigh 15–20 g.

This Cozumel Spear-nosed Bat weighing 20–25 g was roosting in a chultun, *an underground Maya storage area. This species lives in forested areas of Central and South America. These bats eat insects and small vertebrates like lizards.*

leads to the sealing of caves in the interests of human safety, for unfortunately, caves can be dangerous for a variety of reasons. Sealing them is an expedient solution for local authorities.

Increasing habitat destruction will cause the extinction of more bats in the immediate future than any other single agent. Conservation strategies that set aside and preserve large tracts of habitat are the only hope for halting this trend.

HUMAN ATTITUDES

Many people fear bats because of their popular association with blood-feeding and rabies. Others find house bats a nuisance because of their urine, droppings and sounds. The combined effect of these attitudes is that many people do not hesitate to kill bats, and others do not think twice about evicting bats from building roosts. In some countries, such as Great Britain, killing or evicting bats brings substantial fines. In the majority of countries, however, bats do not have enough supporters.

What happens to the bat that is evicted from its building roost? From radio tracking studies in Southeastern Ontario we have learned that Big Brown Bats excluded from their nursery colonies in summer move to a nearby building. Active tags such as radio transmitters allow researchers to find the bats in their new roost sites. In urban settings, the evicted bats usually have found new quarters within 100 m of their old roost. In rural settings, they sometimes had to travel 500 m. Eviction is not a death sentence for Big Brown Bats. But what happens when they can no longer find building roosts? We must remember that not all Big Brown Bats roost in buildings. In southern British Columbia they roost in hollow trees.

Little Brown Bats are different. The work with these bats has involved banded animals because they are too small to carry radio transmitters. The difference between an active and passive tag affects the information available from the research. During the Chautauqua study (Box 14), renovations sealed five buildings that previously had housed bat colonies. A total of 545 bats had been banded in these closed colonies, and none of them was found later in other colonies on or off the institution grounds. Although more than 6,000 bats were banded at Chautauqua in the summers of 1988, 1989 and 1990, only about 20% of these bats have been recaptured, and more than 90% of them at their home roosts.

If evicted Little Brown Bats really do disappear from the population, then sealing them out of a building roost may be an indirect death sentence. The advent of smaller radio transmitters may shed more light on this important question. Information about the responses of other species of house bats to eviction would clarify the effects of this control measure.

A human view of bats as nuisances or, worse, dangerous animals, identifies an immediate challenge for those concerned about bats. The challenge is setting about to change people's attitudes.

HUMAN CONSUMPTION

On some South Pacific islands, notably those in the Marianas Archipelago, the Marianas Fruit Bats are traditional festival food for the Chamorros people. Originally, the locals used nooses on the ends of long poles and traps to catch the bats. With this simple technique the bats' reproduction more than compensated for the human depredations. The advent of firearms, particularly shotguns, changed the balance. Suddenly, the rate at which people could harvest the bats greatly exceeded the bats' reproductive output and the population began to decline. In 1970, the population of Marianas Fruit Bats was estimated at 3,000 individuals, and by 1989 only 400 to 500 survived. Another species, the Little Marianas Fruit Bat, is now believed to be extinct. Furthermore, the demand for bats as food for special occasions produced a market that put hunting pressure on bats elsewhere in the South Pacific.

Meanwhile, in the southern part of China, some caves harbor large populations of Fulvous Fruit Bats. The bats are unpopular with some fruit farmers because of their depredations on some fruit crops. Fruits known as dragons' eyes are particularly favored by both bats and people. The bat colony in at least one commercialized cave northeast of Nanning is a case in point. There some bats are harvested and appear as special treats on bill of fare at the restaurant in the tourist complex. Arguably, Fulvous Fruit Bats are just "paying their way." The small species that dominate the local bat fauna are not worth the effort to harvest and do not appear on the menu.

Since most bats are small mammals, their value as food for humans has not generated problems for the survival of most species. Their small size also means that there is little demand for skins! Nevertheless, larger bats are often part of the human menu, and the larger flying foxes are obviously affected. In some parts of Africa, too, people sometimes eat Old World Fruit Bats.

THE SCIENCE AND EDUCATION MARKET

Two other kinds of human activity threatens bats. Some scientific research is fatal to bats. Many studies of the distribution and classification of bats require specimens which usually are added to museum collections. Specimen records permit evaluation of the patterns of distribution and geographic variation in certain species of bats. For poorly known bat species, identification is possible

BOX 17

BAT HOUSES

Like some species of bats, there are birds that live in and around buildings. In some human cultures there is a tradition of encouraging birds by putting up houses in which they can nest. Indeed, birds such as Purple Martins in North America nest mainly in bird houses. The survival of other species, such as Eastern Bluebirds, also has been enhanced by nest box programs.

Some people have tried to encourage bats by putting up bat houses or bat boxes. A variety of designs has been used in different parts of the world, and in Europe, Australia and South Africa bat houses have met with some success. In Europe, species such as Pipistrelles and Brown Long-eared Bats live in bat houses; in South Africa, Little Free-tailed Bats sometimes roost in bat houses, as do some Australian Bats. In the early part of the 20th century, bat towers were erected at some locations in Texas to encourage local bat populations in the hopes of controlling insects such as mosquitoes.

In February 1987, *National Geographic* ran a brief piece suggesting that bat houses could play an important role in bat conservation. People who like bats but object to sharing homes with them could now consider providing alternate housing for evicted bats. By 1991, bat houses or bat boxes were listed in catalogs of several American and Canadian garden supply companies, reflecting general concern about bats and the environment.

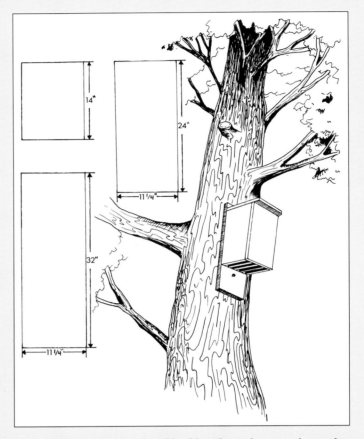

Some bat houses are small and boxlike. Shown here is a design that can be mounted on a tree or the side of a building. The measurements are in inches. The lower panel provides a landing platform for the bats, and the partitions give them small crevices in which to roost. Drawing by Max Licht.

Do bat houses work? On the grounds of the Chautauqua Institution in New York State (see Box 14), members of the Bird, Tree and Garden Club were concerned about their local populations of Little Brown Bats. From 1987 onward, more and more bat houses appeared around Chautauqua, reflecting the full range of designs. Some bat houses were constructed from wood taken from attics that had harbored bats. Others made of new wood were smeared with bat droppings and bat urine to make them smell like home. By the summer of 1991, there were more than 100 bat houses around Chautauqua. During the summers of 1989, 1990 and 1991 occasional solitary

only after careful examination of cranial or dental characters. In other cases chromosome preparations, tissue analysis and morphological studies are required for accurate identification. But other species, for example Spotted Bats or Pallid Bats, are distinctive and easily identified in the hand by a trained observer. There should be no need to kill species like these just to identify them.

Some studies of bat echolocation use procedures that are fatal to bats. This is particularly true of research into information processing in bats' brains. Popula-

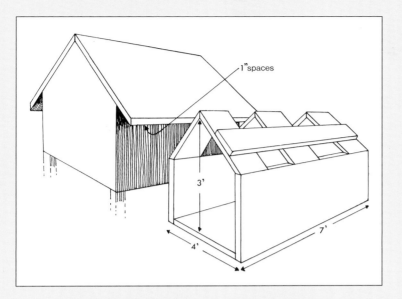

Larger, "Missouri" style bat houses are supposed to provide accommodation for larger groups of bats. These may be placed on the roofs of buildings, or be free-standing atop legs long enough to keep the bats out of reach of predators. Measurements are in feet and inches. Drawing by Max Licht.

Little Brown Bats occupied two or three of the bat houses. The majority of Chautauqua's 10,000 Little Brown Bats, however, avoided these new roost opportunities.

Studies of the temperature profiles in bat houses and those in attics housing bats revealed no statistically significant differences. There was a trend for larger attics to give the bats more protection from extremes of temperatures than small bat boxes could. Larger bat houses, however, seemed to offer the same thermal conditions as attics.

But then consider the situation on the shores of the Toledo Bend Reservoir in Louisiana. There, after six years of experimentation three back-to-back bat houses are used year-round by both Mexican Free-tailed Bats and Big Brown Bats. In 1999, over 800 bats used the houses. This stands in stark contrast to the situation in 1994 when a few flying squirrels but no bats used the two bat houses that were erected. In the intervening period several variations on the bat house theme were used before the 1999 model was perfected. The crowded, multichambered bat houses stand 7 m above the ground. On the outside, the west-facing bat houses are painted white, the east-facing houses dark purple, and all are painted black inside to absorb heat. For more stories about successful bat houses see www.batcon.org/bhra/bhmaster.html.

So, what's the rule and what's the exception? In 2000, no bat house design or situation is guaranteed to attract bats. Bat houses that are painted black, located in sunny locations atop poles or on the sides of buildings, are most likely to succeed. Placing a bat house immediately beside the entrance the bats use to a building also encourages bats to move into the bat house (their preferred entrance would have been sealed after the bats left). But, some bat houses may be up for several years and attract no occupants even in areas where bats are common. In North America, low rates of occupancy provide few clues about just where to situate a bat house to please bats. The Little Brown Bats at Chautauqua seem particularly reluctant to avail themselves of alternative housing. During late summer in the Okanagan Valley in British Columbia, Big Brown Bats occasionally roost in Purple Martin houses. In Arizona, Pallid Bats sometimes roost in cliff swallow nests after the birds have left them for the season.

The success stories indicate that bat houses offer great promise as a means for conserving bats. Bats seek out and exploit new roosting opportunities. During the summer of 1990, a group of Little Brown Bats roosted in a pair of chest waders suspended by the feet from the rafters of a garage. This unusual bat roost was located just across the lake from Chautauqua! It seems that bats do have a sense of humor.

tions of preferred study species, such as the Greater Horseshoe Bat, have dwindled alarmingly in some areas. It is difficult to determine how much of the decline is attributable to consumption of bats in research as opposed to disturbances and habitat destruction. Other species, notably Parnell's Mustached Bats, are used in many research operations although we do not know the status of their populations.

In considering this loss, however, we must remember that these studies of bat biology have produced some exciting findings. They have increased our

This flying fox was for sale in the market of Lae, Papua New Guinea. Flying foxes are among the largest of New Guinea's native mammals, so it is little wonder that they should appear on the human menu.

basic understanding of how mammals' brains work. Other studies of bat anatomy and physiology have also contributed to general and specific knowledge. For instance, studies of blood flow in bats' wings have improved our understanding of circulation; work on sound processing in bat brains has told us more about how our brains work.

Specimens of bats are often listed among the material available from biological supply companies. The bats are usually preserved in fluid and can be used in class dissections. Many students study biology to learn about anatomy. This means working with species, sometimes by dissection. Bat species are exciting alternatives to more usual dissection studies of cats, rats, mice and dogfish. The educational use for bats may be important in the development of new biologists.

Whatever the end or the means, any project that involves harvesting bats must ensure that the rate at which bats are collected does not imperil the population. We know that bats have disappeared from many well-known caves where they used to live. In some cases, over-harvesting probably contributed to their disappearance.

HUMAN RECREATION: CAVING

Cave exploring, or spelunking, while a popular and exciting pastime for a growing number of people, can threaten the survival of bats. Species that establish nursery colonies in caves or those that use caves as hibernation sites are particularly vulnerable to the disturbances associated with caving.

Females disturbed in their nursery roost may drop their young or abandon their preferred sites. Conditions in alternative sites may be less than ideal. If other sites are cooler than the preferred ones, the young will grow more slowly. Slower growth, in turn, decreases the chances of the young surviving their first winter.

Hibernating bats are notoriously sensitive to disturbance. They will arouse from hibernation in response to mechanical disturbances, such as someone touching them. Changes in temperature or even sounds also cause some bats to arouse from hibernation. To arouse from hibernation, bats use energy intended to see them through the winter. The more hibernating bats are disturbed, the more rapidly they lose weight and the less their chance of surviving winter. Disturbing hibernating bats can be deadly for them. In Little Brown Bats a single arousal from hibernation uses the energy that could be used for 60 days of hibernating.

The threat of spelunkers to bats living in caves can be avoided by rescheduling human underground expeditions. Staying out of caves when females are pregnant and nursing can reduce many of the adverse effects of human disturbance. Similarly, avoiding caves when bats are hibernating in them eliminates disturbances that could be fatal. Local authorities or Bat Conservation International should be able to provide this information.

Some caves have been gated to protect bats and other components of cave systems. The gates are designed to control human access, but flying bats must slow down to negotiate the now restricted openings. Recent studies in southeastern Ontario involved a Doppler radar gun (like those used in the enforcement of speed limits on highways) and demonstrated that bats do slow down as they approach gates. Furthermore, bats usually make several approaches to a gate before flying through it. At some gated American caves, predators such as snakes, raccoons and skunks exploit slow-flying bats as they negotiate their way past the barrier. But, appropriately designed gates can protect bats.

It is important to note that many spelunkers are extremely considerate of bats. They find ways to minimize their impact on bats and have contributed immensely to our knowledge of bat distribution. Cavers often have provided specific records of banded animals, documenting patterns of movements or migrations. Responsible caving is compatible with bat conservation.

PESTICIDES

Bats, particularly insectivorous species, are sometimes hapless victims in the war humans wage to control insect pests. Throughout the world, may chemicals are applied every year to minimize the damage done by insects. This chemical warfare is conducted in buildings and gardens as well as in agricultural operations. The insect targets may be dangerous because of diseases they transmit, economically important because of their food, or nuisances with no particular economic or health connections. Some chemicals are specifically designed to affect certain insects or insects in general, while others are toxins with more widespread effects.

Insectivorous bats are exposed to pesticides used against insects. Some of these pesticides have no effect on the bats. Others that are toxic to bats are neutralized when stored in body fat. As long as the bat remains in good condition, the pesticides have no effect. However, when the bat uses its fat reserves, it is exposed to concentrated doses of pesticides.

Some die-offs in bats have been directly attributed to pesticide poisoning. They have occurred in three situations—weaning, migration and hibernation—times when bats have used virtually all of their fat reserves. Nursing bats acquire pesticides from their mothers' milk. While milk is their main food, young put on weight, including body fat. At weaning the fat reserves are consumed and the young are exposed to any pesticides they have accumulated. Migrating and hibernating bats also consume their fat reserves and may show signs of pesticide poisoning.

Bats may also be directly exposed to pesticides used in bat control. Pesticides that kill bats also affect other mammals, including humans. The nuisance presented by house bats hardly justifies the direct risks to people associated with the chemical control of bats. Other chemicals, such as DDT, have been used in bat control. Since they are not very effective against bats, their use is unwarranted.

In parts of the New World tropics, anticoagulants have been used to control populations of vampire bats that feed on cattle. Bats flying near cattle are captured in mist nets, painted with anticoagulants and released. The bats ingest the chemicals while grooming themselves or their roost-mates, and then die. This approach to vampire control can be very specific when applied by people who know their bats. Then it probably affects no other bats. From the standpoint of bat conservation it is infinitely superior to earlier vampire control programs that depended upon napalm and explosives.

THE DANGER OF LABELS

People who are concerned about the survival of bats always ask whether or not any species are immediately threatened with extinction. The International

Although Lesser Woolly Bats are widespread in Africa, they are uncommon in collections. There is no reliable information about the size of their population, the location of their roosts or the details of their insect prey. Applying IUCN labels such as "rare" or "common" to this species is a meaningless exercise. Their survival depends upon habitat conservation. Note the tufts of hair along the bat's forearm, which is 31 mm long.

Union for Conservation of Nature (IUCN) introduced a set of labels designed to identify the status of different animal species. "Endangered species" are those threatened by immediate extinction, while "common species" exist in good numbers and their survival is not threatened. Other labels, such as "rare" or "vulnerable," can be used to identify species whose future is questionable.

How do bat populations stand? The very fact that some species have been identified as "endangered" demonstrates real concern about their future. But the picture is not clear and there have been very few long-term studies. In central Arizona the bats at some study sites were compared between 1972 and 1997. A nursery colony of Cave Bats present in 1972 was not to be found in 1992. Meanwhile, although not found in 1997, lactating Western Big-eared Bats were caught in 1997. Other species, Big Brown Bats, California Myotis and Western Pipistrelles were found both in 1997 and 1972. Most of these bats also had been recorded in the area in 1931.

Applying these labels to bats poses a difficult problem because too often they assume knowledge about bats that simply is not available. There are few accurate figures about population sizes, even those living in areas where bats have been extensively studied. In part, this is because we do not know where most bats roost and have no dependable way of counting them. If the size of the population is unknown, it is impossible to demonstrate that the numbers of bats is increasing, decreasing or remaining the same. Furthermore, when we do not know the location and nature of bats' roosts and feeding areas, it is difficult to organize a plan to protect them. What should be protected? Pick almost any of the 900 or so species of living bats and ask the following questions: How many are there? Where do they roost? Where do they forage? What do they eat? What is the rate at which they produce young? The answers are usually unknown, so applying the IUCN labels is often a meaningless exercise.

PROTECTING BATS

Too many people see no reason to protect something that has no tangible economic or other value. For the most part, bats are perceived to have no value and so they are not worth protecting. Some people appreciate bats' importance as consumers of insects, dispersers of seeds and pollinators of plants. These benefits, however, are often intangible and unlikely to sway opinion in a court of law. Influencing legal opinion may be critical when preservation of habitat hinges on a cost-benefit analysis. Many other people see no reason to protect animals, such as bats, that they consider to be nuisances. Bats that live in human structures such as buildings or old mines pose an interesting question. What did these bats do before humans provided roosts for them? Should we protect the "unnatural" interaction of bats and humans?

One main argument in favor of protecting bats is that they are part of our natural heritage, even the species that live with humans. Countries such as Great Britain have moved to protect bats, including the ones that roost in buildings. Although their regulations may not be as sweeping, other European countries have followed suit, clearly moving to protect bats. The United States has identified some species of bats as "endangered," and in many parts of the world there is a growing awareness of the need to conserve them. Protection, however, is only effective when it is real. Putting bats on a list of protected organisms and doing nothing to protect them is not active conservation.

The Egyptian Fruit Bat, this one a denizen of the Metropolitan Toronto Zoo, is a gentle and trusting animal, well accustomed to people. Bats like this are one central key to public information programs designed to change people's view of bats.

BOX 18

BATS AROUND THE WORLD

Since bats are mainly tropical animals, the closer you are to the equator, the mores species and individuals you are apt to encounter. Across the tropics, richer bat faunas occur in South and Central America, where there are approximately twice as many species as there are in comparable sites in Africa, Southeast Asia or Australia. Numbers of species are one way of illustrating these general trends in bat distribution. Other indicators are the numbers of families of bats or the variety in bats' food habits.

At tropical locations in South and Central America, Africa, India, Southeast Asia and Australia, there usually are seven or eight families of bats even though numbers of species differ markedly between the New World and the Old World. Insectivorous species are found throughout the world wherever there are bats, but blood-feeders are found only in South and Central America. Fruit-eating species occur throughout the tropics, but nectar- and pollen-feeding forms are less widespread particularly in the Old World. In the New World, some nectar-feeding species occur in California, Arizona and Texas, but not in Florida.

Species of bats in three families have colonized the world's temperate zones. In the Old World, Pallid Bats, Horseshoe Bats and Plain-nosed Bats occur from the equator to the most northerly and southerly limits of bats, while in the New World, temperate zone bats are either Pallid Bats (one species) or Plain-nosed Bats species. Throughout the world, some species of Free-tailed Bats penetrate some distance into the temperate zones, whether one considers the situation in the United States, Spain, Kyrgyzstan or Tasmania.

The number of bat species in any location also reflects other factors. One of the most obvious of these is the ameliorating effects of the warmer temperatures of maritime climates. This phenomenon is obvious when you compare the numbers of species of bats in Alaska (6) and southwestern Labrador (1), and Britain (14) or Sweden (16) and Khabarovsk, Russia (3). The numbers of species of bats known from Chile or the Western Cape Province in South Africa reflects the length of these political units and their maritime climates.

Since the first edition of this book appeared in 1992, there has been a dramatic increase in the number of books about bats of different parts of the world (see bibliography).

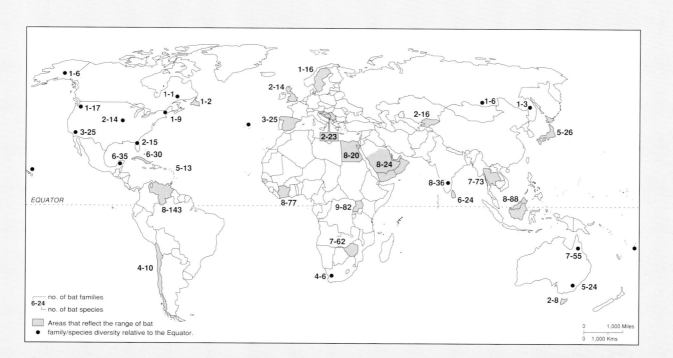

The worldwide diversity of bats. On this map, pairs of numbers separated by dashes indicate the numbers of families (first number) and the number of species (second number) at selected locations around the world.

Even in countries with strong conservation tendencies, people see little reason to protect Common Vampire Bats, which they consider to be economically harmful. Common Vampire Bats can spread rabies among cattle and other domestic stock, representing a costly problem for some Central American and South American ranchers. To fully appreciate the role that Common Vampire Bats play in spreading rabies to cattle, we need some answers to the questions: How much do vampire bats depend upon livestock for blood? What proportion of the Common Vampire Bat population feeds on livestock? Does vaccination adequately protect cattle from rabies spread by vampire bats? Animals as distinctive and intriguing as vampire bats should be protected, but arguing this point would be helped by more specific information about the size of the problem they represent.

In Israel, Turkey, in parts of South Africa and Australia, and in southwestern China, some fruit farmers complain about depredations by fruit bats on their crops. Geographically, these complaints coincide with areas inhabited by large numbers of Old World Fruit Bats. At places where the diets of fruit bats have been studied in detail, the bats make little use of commercial or even introduced fruits. However, Gray-headed Flying Foxes tend to exploit fruits that ripen synchronously in large numbers. This behavior makes commercial fruit crops a natural choice for them. Elsewhere, other fruit bats depend mainly on native fruits that are not commercially important. Harvesting fruit before it is fully ripe is one way to thwart fruit bats, but some fruit bats will always pose a problem to some farmers.

THREE STEPS

The effective protection of bats requires three steps. The first is to change the public image of bats. This should not involve a campaign designed to make people love bats, but rather an educational program enhancing appreciation of bats. A good initial step is to make it clear that bats are not dangerous.

The second step is to learn more about bats. If we knew which resources were critical to their survival, it would be easier to make conservation plans that could have an immediate positive impact on bat populations. Knowing more about bat populations would help us to identify species with low chances of survival.

The third step is to illustrate the importance of bats in natural habitats. Throughout the tropics, fruit bats play a vital role by dispersing the seeds of their plant food. In West Africa, most regeneration of forest occurs via seeds dispersed by bats. Bats that feed on nectar and pollen are important pollinators of many plants, playing a central role in tropical systems. This third step may be more difficult because it involves increasing people's appreciation of natural systems.

The diversity of life in general and bats in particular is one of the most important assets of our world. People tend to forget that we, too, are part of the global system, depending upon it for the production of oxygen and food, and relying on it to dispose of our wastes. Bats offer educators a way to explore diversity and demonstrate the interconnectedness that makes our own species part of the larger system (see page 177).

LEARNING AND BATS

Bats can play a dual role in learning—both enriching educational programs in a wide variety of situations and providing examples of how we continue to discover new things about the world around us. As the subjects of classroom and library study, bats can be used to introduce students at different academic levels to many topics. Bat-focused projects can be done by individuals, by teams of students, or by whole classes. Obvious examples involve basic biology such as form and function (Chapter 1) or conservation and the environment (Chapter 12). But research on bats, for example, the human discovery of echolocation, also illustrates the basic processes and procedures of science, as well as the history of science and its interdisciplinary nature. The study of bats also can educate us about ourselves and the ways we view the world.

Pursuing the example of echolocation, knowledge about the biology and behavior of bats was just part of the discovery of this behavior. A knowledge of physics also was important, as well as technical information about equipment such as a bat detector ("Pierce's sonic detector" of Griffin's work—see Chapter 3). But the attitudes of people affect the dissemination of discoveries in science. In the 1790s this was demonstrated by the response of the scientific community to the work of Spallanzani and Jurine. No matter how strong the supporting evidence, people tend to dismiss ideas that are beyond their experience and imagination—for example, the proposal that bats can "see with their ears." The progression from a basic question (how do bats find their way in the dark?) to experiments that allow the observers to eliminate some possibilities (such as touch or vision) is common throughout science, as is the use of appropriate instrumentation (a bat detector). But, never underestimate the role of good fortune in science. It is interesting to see what started scientists on the road to discovery.

Other aspects of bats further enrich the educational opportunities they present. The sound-based interactions between echolocating bats and many of their insect prey will intrigue students interested in electronic warfare. In the same way the basics of the designs of bats' echolocation calls can appeal to engineers interested in signal design and function. Meanwhile, the role of bats in human mythology and symbolism brings science back into the domain of the humanities and social sciences.

Perhaps the most important role for bats in the education of younger students is putting them in touch with their connections to the biological world. Work in Canada has demonstrated that five-year-old schoolchildren are curious about bats and receptive to information and ideas about them. By age 10, boys and girls differ in their attitudes to bats. Girls seem to have "learned" that it is appropriate to be afraid of or repulsed by these animals while boys have not.

Everywhere people demonstrate over and over again that presenting young children with opportunities to meet live animals enriches the experience, whether the focus is on snakes, owls, fish, insects or bats. The experience with the live animal can be instrumental in influencing a child's view of issues relating to conservation and the environment. A side benefit, is that a positive experience with a live animal may help to set the career paths of many students.

But those who would use live bats in educational programs must be keenly aware of the susceptibility of bats to rabies. This reality is complicated both by the public perception of bats' role in rabies and the litigious nature of some societies. Together these realities mean that involving live bats in educational programs may be easier said than done.

The study of bats illustrates the dynamic and changing face of science. Since the first edition of this book appeared, our knowledge of many aspects of bat biology has changed substantially. Three examples were addressed earlier. The first was new information about the evolutionary relationships between groups of bats. The second was the role that leaf-eating plays in the lives of bats previously thought to be fruit-eaters. The third was the discovery of ultrasonic nectar guides in some bat-pollinated flowers. There are other examples.

WHAT'S IN A DIET?

Chapter 5 considered the variations in the diets of bats. In the early 1970s evidence from Big Brown Bats and Hoary Bats and some other species suggested that different species of insectivorous bats fed mainly on either moths or beetles. This led to the suggestion that while some bats ate mainly soft prey (moth specialists), others more often ate hard prey (beetle specialists). This proposal appeared to be supported by the morphology of bats' jaws and skulls and by the prevalence of beetles or moths in the diets of Big Brown Bats and Hoary Bats, respectively. But how can a Large Slit-faced Bat fit into this picture given the range of prey that it takes (Chapter 5)? We need to address the fundamental question of how the proposed categorization of bats as moth or beetle specialists is complicated by variation in the food eaten by one species. Pallid Bats illustrate the problem.

Near San Jose, California, an observant biologist found dead, chewed slugs among the discarded pieces of prey that had accumulated beneath a feeding roost used by Pallid Bats. There were no previous records of Pallid Bats eating slugs and to be sure, although bitten and dead, the slugs below the roost had not been "eaten" by the bats. Slugs use copious amounts of mucus to make themselves distasteful to many predators. Perhaps this defense had caused the bat(s) to discard them, even if it was too late for the individual slugs in question.

This finding generated a detailed study of the diets of Pallid Bats. The focus was a comparison of what was eaten by the bats in the San Jose area with a site in Death Valley. The two areas were strikingly different in climate. While rainfall and moderate temperatures prevailed on the coast, extremes of temperature and no rain were typical of the desert.

Collecting and analyzing droppings obtained from beneath the bats' roosts showed that the average diet of the bats differed between the two study areas. Indeed, field crickets were the only prey species in common between the two areas. At the coastal site, Pallid Bats ate grasshoppers, Jerusalem crickets, katydids, a variety of carabid and cerambycid beetles, as well as occasional sun spiders and jumping spiders. In Death Valley, Pallid Bats ate ant lions, tenebrionid, scarab and buprestid beetles. Sampling the potential prey in the two areas showed that the differences in diet coincided with differences in the arthropods there. It was no surprise that what Pallid Bats ate reflected what was available to them where they lived. On the coast some prey species were more consistently available over longer periods of time. In the desert there were more dramatic changes in the actual prey available to the bats at any time. But the exciting story was concealed by the averages. It emerged when the diets of individual bats were examined.

By catching bats after they had fed and holding them individually in cloth bags for an hour or so, it was possible to obtain droppings from specific individuals. The diets of these bats could then be compared with the picture presented by the average incidences of different prey in the diet as indicated from analysis of droppings collected from beneath the roost. On any night in Death Valley, the diet of any individual did not differ statistically from the average diet of the group. On the coast, however, none of the individuals sampled ate the average diet. Each of the coastal bats ate only a small subset of the colony's diet. Some individuals fed more on Jerusalem crickets, others mainly on field crickets or katydids. So, how would you classify Pallid Bats by their diets? Over the summer, some individuals appeared to specialize on Jerusalem crickets, others on field crickets or katydids. But others took a greater variety of prey. Pallid Bats feed mainly on arthropods, with occasional excursions beyond this phylum. In California, Pallid Bats specialize on neither moths nor beetles.

The study raises more questions. How do the diets of the Pallid Bats on the coast reflect individual differences in foraging behavior? Are differences in diet passed from one individual to another, either by observational learning (see page 36) or by some facet of interactions between mothers and their dependent young?

The distinction between aerial-feeding and gleaning bats seems quite pervasive, the difference between taking flying insects in the air or snatching non-flying prey from surfaces such as the ground or vegetation. Pallid Bats added an additional wrinkle to the story. In captivity, some individual flying Pallid Bats used their wings to push flying insects such as ant lions against the walls or ceiling where the victim was caught, dispatched and eaten. Was this aerial foraging or was it gleaning?

The feeding behavior of bats will continue to be a treasure trove of interesting discoveries. For example, although we know that Pallid Bats visit plants and eat nectar and pollen, this aspect of their foraging behavior remains little studied. As usual, the results of one study generate more questions than answers.

LIGHT POLLUTION!

The advent of street lighting changed the nocturnal atmosphere of many countrysides. With the spread of street lights, astronomers who observed the night skies through telescopes were more and more obliged to use remote locations where street lights did not reduce their ability to perform their studies. Astronomers often consider street lights to be a main source of light pollution. The same lights that pollute the night skies for astronomers attract insects and thus bats!

Many species of nocturnal insects are attracted to lights, making an isolated streetlight an excellent place to watch interactions between bats and their prey. From Hawaii to Africa, Australia to northern Canada, Sweden, and Israel, bats often feed among the clouds of insects attracted to lights.

In southwestern Ontario, studies of foraging Red Bats and Hoary Bats were expanded following a chance conversation between biologists. As a result, ongoing work on Red Bats and Hoary Bats was expanded by colleagues with the expertise in flight speeds and flight costs. Now, in addition to observations of marked Red Bats and Hoary Bats and their interactions with moths, the aspect ratios and wing loadings (see page 19) of the bats were measured. A Doppler radar was used to measure the flight speeds of foraging bats.

Information about flight speeds and the wing features allowed calculation of the costs of flight for the Red Bats and Hoary Bats. The flight speeds of Red Bats ranged from 3 to 10 m (average 6.7) per second; those of Hoary Bats 4 to 12 (average 7.7) m per second. There was no statistical evidence that flight speeds in either species varied significantly over time of night, date or location. The average flight speeds of the bats were not those predicted if the bats minimized the power required for flight. Nor were the flight speeds what would have been expected to maximize the distance the bats covered on a given amount of fuel.

**This table presents the comparative information for
Red Bats and Hoary Bats foraging at streetlights.**

	Red Bat	Hoary Bat
Mass in g	13	31
aspect ratio	6.7	8.1
wing loading in Newtons per m²	10.55	15.62
Flight time in min	127	222
cost of flight in kiloJoules (kJ) per gram per sec	1.14	5
attack rate in sec	20.3	17.5
success rate (percent of attacks)	39	50
energy value of moths in kJ per gram		
0.1 g moths	0.648	
0.3 g moths	1.944	
cost of lactation in kJ per day	22.02	55.9
cost of commuting in kJ	33.1	58.7

When the bats' costs are considered along with the information about their attacks on moths and the successes of these attacks, the following picture emerges. Red Bats must catch and eat 275 small (0.1 g) moths each night to cover their costs. If they were to eat bigger moths (0.3 g), they would need 92 of them. Since Red Bats succeeded on about 39% of their attacks, this means making 702 attacks per night on small moths, 233 on bigger ones. Meanwhile, the larger Hoary Bats would have to eat over 1,800 small moths a night (3,600 attacks), or 601 bigger moths (over 1,200 attacks). The effect of the lights, namely concentrating the prey, is significant. If the Hoary Bats (for example) were only attacking prey once a minute (as they do when feeding away from lights in Manitoba), they would have to fly more (almost 700 min), increasing their costs and probably forcing them to concentrate on larger moths.

Information from Hoary Bats carrying temperature-sensitive radiotransmitters added another dimension to the picture. On nights with minimum temperatures from 13–21° C, bats showed two patterns of behavior. Some bats left their roosts, flew to the lights and hunted there briefly before taking off, quickly moving out of range. Others entered torpor and just remained in their roosts. At temperatures were below 13°C, there were very few insects at the lights and the radio-tagged bats always entered torpor.

The coincidence of a combined approach to the research and a situation where the bats were readily captured and observed was central to the overall study. The results demonstrated how light pollution could be a good thing for bats that hunt flying insects.

ROOSTS

The variety of roosts used by bats was explored in Chapter 6. Many lines of evidence point to roosts as factors that could limit the distributions and populations of bats. The reluctance of Little Brown Bats at Chautauqua to use bat houses does not support the view that roosts were limiting for bats there. But one study in Sweden reported that several species of bats moved into a marshy area when bat houses were provided. The behavior of Little Brown Bats at Chautauqua could reflect an abundance of other roosts, obviating the need to use bat houses.

Biting leaves or other plant structures to form roosts (tents) is an exciting behavior of some bats, even though we usually lack details about which bats

Two Jamaican Fruit Bats roosting in a tent made from the frond of a palm.

An unoccupied tent in a palm leaf.

actually build the tents. A visit to the neotropics, where most species of tent-roosting bats occur, reveals that tents are more common in some areas than in others. Near Tortuguero on the Caribbean coast in Costa Rica, tents are very common. Further north near Lamanai in Belize, they are uncommon. It is easy to overlook tents when you are not sure what to look for, but at Tortuguero they are obvious, and after seeing them you are much less likely to overlook them.

Inconspicuousness is key to a tent's value as a bat roost. If making the tent made the leaf more obvious to a predator, then tents would not be good places to roost. In reality, tents, even ones that are three months old, are not conspicuous. One reason the tents are inconspicuous is that the portions of leaves away from the bites remain green just like the rest of the leaves and other leaves. To a botanist interested in the anatomy of plants, the maintenance of connections between the plant and the partially severed leaves raises an interesting question: How is this achieved?

A red dye (Safranine) dissolved in water moved through the leaves and revealed the answer. Water and dissolved materials move through vascular plants in vessels made of specialized cells called xylem elements. By placing freshly cut stems of leaves (called petioles) in a solution of the red dye in water and making another fresh cut of the petiole below the surface of the solution, the xylem vessels in the leaf were exposed to the dye. The vessels took up the dye and moved it through the leaf. Observers could watch the progression of the red dye through the leaves and observe what happened at bite sites.

In plants, there are different-sized xylem elements in different-sized veins. The smallest (10 microns in diameter) xylem elements occur in minor transverse vessels. In leaves not modified as tents, the dye moved down the progression from larger to smaller xylem elements, and the 10 microns diameter transverse veins delivered water and other materials to leaf tissue. In leaves modified as tents, the dye followed the same progression of vein size until it reached the damaged areas. There the minor transverse vessels with single xylem elements conducted the water flow around the damaged areas to the partly severed sections of the leaf. This was surprising because the 10 microns diameter xylem elements in the minor transverse veins were thought to be capable of only very local transport of water and materials. The small vessels had a greater capacity for transport than predicted by models of water flow in tubes.

A close up showing how a red dye (Safranine) dissolved in water moved in a leaf, around the bites made by bats constructing a tent. By moving through minor transverse veins, water supply was maintained to the parts of the leaf on the other side of the sites of the bat bites. Photo by Ewa Chulewa.

The findings present information about tents from the plants' point of view but do not explain how or why bats began to make tents. Did bats first make tents by biting leaves to give them purchase on otherwise slippery surfaces?

SPIX'S NEW WORLD DISK-WINGED BATS

Although interlocking between their toenails and the roost surface allows most bats to hang, some have specializations for adhering to slippery surfaces. Adhesive or suction disks are the best example. They occur on the wrists and ankles of four species of bats: three New World Disk-winged Bats and one Old World Disk-winged Bat. The disks allow the bats to cling to smooth, slippery surfaces such as those of new and as yet unfurled leaves. In Spix's New World Disk-winged Bats the wrist disks are 3.5 to 3.9 mm in diameter.

The silhouette of a Spix's New World Disk-winged Bat roosting in a partly unfurled Heliconia leaf. Note the obvious disks.

But how do the disks actually work? Other animals from frogs to limpets, octopodi to starfish also have disks and use suction, wet adhesion or glue to stick to smooth surfaces. As the name implies, suction is involved when a vacuum holds the disk to a surface. Wet adhesion is the phenomenon responsible for a wet piece of paper sticking to a smooth surface such as a window pane or wall. Glue involves the secretion of glue-like substances that stick a bat's disks to the surface.

Testing the various possibilities involved a platform that could be rotated to put a roosting bat in different positions. At the beginning of any trial, each bat sat on a horizontal surface with its belly facing the ground. By rotating the platform the sitting bat could be moved through various stages until it had been rotated 180° from its original position. Now the bat's belly faced skywards. Furthermore, the surfaces on which the bat sat could be changed. Trials with this apparatus showed that Spix's New World Disk-winged Bats could adhere to smooth surfaces such as Plexiglas or polished aluminum through 180° of rotation. The same bats could not stick to polished aluminum pierced by 0.45 mm diameter holes when the surface was rotated even to 90°. Now holes under each wrist disk of a Spix's New World Disk-winged Bat prevented the bat's establishing a vacuum. The same bats usually could not adhere to rough sandpaper rotated beyond 90°. Some individuals, however, used their thumbnails to interlock with the rough surface, behaving like bats without disks.

These results supported the earlier suggestion that New World Disk-winged Bats used suction to adhere to smooth surfaces. Tested in the same apparatus, other small species of bats (Sheath-tailed Bats, New World Leaf-nosed Bats and Plain-nosed Bats) readily clung to the sandpaper, apparently interlocking their toe claws with the irregularities on the sandpaper. The other species of bats slid off of the polished aluminum or Plexiglas surfaces when they were rotated beyond about 60°. There was some evidence that wet adhesion might also be involved with the Spix's New World Disk-winged Bats. Do Old World Disk-winged Bats show the same abilities? It seems likely, but we do not know. So few of them have been caught and studied that most aspects of their biology remain a mystery.

The unfurling of their leaf roosts means that Spix's New World Disk-winged Bats must change roosts almost every day, certainly every second day. Other species of bats (e.g., Big Brown Bats and Lesser Yellow House Bats) also change roosts often. The difference, of course, is that for Spix's New World Disk-winged Bats, the roost disappears when the leaf unfurls. For the other species, the hollow tree remains. Banded Spix's New World Disk-winged Bats

A Spix's New World Disk-winged Bat roosts in an empty drinking glass sitting with its head up, adhering to the glass surface with the disks on it wrists and ankles.

A close-up view of a wrist disk of the Spix's New World Disk-winged Bat in the glass. This disk was 3.6 mm in diameter.

typically moved less than 500 m between leaf roosts. Within any leaf roost, groups of Spix's New World Disk-winged Bats ranged from 2 to 11 individuals. The average group size was 4 bats. Over the course of a month, up to 6 animals were found roosting together. It remains to be seen what DNA fingerprinting will reveal about the genetic structure of these groups.

While we know that Spix's New World Disk-winged Bats move roosts because the roost disappears, we are less clear about why other bats change roosts.

A "SOLITARY" BAT BECOMES COLONIAL

In their classic 1969 book about bats of the United States, Barbour and Davis noted that Silver-haired Bats were migratory like Red Bats and Hoary Bats. Furthermore, Silver-haired bats were thought to roost alone in trees, a view of this common and widespread species that did not change until 1986. Then a publication described a nursery colony of Silver-haired Bats that had been found in 1979. The bats had been roosting in a hollow basswood tree in southern Ontario. The colony was discovered by accident when the some of the bats flew out of the tree as it was felled. The roost tree had been right beside an interpretive center in a busy park but the bats had gone unnoticed. A search of the literature revealed an earlier (1953) indication that Silver-haired Bats were colonial—but the idea had not caught on.

Today radio-tracking studies have revealed much more about the roosting habits of Silver-haired Bats. Females form nursery colonies, usually in hollows in trees, but sometimes under pieces of loose bark. In southern British Columbia, tagged Silver-haired Bats that roosted together moved as a unit usually every few days. Radio-tagged Silver-haired Bats moved from 100 to 900 m between hollow trees (average 300 m). The same tagged individuals covered much larger distances when foraging. The importance of this group cohesion is highlighted when we remember that Silver-haired Bats are migratory, spending the winters in more southern parts of their geographic range. Furthermore the groups returned to the same roost trees year after year. Genetic

A Silver-haired Bat about to take flight from a tree trunk outside its roost.

studies of female Silver-haired bats that roosted together in hollow trees revealed that a colony consisted mostly of genetic relatives. Colony members were mainly mothers, daughters and granddaughters.

Our views of this bat have changed substantially since 1986.

FORESTS AND BATS

In many parts of the world, the forest industry is an important economic engine, providing many direct and indirect jobs partly because forest products are used in so many different ways. Therefore forests throughout the world are under pressure from people armed with the technology that allows harvesting trees on a grand scale. As noted in Chapter 12, logging operations can jeopardize the survival of many forest organisms, including bats.

Understanding how bats respond to logging operations is essential if we are to ensure that deforestation exercises do not leave too many bats without suitable habitat. For bats, suitable habitat must meet their requirements for foraging and roosting. The last decade has seen an upsurge in interest about bats and forests. This was the topic of a two-day symposium held in Victoria, British Columbia, in 1996.

Traditionally, various species of bats in forests were studied by catching them or finding them in their day roosts. Captures of bats in mist nets or in Tuttle traps indicated which species occurred in woodlands, but some bats are easier to capture than others so the picture was often incomplete. Meanwhile, finding bats in their day roosts appeared to be entirely quixotic, giving little assurance that we had an accurate picture of which species roosted where. Bat detectors (Box 8) and small radio transmitters (Chapter 2) provided additional tools for studying bats in forests and woodlands.

Capturing bats and monitoring their echolocation calls revealed changes in bat faunas between forested areas and adjacent areas from which most trees had been removed. Some studies suggested that flying bats traveled beyond forest borders, perhaps commuting from roosts in forested areas to adjacent open spaces. Some foraging bats were more active in clear-cut or disturbed areas than they were in forests or woodlands, whether the agent responsible for removing trees was humans or elephants. These differences in activity often reflected the relative abundance of flying insects.

Even when concerted efforts were made to find bats in their roosts, many species remain unfound. For example, 73 species of bats have been recorded from one area in French Guiana. In spite of systematic and careful searching, the day roosts of over half of these species remain unknown. Radio tracking can be a key to finding the day roosts of bats, but this technique is limited by the sizes of bats and transmitters. Furthermore, the signals from transmitters placed on bats that roost underground may not be detectable from the surface. This was clear during studies conducted in January 1999 and January 2000 studies in Belize. There Wrinkle-faced Bats and Heller's Broad-nosed Bats that roosted in foliage, or Common Yellow-shouldered Bats that roosted in foliage or in tree hollows, were readily located by signals from their transmitters. The day roosts, presumably underground, used by radio-tagged Parnell's Mustached Bats and Cozumel Spear-nosed Bats never were located.

One excellent example of the impact of radiotracking on our knowledge of forest-roosting bats comes from New Zealand. There, radio-tagged Long-tailed Bats roosted in tree hollows in a temperate rain forest. These bats typically selected cavities that were at least 16 m above the ground. Normally they used trees at least 1 m in diameter at breast height, most often red and silver beeches. Radio-tagged bats repeatedly switched roosts, over 70% of the time occupying any tree hollow for just one night. Bats roosting alone (adult males) tended to switch roosts less frequently (on average 2.2 days) than communal roosts, typically nursery colonies (average 1.4 days). The bats covered varying distances between their day roosts, from 3 m to 3,400 m.

By following radio-tagged individuals, many studies have demonstrated the range of forest roosts used by bats. In southern British Columbia, radio-tagged Long-eared Myotis roosted under pieces of loose bark on stumps in clear-cut areas. In the same and other areas, bats may roost in hollows in snags (dead limbs) that extend beyond the canopy. These bat-occupied roosts often are exposed to direct sunlight, suggesting that roost temperature is important. Bats may enter such hollows through openings made by birds ranging from chickadees to woodpeckers and nuthatches.

Many studies also demonstrate that all too often day roosts used by the bats are not conspicuous from the ground, and without the signals from radio transmitters, the bats would go unnoticed by humans. As noted above, Silver-haired Bats are an example of this phenomenon, as are Long-tailed Bats and many other species. In the forest around the Cypress Hills in Saskatchewan, Canada, Big Brown Bats roosted in almost all of the hollows available in poplar (aspen) trees but not in hollows in coniferous trees. Roosts in hollows or under loose pieces of bark are threatened by forestry practices which remove such "snags," sometimes in the interests of public safety.

Meanwhile, a few species roost in foliage, whether the setting is New York State (Red Bats and Hoary Bats), Belize (e.g., Northern Ghost Bats, Heller's Broad-nosed Bat, Wrinkle-faced Bats), French Guiana (Heller's Broad-nosed Bats, Western Red Bats), or South Africa's Kruger National Park (Wahlberg's Epauletted Fruit Bats, Butterfly Bats). A comparison between different areas of the breakdown of bat species by the roost type they use suggests little difference. For example, when the roosts used by different species are compared between Belize, French Guiana and Kruger National Park, most species roost in hollows that may be in trees, on the ground or in buildings. When available, caves are often used as day roosts by some bats of the tropics and subtropics. As one goes farther from the equator, however, caves become progressively cooler and are less often used as summer day roosts by bats.

The importance of forests per se to foraging bats often is less clear. While gleaners may be most active in forested areas (e.g., Mouse-eared Bats, Fringe-lipped Bats and Davis' Round-eared Bats), aerial foragers appear to be less habitat-specific. Therefore, in Europe, foraging Noctules may be seen (or heard via bat detectors) foraging over forest or garbage dumps, while in parts of Israel they forage over open woodlands, scrub and agricultural areas. Throughout their range, Hoary Bats forage well above forest canopies or over lakes, prairies or deserts. In the Galapagos Islands, Hoary Bats forage over the scrub woodland. In any of these areas, smaller species with broader wings may be most active along the margins of forests or along trails and roads and streams that cut through them. Long-legged Myotis from western North America are good examples.

But in some forests, for example the interior rain forest in British Columbia, monitoring echolocation calls reveals that bats are much less active in the depths of the forest than they are along their edges or trails and streams in the woods. In one sense this is surprising because insect abundance is relatively high in the forests. In the boreal forest in central Saskatchewan, several

species of Mouse-eared Bats are more often active below the canopy, while Hoary Bats are most active above it, corresponding to differences in wing shape and flight performance. In temperate rain forest on Vancouver Island, foraging bats were more active below the canopy on nights with less moonlight. On bright, moonlit nights, bats were more often active higher in the canopy. Meanwhile in central Ontario, Silver-haired Bats, Little Brown Bats and Northern Long-eared Bats are more active in old growth white pine and mixed woods, while Hoary Bats show less effect of habitat. This difference appears to correspond to the dichotomy between species roosting in foliage (Hoary Bat) and those using cavities or crevices (the others).

Hemprich's Long-eared Bats roost in crevices and do not depend on trees.

HIGH-FLYING BATS

Observations using radar indicated that in parts of Texas, Mexican Free-tailed Bats often left their cave roost and then proceeded to gain altitude and fly up to 10,000 feet above the ground (see page 146). It was not immediately clear just what these bats were doing at that altitude and getting up there to monitor their behavior was a challenge.

In the 1980s, the outputs of bat detectors suspended from helium-filled kite balloons indicated that several species of Free-tailed or Sheath-tailed Bats flew 1,950 to 2,600 feet above the ground over savannah woodland in North Queensland (Australia) or in Zimbabwe. Species-specific echolocation calls provided evidence that different species of bats were involved. Feeding buzzes, the high pulse rates associated with attacks on flying insects, demonstrated that the bats were foraging up to at least 1,950 feet above the ground. The high flying bat species in the Australian or Zimbabwean location were not the Plain-nosed, Horseshoe or Old World Leaf-nosed Bats common in the areas.

The scene shifts back to the American southwest, where a combination of bat detectors on helium-filled kite balloons and radar observations revealed more about what was happening at altitude in the night skies over Texas. Agriculture researchers used radar to track the dispersal flights of tens of thousands of corn ear-worm-sized moths. The clouds of moths occur at densities of over 1,000 insects per million cubic meters of airspace (equal to at least 1 moth per cube of air 32.5 feet on a side). The moths set out from locations in Mexico and headed north, moving into Texas where their caterpillars would present an important economic problem. Some of the moths flew 650-2,600 feet above the ground.

Radar images of migrating moths also showed that occasionally, larger flying objects passed through the swarms of flying moths. Bats were suspected, and monitoring with bat detectors indicated that bats were feeding among these groups of moths. It appears that the bats are most often Mexican Free-tails previously known for their high altitude flights. Depending upon the flights speeds of the bats and their rates of success in attacking these moths, researchers estimate that hunting in these clouds of migrating moths, Mexican Free-tailed Bats could meet their daily energy needs in less than 10 minutes. At these altitudes, the echolocation calls of the Mexican Free-tailed Bats differ from those usually associated with this species. The calls of the high-flying bats searching for targets are 20 ms long and dominated by 20 kHz sounds. The bats produce these calls about every 350 ms. In short, the calls are longer, lower in frequency, and produced at longer intervals than those recorded from Mexican Free-tailed Bats flying at lower altitudes.

ECHOLOCATION

There is no doubt that the ready commercial availability of bat detectors (Box 8) has fundamentally changed the approach that many biologists take to the study of bats. By 1979 we knew that it was possible to distinguish between some different species of Mouse-eared Bats by their echolocation calls. Two papers published in 1981 expanded the scope of this discovery, reporting work from different parts of Europe, the United States, Canada and Zimbabwe. This demonstrated the general utility of bat detectors to monitor the echolocation calls of some bats. As Griffin predicted in 1958, echolocation provides a window on the behavior and ecology of bats.

One exciting development growing out of studies of bats' echolocation was the discovery in Britain that Pipistrelles showed two distinctive patterns of echolocation calls. These two phonic types, one producing echolocation calls with most energy at 45 kHz, the other with most energy at 55 kHz, are widespread in Britain. Pipistrelles often roost in buildings, and in any colony there is just one phonotype or the other. Meanwhile, listening with a bat detector reveals both phonotypes foraging at the same time in many places.

The differences between the two types of Pipistrelles extends to the vocalizations used in social interactions. During the mating season, some adult male Pipistrelles perform songflights from their roosts. These displays are thought to attract females, which then mate with the males in the roost. The 45 kHz and 55 kHz phonotypes produce different songs during songflights. The 55 kHz bats produce their songs at faster rates than the 45 kHz bats, coinciding with differences in size. The 55 kHz bats are smaller than the 45 kHz bats and larger bats tend to produce vocalizations at slower rates than smaller ones. The differences extend to other vocalizations as well. Foraging Pipistrelles use different vocalizations to advertise their presence to other bats of the same species. Playback experiments demonstrated that while 45 kHz Pipistrelles avoided areas where 45 kHz calls were broadcast, the 55 kHz Pipistrelles showed no such avoidance behavior.

Techniques from molecular biology were used to examine the DNA of bats of the two phonotypes. Specifically, 630 base pairs of aligned cytochrome b gene sequences were compared from four bats of each phonotype and from other related species. The two phonotypes of Pipistrelles were almost as different in their DNA as either was from two other species of European pipistrelles, Kuhl's Pipistrelle and Nathusius' Pipistrelle.

Echolocation and other behavior strongly suggested that the two phonotypes represented two different species. This position was supported by the DNA work. While we can expect to hear of new species of bats being described from the tropics (e.g., Brosset's Big-eared Bat from French Guiana in 1998) the discovery of a "new" species in Europe, let alone in populations of one of the world's most studied bats, was surprising.

The Pipistrelle story suggests that we will see more such examples of "new" species of bats hidden right under our noses.

COMMUNICATION

Meanwhile, other work with Pipistrelles in Britain had suggested that individuals use odor to recognize their home roosts. This was to be expected given the importance of odor in other aspects of the lives of bats (Chapter 7). Still, expecting something is not the same as being able to prove it experimentally.

The sac-like structures in the wings of some species of Sheath-tailed Bats that occur in the New World had been called "glands." Anatomical studies of several species demonstrated that they were not glands because they lacked glandular tissue. Early studies of Greater White-lined Bats had revealed that males could evert the sac and shake its contents over females or roosting areas-behavior called "salting" (see Chapter 7). More recently, further observations showed that male Greater White-lined Bats spat into their wing sacs and transferred to them glandular secretions from elsewhere on the body. The sacs served as fermentation chambers, generating a potent olfactory signal which was used in communication.

Salting behavior showed how the placement of sacs on the wings facilitated spreading the contents of the gland. Indeed, one could argue that this was an alternative to specialized hairs (osmetrichia—Box 13). By their design and nature, sacs weigh less than glands, which explains how they can occur on bats' wings. Furthermore, differences in the position and orientation of the sacs between species suggests that wing sacs have evolved more than once in the Sheath-tailed Bats.

Not surprisingly, the scent glands of bats are typically mammalian, producing some substances that are volatile and whose odor lingers for a short time. Other glandular secretions are oilier, making them less volatile and capable of leaving a long-lasting odor. When scent glands differ markedly between males and females, it follows that they are presumed to serve a role in mating choice and perhaps mating behavior. Most of the time when we have information about the structure of the glands, we lack corresponding data about behavior. One prime example comes from the Yellow Bat of Central

The wing sac of a male Greater White-lined Bat acts like a fermentation chamber. In the field, the bat spit into these sacs and move to them secretions from glandular areas elsewhere on the body. The sacs are eversible.

Glands on the lower half of its ears are conspicuous in this male Yellow Bat from Belize. Females lack these glands suggesting that they play a role in male-female interactions.

America. In 1993 it was first noted that while male Yellow Bats had conspicuous ear glands, females did not. Comparable ear glands also occur on Van Gelder's Bats. In either case we know about the glands but not about the roles they may play in the bats' lives. The same is not true of some other species.

As noted earlier (Box 13), males of some Free-tailed Bats have erectile crests of long hairs between their ears. In males the crest hairs grow out of a large gland located between the ears. The gland is present in a smaller form in females, and the hairs associated with it are not as long or as specialized as those of the males' crests.

Observations of interactions between males and between male and female captive Little Free-tailed Bats provided information about how males used the crests. Inside roosts, male Little Free-tailed Bats marked and defended spaces around their preferred sites. The roost sites used by the most females were the ones most sought after by males. The males scent-marked the surfaces where they roosted alone or with females. When two males met on the border between their territories, first they moved their ears down and then

A young Proboscis Bat sits on its mother's back. When the photograph was taken, the young weighed 6 g, compared to its mother's 8 g. Photograph by Enrico Bernard.

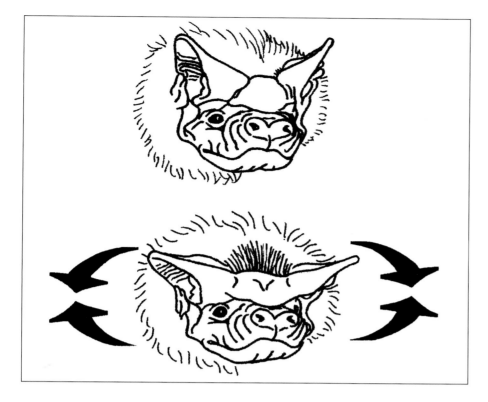

bowed. This results first in erection of the crests and then directing to the other male. Then each male rapidly shook its head while rotating it back and forth and directing the erected crest at its rival. In roosts these territorial encounters ended abruptly when one bat turned and left the contested territory. If the animals were more confined, however, the interaction escalated into a fight as the bats bit one another on the lips. In Little Free-tailed Bats, the crests and associated glands appear to have more to do with male-male interactions over space than with male-female behavior around mating.

Angola Free-tailed Bats lack the erectile crests but show similar territorial behavior within their roosts. Again, by defending areas preferred by females, male Angola Free-tailed Bats have more opportunities for mating than individuals defending spaces not used by females. During mating, male Little Free-tailed Bats or Angola Free-tailed Bats literally jump on the backs of females, grasping them firmly with hind feet, wings and thumbs and biting the backs of their necks. Females usually struggle and resist these attempts, which attract the attention of other males. When another male attempts to mate with females in its territory, the resident male interrupts the proceedings and chases away the intruder.

Angola Free-tailed Bats and Little Free-tailed Bats breed several times a year. Their colonies, which occur in buildings, bridges and hollow trees, include adult males and females. In both species, experiments revealed that bats could distinguish males from females by scent alone. The observation of territorial and mating behavior in captive Angola Free-tailed Bats and Little Free-tailed Bats gives us some clues about how their colonies are organized.

YOU ARE WHAT YOU EAT

Experience with many animals, notably raptors such as Peregrine Falcons or Bald Eagles, demonstrated how pesticides and other contaminants accumulated as one moved up the food chain. Bats are no exception to this and we know that some species ingest pesticides with the insects they consume (see page 173). Raised levels of pesticides appear to account for some bat die-offs that have been reported from various locations, usually in the American southwest.

The fact that bats are small, long-lived, mobile and eat insects makes them likely candidates as bioindicators, species that can be used to monitor the overall health of ecosystems. Samples of fur clipped from the backs of bats caught during fall swarming behavior (see page 139) were analyzed for the presence of different metallic contaminants. Fur is a useful indicator because it is shed (molted) each year and can be clipped without harming the bats. While most metals, for example, antimony, arsenic, cadmium, copper, molybdenum, silver, strontium and tin, had not accumulated in the bats' hairs, other metals were present in elevated amounts.

Some of the Little Brown Bats, Northern Long-eared Bats, Small-footed Bats and Big Brown Bats had fur containing elevated amounts of mercury, aluminum, lead, iron, zinc and selenium. Bats from various areas showed different levels of elevation of these metals, but Little Brown Bats from different areas showed no statistically significant differences in the amounts of these metals in their fur.

The levels of mercury in Little Brown Bats ranged from 2 to 7.6 mg/kg, resembling the data obtained from fish-eating mammals and birds. The mercury values from bat fur are lower than those obtained from the hair of people consuming mercury-contaminated fish (6.5 to 26 mg/kg). Earlier studies had indicated relatively high levels of mercury in some bats from Japan. Presumably these levels of mercury accumulation will occur in bats that feed on aquatic insects emerging from water contaminated by mercury. Other studies had indicated that bats sometimes showed elevated levels of lead, zinc and selenium.

LACTATING MALE BATS

The final anecdote for this chapter arises from research done in the early 1990s. One of the most newsworthy discoveries about bats in the last 10 years was the report from Malaysia of lactating male bats. Some adult male Dyak Fruit Bats caught in mist nets in July and August had mammary glands from which small amounts of milk could be expressed by manual palpation. The amount of milk produced by males was small (4–6 μl) compared to the amounts expressed from females (350 μl). The nipples of lactating males were smaller and less cornified than those of females, suggesting little, if any, suckling by young. The extent of this finding, in Dyak Fruit Bats and other species remains unclear. It is possible that secondary compounds ingested by Dyak Fruit Bats eating leaves could have triggered the development of functional mammary glands in males. The social significance of lactation by male Dyak Fruit Bats also remains unknown.

IMAGES OF BATS

The public impression of bats can be prejudiced by at least two factors. The first is the way bats are portrayed. Pictures may show bats with bared teeth, supporting the view that bats are something to be feared. Like other animals, including humans, a bat's facial expression affects our impression of its disposition. The two accompanying pictures of a Schlieffen's Bat eloquently make this point.

The second factor is the combination of vampires and rabies. It is common to meet people who think that all bats feed on blood. It is even more common to encounter otherwise educated people who are convinced that bats are asymptomatic carriers of rabies. This is a powerful combination of negative images that can be redressed only by providing correct information. Nonetheless, many humans are fascinated by bats.

The combination of the world's varieties of people and bats makes it hazardous to generalize about human attitudes toward bats. As noted earlier, different human names for bats reflect a variety of views of the Chiroptera. In China, for example, at least five different symbols represent bats. Approximately translated, they mean "embracing wings" (*fu i*), "heavenly rat" (*t'ien shu*), "fairy rat" (*hsien shu*), "flying rat" (*fei shu*), and "night swallow" (*yeh yen*). Images of bats abound in Chinese art and on items such as clothing and utensils.

Chinese representation of bats are usually done in red, the color of joy. The bats are symbols of happiness and joy, and the five-bat design, the *wu fu*, represents the five blessings: old age, wealth, health, love of virtue and a natural death. Look for five stylized bats on rice bowls in Chinese restaurants everywhere.

In Chinese art, bats may be presented with other positive symbols. Two examples are dragons, the spirit of change and of life itself, and peaches, signs of marriage, immortality and springtime. A variety of flowers also accompanies many bat symbols, conveying a number of positive images whose specific meaning changes according to the flowers and the context. It is jarring to see

This Schlieffen's Bat may weigh just 5 g but it looks very ferocious and hostile in this view.

In a more relaxed pose, another Schlief-fen's Bat looks much less formidable.

Chinese bats accompanied by swastikas, a strongly negative symbol for many people since the 1930s. Its association with bats, however, makes sense because many human societies traditionally consider the swastika to be a powerfully positive image. For the Chinese it represents resignation of spirit, luck, truth and eternity. Furthermore, the word for swastika sounds the same as the word for ten thousand, so a bat carrying a swastika represents ten thousand blessings.

Wings are the major distinctive feature of bats in Chinese art. The array of wing shapes and attitudes could indicate either an appreciation of the diversity

This cartoon by Max Licht portrays five different Chinese names for bats.

This Chinese bowl epitomizes the Embracing Wings name for bats.

of bats, or the artistic demands of setting and design. Eyes dominate the facial features of bats in Chinese art, so it is evident that the artists did not think of them as blind. Occasionally both Chinese and Japanese images of bats distinguish between Old World Fruit Bats and other bats.

On the other side of the world in the parts of Central America and South America known as Mesoamerica, bats are commonly portrayed along with other animals such as jaguars, hummingbirds and snakes. In some cases, ceramic bat faces are portrayed with enough accuracy to permit a bat biologist to recognize the genus or even the species of bat involved. Here, bat faces are usually shown on human bodies. Leaf-like ornamentations on the face and nose commonly identify the bats as New World Leaf-nosed Bats. In other cases, some distinctive anatomical feature identifies the bat basis behind the image. For example, Zotz, the Maya god of the underworld, has upper incisor teeth that are either large and triangular-shaped or hooked. The triangular teeth are those of an adult vampire bat, the hooked teeth those of a very young vampire. Zotz has a vampire bat's head on a human body and sometimes he is shown carrying a heart that is dripping blood.

Other bat faces also appear among the array of deities. Species of Ghost-faced Bats, members of the Mustached Bat family, have very distinctive faces. The look is a combination of ears, eyes and lips, but also nostrils. It is the nostrils that make it easy to recognize the Ghost-faced Bats' images on ceramic pieces. These are evident in the photographs, one from the Tairo-nan culture in northern Colombia, and another from a Maya vessel. Some faces are said to represent bats, but the precise association is unclear. To

A small Chinese bat in jade.

This Chinese bat is embroidered on a 12-symbol satin robe dating from the Ch'ing period. The bat carries a peach, a positive symbol in Chinese culture. Red is the color of joy.

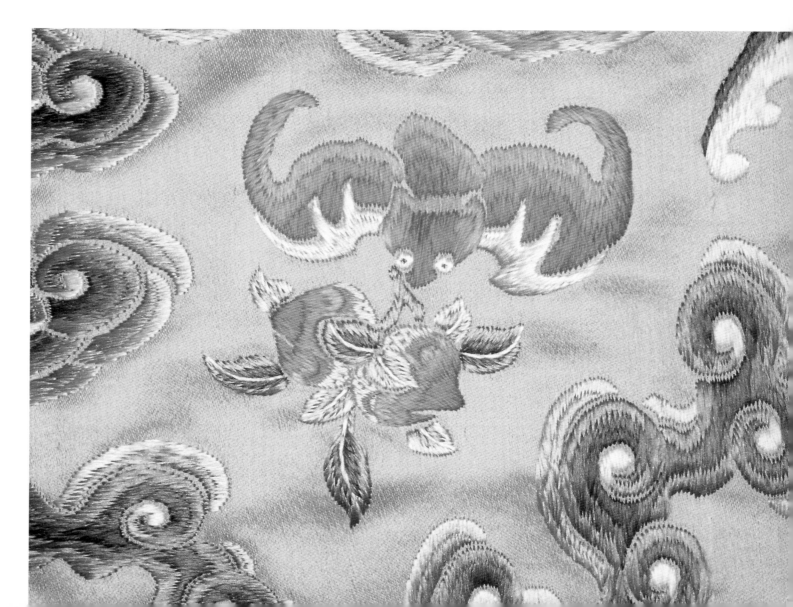

BOX 19

HOLY BATS

In many parts of the world, places of worship are sanctuaries for people. In some places the protections extends to other creatures, even bats. In India, for example, bats often roost in temples, occupying darker, sheltered places, more or less out of the human traffic. Black-bearded Tomb Bats and Indian False Vampire Bats are common temple residents in southern India. In spite of their often noisy comings and goings, and the mess associated with their droppings, the bats usually are tolerated.

The main temple in the town of Madurai in southern India harbors many Schneider's Round-leafed Bats. This species normally roosts in caves, making the dark, open areas of the temple ideal for them. Hundreds of these bats roost in the temple in no obvious conflict with the people who flock there. This species is a common temple resident in many other parts of India.

Short-faced Fruit Bats usually roost in foliage. However, several of them roost in a dimly lighted area in the temple in Thirupparankunram Town, in southern India. When I visited the temple, some bats were flapping around above the many human visitors to the temple. In another part of the temple several Sheath-tailed Bats, probably Black-bearded Tomb Bats, roosted above business stalls.

It may not be surprising that bats are safe in some places of worship, particularly in India where many religious traditions protect

This view inside the Thirupparankunram town temple is taken from just below the roosting site of a colony of Short-faced Fruit Bats.

The bats roost in a small raised area of ceiling.

further complicate matters, some Taironan pieces combine the features of several bats.

In Maya culture, the vampire image portrayed in teeth and blood was used to symbolize the underworld. To the Kogi people, descendants of the Tairona of northern Colombia, the vampire bat is associated with human fertility. A girl who has been "bitten by the bat" has begun to menstruate, signifying the onset of puberty and adulthood. It is hard to reconcile this association with the Kogi account of the bat's origin. According to Kogi mythology the bat was the first animal in creation, arising from an incestuous and homosexual relationship between the solar lord and his own son.

Elsewhere in the world, people's perceptions of bats vary considerably. There are tribes in New Guinea for whom bats are also fertility symbols, apparently because of the prominence of the penis in certain bats. In Western civilization, bats appear on the coats of arms of specific families. Examples include Chauvet and Le Corré from France, Batzon from Belgium, Bateson from Ireland, Wengatz and Krüdener from Germany and Trippel from Switzerland.

Gigantic Flying Foxes fly around their roost tree, near the village of Piliangu-lam in southern India.

A view of a roosting Short-faced Fruit Bat. These 40-g bats are common in parts of India.

animals. The situation there contrasts sharply with the attitudes encountered in many churches in North America. There, in some cases any means of exterminating bats seems acceptable to both the administration and the congregation.

In India the protection may extend beyond artificial places of worship. Near the village of Piliangulam, a huge banyan tree is home to about 500 Gigantic Flying Foxes. The villagers say that the bat colony has been there for at least 80 years. These bats, they believe, are protected by a god.

Under the banyan tree is a shrine to a god named Muni. By protecting the bats in the tree, the villagers maintain favor with Muni. They fear his retribution should they fail in their duty; and they do not tolerate others who would harm the bats. Gigantic Flying Foxes also are protected in at least three other villages in southern India: Keelarajaku-laraman, Sri Vaikundam and Ramanathapuram.

Gigantic Flying Foxes are not so fortunate everywhere in India. Elsewhere they may be harvested as a source of protein or medications. Because these bats eat some commercially important fruits, they have been classed as vermin along with poisonous snakes and rats. Biologists are petitioning the government of India to change the status of these bats and overtly recognize their value to ecosystems and ensure their survival.

From Great Britain the list is longer, including Baxter, Martyn, Steynings, Bascom, Wakefield and Heyworth.

Bottles of Bacardi alcoholic drinks bear a distinctive label that is dominated by a bat. This Bacardi bat, "the most famous bat in the world" according to Bacardi, traces its history to the bat on the coat of arms of the Spanish city of Valencia. The bat was added to that coat of arms because of the timely appearance of a bat in the royal tent just before a battle involving James I of Aragon (1208–76) and the Moors. Montsevelier in Switzerland and Gretz-Armainvilliers and Brétigny-sur-Orge in France are other cities that portray a bat on their coats of arms.

Traditionally, in some parts of Europe (rural France, Holland and England) bats have been used to ward off misfortune. To protect a household or building, a bat must be nailed head down above the door. Other uses are less harmful to the animal. Bat droppings were commonly used as ingredients in some Arabic medicines. Bat droppings could be mixed with vinegar and taken internally or applied externally on tumors. The ashes of a bat or an owl could be drunk with wine to promote milk production in women.

This vessel bearing the image of a leaf-nosed bat was found in the grave of a Maya child at Altun Ha in Belize. Dating from about A.D. 650, the bat has stylized wings, and its face bears conspicuous eyes, ears and nose-leaf. The prominent ridges probably represent white facial stripes.

Bats have been involved with a number of military operations. During the war of 1812 between the United States and Great Britain and again during the American Civil War, bat guano was an important source of saltpeter. This essential ingredient in gunpowder was obtained by mining deposits of guano in caves. During the U.S. Civil War some of the bat caves were important enough

Three bats adorn this side of a Japanese sword hilt. Two are obviously small, insectivorous species, while the third is clearly a flying fox. Flying foxes occur on some of the southern Japanese islands.

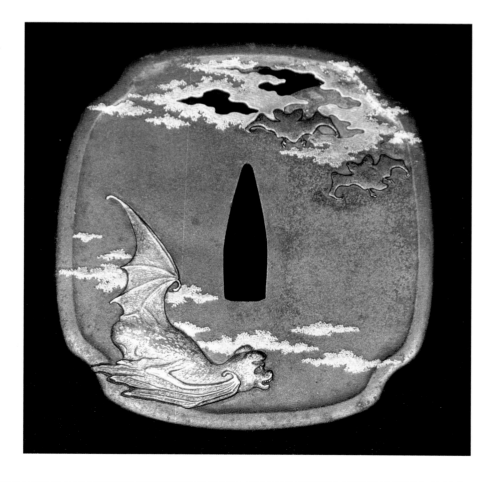

The nostrils on the bat face adorning this Maya plumbate pot from the collections of the Royal Ontario Museum suggest a Ghost-faced Bat as a model. The pot dates from the mid-10th to mid-11th century A.D.

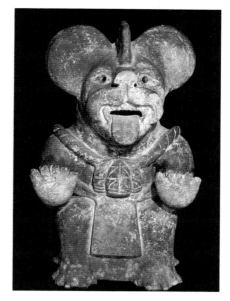

strategically to warrant a substantial guard. It is not very romantic, however, to think of northern casualties during the Civil War falling from an onslaught of lead propelled by rendered bat droppings!

During the Second World War, bats were to have been instrumental in one U.S. operation against the Japanese. The plan was to attach small incendiary bombs to Mexican Free-tailed Bats. The bats and their bombs would be placed in large cages that were to be dropped by parachute over large Japanese cities. A pressure sensor would open the cages at an appropriate altitude. The bats would leave the cages and fly away, eventually seeking shelter in buildings. In the buildings, the planners assumed that each bomb would ignite when the bat shed it. As designed, "Project X ray" would have placed incendiary bombs in many buildings. Fortunately for the bats, the plan was abandoned.

Today a number of military units use bats as symbols on regimental badges. From Great Britain, the list includes the 9th, 153rd and 162nd Squadrons of the Royal Air Force. The Spanish 252nd Legionary Air Squadron of the San Juan airbase also has a bat emblem, along with the Swiss Group moyen de DCA 52, and the Appareil de conduite de tir Fledermaus. The Belgian medical service, Service Militarie de Transfusion Sanguine, and the American 45th Tacti-

Left: This Antillean Ghost-faced Bat is a member of the Mustached Bat family. The distinctive face, with eyes located back inside the ears, and leaf-like growths on the lips, appears to be represented on different Mesoamerican ceramic pieces. Note the striking similarity in nostrils.

These three views show the Ghost-faced Bat-like head on a distinctively male human body, the main decoration on a Taironan tetrapod vessel. The piece, part of the Gardiner Collection, dates from A.D. 1000–1500.

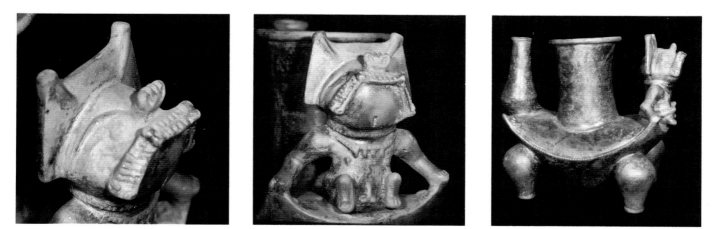

BOX 20

TWO COMMON MYTHS ABOUT BATS

There are many myths about bats, and for the most part they are stories that portray bats in a bad light. Here are two myths, along with explanations about how they might have developed.

"BATS ARE BLIND"

As we have seen in Chapter 4, bats are not blind and many have keen vision that compares well with our own or that of owls. Why, then, do we have the myth?

Virtually all bats are nocturnal, conducting most of their business in the hours of darkness. The eyes of most bats are specialized for nighttime operation, so in bright sunlight bats tend to squint. Since bats are small to begin with, small eyes squinted shut are hard to see unless you look very closely. A casual glance at a bat held in bright light leaves the impression that it has no eyes. Many of the photographs and illustrations in this book, however, show that bats do have eyes.

Echolocation (Chapter 3), well known from many bats, contributes to the general impression that bats are blind. Almost everyone has heard of the "radar" or "sonar" of a bat, so it seems natural to assume that animals with this elegant specialization would not need vision at all.

Bats are not blind; they see very well and many species use vision as well as echolocation.

"BATS GET IN YOUR HAIR"

Almost everyone's Great Aunt Mildred has had at least several bats caught in her hair at some time. While I have seen bats trained to land in people's hair, there is little evidence to support the view that hair-seeking is normal bat behavior. What natural behavior could account for this myth?

In two common situations insectivorous bats fly close to people. The first occurs when someone is standing outside on a summer evening surrounded by a hoard of mosquitoes. To a passing bat, these insects are a rich patch of prey. To exploit them, the bat flies into the cloud of insects, sometimes closely approaching the person who attracted them. The bat's behavior could suggest that it is trying to get in someone's hair.

The second occurs when a bat is flying in a room. As it approaches the wall, it slows down. In slowing down, it eventually reaches the point when it stalls in flight. To counter the stall, the bat swoops low and regains airspeed. To the human observer, the bat may appear to dive for one's hair.

In either situation, there is a simple explanation for the bat's behavior which does not involve any intent to become entangled in someone's hair. Perhaps bats have a comparable myth, that people try to catch them in their hair. If this were true, it would put a different light on an old French story about bats and hair.

In French, one word for bat is *chauve-souris*, which means "bald mouse." In French folklore, the bat is said to try to steal hair from people's heads to put on its wings. Alternatively, bats may have lost the hair on their wings because of some disease which they try to spread to other animals, such as people. Perhaps bats consider baldness an advanced state and want to share it with people!

cal Reconnaissance Squadron, the 105th AC&W Squadron and the 353rd Organizational Maintenance Squadron also show bats on their badges. Some of the units showing bat emblems are involved in electronic warfare, but at least one is medically oriented. One unit, the 360 Squadron of the joint Royal Navy/Royal Air Force Squadron shows an arctiid moth. This unit provides electronic countermeasures training for users of Air Defense radar systems. The emblem recognizes the "electronic warfare" between echolocating bats and arctiid moths (see page 49).

There is no set human view of bats. The diversity of names for these animals reflects a varied fascination. The connections range from obscurity (the Greek *nycteris*) and evening (the Italian *pipistrello*) to droppings or urine (the

Old French *pissaratta*). Other names recognize bats' combinations of mammal and bird-like qualities (the Irish *sciatham leathair*), their fluttering flight (the Old French *ratapignada*) or their resemblance to mice (the German *Fledermaus* or the French *chauve-souris*). Hungarian and English provide especially apt names—*denever* and *bat*—because they do not rely on other animals or a single bat trait to identify these unique creatures.

• • •

Bats are intriguing and have a history that goes back over 50 million years. The members of the Chiroptera have adopted an amazing array of lifestyles and habits, reflected in their appearance and by remarkable specializations such as echolocation. Human uses for bats and their images are also diverse, reflecting the variety of bat habits and lifestyles.

It is easy to admire the many species that exploit human-wrought changes in the environment. We can learn from their flexibility. And yet the sensitivity of other bats to environmental changes may make them invaluable to us as indicators of the health of the ecosystems where they occur. Bats offer something for everyone.

John Taylor took this photograph of part of a fresco entitled "The Feast of the Gods." The mural was painted in the Garden Room in the residence of the Bishop of Würzburg in Bavaria. The painting, by Johann Zick, dates from 1750.

APPENDIX

Common and Scientific Names of Bats in Text

° denotes illustration

COMMON NAME	SCIENTIFIC NAME	FAMILY
Angola Free-tailed Bat	*Tadarida condylura*	Molossidae
Antillean Ghost-faced Bat°	*Mormoops blainvillii*	Mormoopidae
Australian Little Brown Bat	*Eptesicus pumilus*	Vespertilionidae
Australian Northern Long-eared Bat°	*Nyctophilus bifax*	Vespertilionidae
Bamboo Bats	*Tylonycteris* species	Vespertilionidae
Banana Bat°	*Pipistrellus nanus*	Vespertilionidae
Bemmeleni's Free-tailed Bat°	*Tadarida bemmeleni*	Molossidae
Bent-winged Bats	*Miniopterus* species	Vespertilionidae
Bicolored Roundleaf Bat°	*Hipposidoros bicolor*	Hipposideridae
Big Brown Bat°	*Eptesicus fuscus*	Vespertilionidae
Big Fruit Bat°	*Artibeus lituratus*	Phyllostomidae
Black-bearded Tomb Bat°	*Taphozous melanopogon*	Emballonuridae
Blackhawk Bat	*Taphozous peli*	Emballonuridae
Brosset's Big-eared Bat	*Micronycteris brosseti*	Phyllostomidae
Brown Fruit Bat°	*Artibeus concolor*	Phyllostomidae
Brown Long-eared Bat	*Plecotus auritus*	Vespertilionidae
Bulldog Bat°	*Noctilio* species	Noctilionidae
Butterfly Bat°	*Chalinolobus variegatus*	Vespertilionidae
Buttikofer's Epauletted Bat	*Epomops buettikoferi*	Pteropodidae
California Leaf-nosed Bat°	*Macrotus californicus*	Phyllostomidae
Cape Serotine	*Eptesicus capensis*	Vespertilionidae
Cave Bat	*Mytois velifer*	Vespertilionidae
Cave Myotis	*Myotis velifer*	Vespertilionidae
Cave Nectar Bat°	*Eonycteris spelaea*	Pteropodidae
Commerson's Leaf-nosed Bat°	*Hipposideros commersoni*	Hipposideridae
Commissaris' Long-tongued Bat°	*Glossophaga commissarisi*	Phyllostomidae
Common Vampire Bat°	*Desmodus rotundus*	Phyllostomidae
Common Yellow-shouldered Bat°	*Sturnira lilium*	Phyllostomidae

COMMON NAME	SCIENTIFIC NAME	FAMILY
Cozumel Spear-nosed Bat°	*Mimon cozumelae*	Phyllostomidae
Darling's Horseshoe Bat°	*Rhinolophus darlingi*	Rhinolophidae
Daubenton's Bat	*Myotis daubentoni*	Vespertilionidae
Davis' Round-eared Bat°	*Tonatia evotis*	Phyllostomidae
Dome-headed Bat	*Phoniscus papuensis*	Vespertilionidae
Dwarf Epauletted Bat	*Micropteropus pusillus*	Pteropodidae
Dyak Fruit Bat	*Dyacopterus spadiceus*	Pteropodidace
Eastern Pipistrelle	*Pipistrellus subflavus*	Vespertilionidae
Eastern Red Bat°	*Lasiurus borealis*	Vespertilionidae
Eastern Small-footed Bat°	*Myotis leibii*	Vespertilionidae
Egyptian Free-tailed Bat°	*Tadarida aegyptiaca*	Molossidae
Egyptian Fruit Bat°	*Rousettus egyptiacus*	Pteropodidae
Egyptian Slit-faced Bat°	*Nycteris thebaica*	Nycteridae
Epauletted Fruit Bat°	*Epomophorus crypturus*	Pteropodidae
Evening Bat	*Nycticeius humeralis*	Vespertilionidae
False Vampire Bats°		Megadermatidae
Flying Foxes°	*Pteropus* species	Pteropodidae
Free-tailed Bats°		Molossidae
Fringe-lipped Bat	*Trachops cirrhosus*	Phyllostomidae
Fulvous Fruit Bat	*Rousettus leschenaulti*	Pteropodidace
Funnel-eared Bats°	*Natalus* species	Natalidae
Gambian Epauletted Fruit Bat	*Epomophorus gambianus*	Pteropodidae
Ghost Bat	*Macroderma gigas*	Megadermatidae
Ghost-faced Bats°	*Mormoops* species	Mormoopidae
Gigantic Flying Fox°	*Pteropus giganteus*	Pteropodidae
Gray Bat	*Myotis grisescens*	Vespertilionidae
Gray-headed Flying Fox°	*Pteropus poliocephalus*	Pteropodidae
Greater Bamboo Bat°	*Tylonycteris robustula*	Vespertilionidae
Greater Bulldog Bat°	*Noctilio leporinus*	Noctilionidae
Greater Horseshoe Bat°	*Rhinolophus ferrumequinum*	Rhinolophidae
Greater Spear-nosed Bat°	*Phyllostomus hastatus*	Phyllostomidae
Greater Tube-nosed Bat°	*Murina leucogaster*	Vespertilionidae
Greater White-lined Bat°	*Saccopteryx bilineata*	Emballonuridae
Hairy-legged Vampire Bat°	*Diphylla ecaudata*	Phyllostomidae
Hairy Slit-faced Bat	*Nycteris hispida*	Nycteridae
Hammerhead Bat°	*Hypsignathus monstrosus*	Pteropodidae
Heart-nosed Bat	*Cardioderma cor*	Megadermatidae
Heller's Broad-nosed Bat	*Platyrrhinus helleri*	Phyllostomidae
Hemprich's Long-eared Bat°	*Otonycteris hemprichi*	Vespertilionidae
Hildebrandt's Horseshoe Bat°	*Rhinolophus hildebrandti*	Rhinolophidae
Hoary Bat°	*Lasiurus cinereus*	Vespertilionidae
Hog-nosed Bat	*Craseonycteris thonglongyai*	Craseonycteridae
Honduran Ghost Bat°	*Ectophylla alba*	Phyllostomidae
Horseshoe Bats°	*Rhinolophus* species	Rhinolophidae
House Bat	*Scotophilus kuhlii*	Vespertilionidae
Indian False Vampire Bat°	*Megaderma lyra*	Megadermatidae
Intermediate Fruit Bat°	*Artibeus intermedius*	Phyllostomidae
Jamaican Fruit Bat°	*Artibeus jamaicensis*	Phyllostomidae
Jamaican Funnel-eared Bat°	*Natalus micropus*	Natalidae
Kuhl's Pipistrelle	*Pipistrellus kuhlii*	Vespertilionidae

COMMON NAME	SCIENTIFIC NAME	FAMILY
Large Flying Fox	*Pteropus vampyrus*	Pteropodidae
Large-footed Myotis	*Myotis adversus*	Vespertilionidae
Large Slit-faced Bat°	*Nycteris grandis*	Nycteridae
Lesser Bamboo Bat	*Tylonycteris pachypus*	Vespertilionidae
Lesser Bulldog Bat	*Noctilio albiventris*	Noctilionidae
Lesser False Vampire Bat°	*Megaderma spasma*	Megadermatidae
Lesser Long-nosed Bat	*Leptonycteris curasoae*	Phyllostomidae
Lesser Rat-tailed Bat°	*Rhinopoma hardwickei*	Rhinopomatidae
Lesser Philippine Fruit Bat°	*Ptenochirus minor*	Pteropodidae
Lesser Tube-nosed Fruit Bat°	*Paranyctimene raptor*	Pteropodidae
Lesser White-lined Bat	*Saccopteryx leptura*	Emballonuridae
Lesser Woolly Bat°	*Kerivoula lanosa*	Vespertilionidae
Lesser Yellow House Bat°	*Scotophilus borbonicus*	Vespertilionidae
Linnaeus' False Vampire Bat°	*Vampyrum spectrum*	Phyllostomidae
Little Big-eared Bat	*Micronycteris megalotis*	Phyllostomidae
Little Brown Bat°	*Myotis lucifugus*	Vespertilionidae
Little Collared Fruit Bat	*Myonycteris torquata*	Pteropodidae
Little Free-tailed Bat°	*Tadarida pumila*	Molossidae
Long-crested Free-tailed Bat°	*Tadarida chapini*	Molossidae
Long-eared Bat	*Laephotis wintoni*	Vespertilionidae
Long-eared Myotis	*Myotis evotis*	Vespertilionidae
Long-legged Myotis	*Myotis volans*	Vespertilionidae
Long-tailed Bat	*Chalinolobus tuberculatus*	Vespertilionidae
MacLeay's Mustached Bat°	*Pteronotus macleayi*	Mormoopidae
Madagascar Large Free-tailed Bat	*Tadarida fulminans*	Molossidae
Marianas Fruit Bat	*Pteropus mariannus*	Pteropodidae
Marinkelle's Sword-nosed Bat	*Lonchorhina marinkelle*	Phyllostomidae
Martienssen's Free-tailed Bat	*Otomops martiensseni*	Molossidae
Mauritian Tomb Bat°	*Taphozous mauritianus*	Emballonuridae
Mexican Fishing Bat	*Pizonyx vivesi*	Vespertilionidae
Mexican Free-tailed Bat°	*Tadarida brasiliensis*	Molossidae
Mexican Long-tongued Bat°	*Choeronycteris mexicana*	Phyllostomidae
Midas' Free-tailed Bat	*Tadarida midas*	Molossidae
Moluccan Naked-backed Bat°	*Dobsonia moluccensis*	Pteropodidae
Mouse-eared Bat°	*Myois myotis*	Vespertilionidae
Mouse-eared Bats°	*Myotis* species	Vespertilionidae
Mouse-[a.k.a. Rat-]tailed Bats°	*Rhinopoma* species	Rhinopomatidae
Mustached Bats°		Moroopidae
Naked Bat	*Cheiromeles torquatus*	Molossidae
Naked-rumped Tomb Bat°	*Taphozous nudiventris*	Emballonuridae
Narrow-winged Pipistrelle	*Pipistrellus stenopterus*	Vespertilionidae
Nathusius' Pipistrelle	*Pipistrellus nathusii*	Vespertilionidae
New World Leaf-nosed Bats°		Phyllostomidae
New World Disk-winged Bats	*Thyroptera* species	Thyropteridae
Noctule	*Nyctalus noctula*	Vespertilionidae
Northern Blossom Bat	*Macroglossus lagochilus*	Pteropodidae
Northern Ghost Bat	*Diclidurus albus*	Emballonuridae
Northern Long-eared Bat°	*Myotis septentrionalis*	Vespertilionidae
Old World Fruit Bats°		Pteropodidae
Old World Leaf-nosed Bats°		Hipposideridae
Old World Disk-winged Bat	*Myzopoda aurita*	Myzopodidae
Old World Disk-winged Bats	*Myzopoda* species	Myzopodidae

COMMON NAME	SCIENTIFIC NAME	FAMILY
Pale Spear-nosed Bat°	*Phyllostomus discolor*	Phyllostomidae
Pallas' Long-tongued Bat	*Glossophaga soricina*	Phyllostomidae
Pallas' Mastiff Bat°	*Molossus molossus*	Molossidae
Pallid Bat°	*Antrozous pallidus*	Antrozoidae
Pallid Large-footed Myotis	*Myotis macrotarsus*	Vespertilionidae
Parnell's Mustached Bat°	*Pteronotus parnellii*	Mormoopidae
Peters' Flat-headed Bat°	*Platymops setiger*	Molossidae
Peters' White-lined Bat°	*Chiroderma villosum*	Phyllostomidae
Pipistrelle	*Pipistrellus pipistrellus*	Vespertilionidae
Plain-nosed Bats°		Vespertilionidae
Proboscis Bat°	*Rhynchonycteris naso*	Emballonuridae
Pygmy Fruit Bat°	*Artibeus phaeotis*	Phyllostomidae
Queensland Blossom Bat	*Syconycteris crassa*	Pteropodidae
Red Fruit Bat	*Pteropus scapulatus*	Pteropodidae
Red Mastiff Bat°	*Molossus rufus*	Molossidae
Rendall's Serotine°	*Eptesicus rendallii*	Vespertilionidae
Rickett's Big-footed Bat	*Myotis ricketti*	Vespertilionidae
Roberts' Flat-headed Bat	*Sauromys petrophilus*	Molossidae
Rufous Hairy Bat	*Myotis bocagei*	Vespertilionidae
Rufous Horseshoe Bat	*Rhinolophus rouxi*	Rhinolophidae
Ruppell's Bat°	*Pipistrellus rueppellii*	Vespertilionidae
Ruppell's Horseshoe Bat	*Rhinolophus fumigatus*	Rhinolophidae
Rusty Pipistrelle	*Pipistrellus rusticus*	Vespertilionidae
Sanborn's Long-tongued Bat	*Leptonycteris sanborni*	Phyllostomidae
Schlieffen's Bat°	*Nycticeius schlieffeni*	Vespertilionidae
Schmidt's Large-eared Bat°	*Micronycteris schmidtorum*	Phyllostomidae
Schneider's Roundleaf Bat°	*Hipposideros speoris*	Hipposideridae
Schreiber's Bent-winged Bat	*Miniopterus schreibersii*	Vespertilionidae
Sheath-tailed Bats°		Emballonuridae
Short-eared Trident Bat	*Cloeotis percivali*	Hipposideridae
Short-faced Fruit Bat°	*Cynopterus sphinx*	Pteropodidae
Short-tailed Bat°	*Mystacina tuberculata*	Mystacinidae
Short-tailed Bats°	*Mystacina* species	Mystacinidae
Short-tailed Fruit Bat°	*Carollia perspicillata*	Phyllostomidae
Silver-haired Bat	*Lasionycteris noctivagans*	Vespertilionidae
Slit-faced Bats°	*Nycteris* species	Nycteridae
Sooty Mustached Bat°	*Pteronotus fuliginosus*	Mormoopidae
South American Flat-headed Bat	*Neoplatymops mattogrosensis*	Molossidae
Spix's New World Disk-winged Bat°	*Thyroptera tricolor*	Thyropteridae
Spotted Bat°	*Euderma maculatum*	Vespertilionidae
Straw-colored Fruit Bat	*Eidolon helvum*	Pteropodidae
Sundevell's Leaf-nosed Bat°	*Hipposideros caffer*	Hipposideridae
Tomb Bats°	*Taphozous* species	Emballonuridae
Tome's Long-eared Bats°	*Lonchorhina aurita*	Phyllostomidae
Thumbless Bats°		Furipteridae
Triple Leaf-nosed Bat	*Triaenops persicus*	Hipposideridae
Tube-nosed Bats°		either Pteropodidae or Vespertilionidae

COMMON NAME	SCIENTIFIC NAME	FAMILY
Vampire Bats°	Phyllostomidae	
Van Gelder's Bat	*Bauerus dubiaquercus*	Antrozoidae
Visored Bat	*Sphaeronycteris toxophyllum*	Phyllostomidae
Wahlberg's Epauletted Fruit Bat°	*Epomophorus wahlbergi*	Pteropodidae
Waterhouse's Leaf-nosed Bat	*Macrotus waterhousii*	Phyllostomidae
Welwitsch's Hairy Bat°	*Myotis welwitschii*	Vespertilionidae
Western Big-eared Bat°	*Plecotus townsendii*	Vespertilionidae
Western Pipistrelle	*Pipistrellus hesperus*	Vespertilionidae
Western Red Bat	*Lasiurus blossevilli*	Vespertilionidae
White-winged Vampire Bat°	*Diaemus youngi*	Phyllostomidae
Woemann's Bat°	*Megaloglossus woermanni*	Pteropodidae
Woolly False Vampire Bat°	*Chrotopterus auritus*	Phyllostomidae
Wrinkle-faced Bat°	*Centurio senex*	Phyllostomidae
Wroughton's Pipistrelle°	*Pipistrellus mimus*	Vespertilionidae
Yellow Bat°	*Rhogeessa anaeus*	Vespertilionidae
Yellow Bats°	*Rhogeessa* species	Vespertilionidae
Yellow House Bat	*Scotophilus dinganii*	Vespertilionidae
Yellow-throated Bat°	*Micronycteris brachyotis*	Phyllostomidae
Yellow-winged Bat	*Lavia frons*	Megadermatidae

BIBLIOGRAPHY

GENERAL WORKS ABOUT BATS

Allen, G. M. *Bats*. Cambridge: Harvard University Press, 1939.

Altringham, J. D. *Bats: Biology and Behaviour*. Oxford: Oxford University Press, 1996.

Baker, R. J., D. C. Carter, and J. K. Jones, Jr. eds. *Biology of Bats of the New World Family Phyllostomatidae*. Lubbock: Museum Publication, Texas Tech University, Vol. 1, 1976; Vol. 2 1977; Vol. 3, 1979.

Brosset, A. *La biologie des chiroptères*. Paris: Masson et Cie, 1966.

Derennes, C. *The Life of the Bat*. New York: Harper Brothers, 1924.

Fenton, M. B. *Just Bats*. Toronto: University of Toronto Press, 1983.

———. *The Bat: Wings in the Night Sky*. Toronto: Key Porter, 1998.

Fenton, M. B. P. A. Racey, and J. M. V. Rayner, eds. *Recent Advances in the Study of Bats*. Cambridge: Cambridge University Press, 1987.

Findley, J. S. *Bats: A Community Perspective*. Cambridge: Cambridge University Press, 1993.

Gebhard, F. *Fledermause*. Basel, Switzerland: Birkhauser Verlag, 1997.

Hanak, V., I. Horacek, and J. Gaisler, eds. *European Bat Research 1987*. Prague: Charles University Press, 1989.

Hill, J. E., and J. D. Smith. *Bats: A Natural History*. London: British Museum (Natural History), 1984.

Kunz, T. H., ed. *Ecology of Bats*. New York: Plenum Publishing, 1982.

Kunz, T. H., and M. B. Fenton, eds. *Ecology of Bats*. Chicago: University of Chicago Press. In press.

Kunz, T. H., and P. A. Racey, eds. *Bat Biology and Conservation*. Washington, D.C.: Smithsonian Institution Press, 1998.

Leen, N., and A. Novick. *The World of Bats*. New York: Holt, Rinehart and Winston, 1969.

Neuweiler, G. *The Biology of Bats*. Oxford: Oxford University Press, 2000.

Nowak, R. M. *Walker's Mammals of the World*. Vol. 1, 6th ed. Baltimore: Johns Hopkins University Press, 1999.

Racey, P. A., and S. M. Swift, eds. *Ecology, Evolution and Behaviour of Bats.* London: Zoological Society of London, Symposia 67, 1995.

Ransome, R. D. *The Natural History of Hibernating Bats.* London: Christopher Helm, 1990.

Richarz, K., and A. Limbrunner. *The World of Bats, The Flying Goblins of the Night.* Stuttgart, Germany: TFH Publications, 1993.

Robertson, J. *The Complete Bat.* London: Chatto and Windus, 1990.

Schober, W. *The Lives of Bats.* New York: Arco Publishing, 1984.

Slaughter, B. H., and D. W. Walton, eds. *About Bats: A Chiropteran Symposium.* Dallas: Southern Methodist University Press, 1970.

Swift, S. M. *Long-eared Bats.* Cambridge: T & AD Poyser Natural History, 1998.

Tuttle, M. D. *America's Neighborhood Bats.* Austin: University of Texas Press, 1988.

Wilson, D. E. *Bats in Question.* Washington, D.C.: Smithsonian Institution Press, 1997.

Wilson, D. E., and D. M. Reeder. *Mammal Species of the World.* Washington, D.C.: Smithsonian Institution Press, 1993.

Wimsatt, W. A., ed. *Biology of Bats*, 3 vols. New York: Academic Press, 1970–77.

Yalden, D. W., and P. A. Morris. *The Lives of Bats.* New York: New York Times / Quadrangle Press, 1974.

WORLD WIDE WEB SITES

Bat Conservation International: http://www.batcon.org/

The London (England) Bat Group: http://www.compulink.co.uk/~peegee/lbg/lbg.html

Chiroptera Neotropical: http://guarany.unb.br/woo/chiroptera

http://members.aol.com/bats4kids

http://www.batbox.org

http://www.batconservation.org

http://www.direct.ca/pestpage/bats1.html

http://www.nasbr.com

Batline, an email discussion group. To subscribe send a message to listserve@unm.edu. The message should read sub batline yourfirstname yourlastname.

BAT BOOKS FOR YOUNGER REARDERS

Appelt, K. *Bat Jamboree.* New York: Morrow Junior Books, 1996.

Arnold, C., and R. Hewett. *Bat.* New York: Morrow Junior Books, 1996.

Bash, B. *Shadows of the Night: The Hidden World of the Little Brown Bat.* San Francisco: Sierra Club Books for Children, 1993.

Cannon, A. *The Bat in the Boot.* Norwich, UK: Grolier, 1996.

Cannon, J. *Stellaluna.* San Diego: Harcourt Brace, 1993.

Conroy, D. *The Bat Who Was All in a Flap.* Dublin: The O'Brian Press, 1995.

Cooper, A. C. *Bats: Swift Shadows in the Twilight.* Schull, Ireland: Roberts Rinehart, 1994.

Earle, A. *Zipping, Zapping, Zooming Bats.* New York: HarperCollins, 1995.

Gallant, R. A. *Limestone Caves.* New York: Franklin Watts, 1998.

Gilson, J. *It Goes Eeeeee.* New York: Clarion Books, 1994.

Glasser, L. *Beautiful Bats.* New York: Millbrook Press, 1997.

Graham, G. L. *Bats of the World*. New York: Golden Press, 1994.

Halton, C. M. *Those Amazing Bats*. Minneapolis, Minn.: Dillon Press, 1991.

Kramer, S. *The Dark Zone: Exploring the Secret World of Caves*. New York: McGraw Hill, 1998.

Lundberg, K. *Bats for Kids*. Minocqua, Wisc.: NorthWord Press, 1996.

Maestro, B.. *Bats: Night Fliers*. New York: Scholastic Press, 1994.

Markle, S. *Outside and Inside Bats*. New York: Atheneum Books for Younger Readers, 1997.

McNulty, F. *When I Lived with Bats*. New York: Scholastic Press, 1999.

Nielsen, V. *Batty Hattie*. London: Cavendish Press, 1999.

Oppel, K. *Silverwing*. Toronto: HarperCollins, 1997.

———. *Sunwing*. Toronto: HarperCollins, 1999.

Quackenbush, R. *Batbaby*. New York: Random House, 1997.

Schindler, S. D. *Bat in the Dining Room*. New York: Cavendish, 1997.

Stanley, S. *Bats on My Brain*. Portland: Oregon Zoo, 1998.

Stuart, D. *Bats: Mysterious Flyers of the Night*. Minneapolis, Minn.: Carolrhoda Books, 1994.

Swanson, D. *Welcome to the World of Bats*. Vancouver: Whitecap Books, 1998.

NEWSLETTERS ABOUT BATS

Bat Research News, published quarterly. Managing editor, Dr. G. R. Horst, Department of Biology, State University of New York, Potsdam, New York 13676.

BATS, published by Bat Conservation International, P.O. Box 162603, Austin, TX 78716.

CHAPTER 1

(in addition to the general works noted above)

Crerar, L. M., and M. B. Fenton. "Cervical vertebrae in relation to roosting posture in bats." *Journal of Mammalogy* 65 (1984):395–403.

Norberg, U. M. *Vertebrate Flight*. Berlin: Springer-Verlag, 1990.

Norberg, U. M., and M. B. Fenton. "Carnivorous Bats?" *Biological Journal of the Linnean Society*, 33(1988):383–394.

Pennycuick, C. J. *Animal Flight*. London: Edward Arnold Series in Biology 33 (1972).

Simmons, N. B., and J. H. Geisler. "Phylogenetic Relationships of Icaronycteris, Archaeonycteris, Hassianycteris and Palaeochiropteryx to Extant Bat Lineages, with Comments on the Evolution of Echolocation and Foraging Strategies in Microchiroptera." *Bulletin of the American Museum of Natural History* 235(1998):1–182.

Teeling, E. C., et al. "Molecular Evidence Regarding the Origin of Echolocation and Flight in Bats." *Nature* 403(2000):188–192.

Wilson, D. E., and D. M. Reeder. *Mammal Species of the World*. Washington, D.C.: Smithsonian Institution Press, 1993.

CHAPTER 2

Hovorka, M. D., C. S. Marks, and E. Muller. "An improved chemiluminescent tag for bats." *Wildlife Society Bulletin* 24 (1996):709–712, 1996.

Kunz, T. H. ed. *Behavioral and Ecological Methods for the Study of Bats*. Washington, D.C.: Smithsonian Institution Press, 1988.

Thomas, D. W., and S. D. West. *Sampling Methods for Bats*. Portland: U.S. Department of Agriculture, Forest Service, Pacific Northwest Research Station General Technical Report, PNW-GTR-243, 1989.

CHAPTER 3

Au, W. W. L. *The Sonar of Dolphins*. New York: Springer, 1993.

Busnell, R. G., and J. F. Fish (eds). *Animal Sonar Systems*. New York: Plenum Publishing, 1980.

Fenton, M. B., D. Audet, M. K. Obrist, and J. Rydell. "Signal Strength, Timing, and Self-deafening: the Evolution of Echolocation in Bats." *Paleobiology* 21 (1995):229–242.

Forbes, B., and E. M. Newhook. "A Comparison of the Performance of Three Models of Bat Detectors." *Journal of Mammalogy* 71 (1990):108–110.

Griffin, D. R. *Listening in the Dark*. New Haven: Yale University Press, 1958.

Nachtigall, P. E., and P. W. B. Moore (eds). *Animal Sonar Systems: Processes and Performance*. New York: Plenum Publishing, 1988.

Pollak, G. D., and J. H. Casseday. *Neural Basis of Echolocation in Bats*. Berlin: Springer-Verlag, 1989.

Popper, A. N., and R. Faye, eds. *Hearing by Bats*. New York: Springer-Verlag, 1995.

Roeder, K. D. *Nerve Cells and Insect Behavior, Revised Edition*. Harvard University Press, Cambridge, 1967.

Sales, G., and J. D. Pye. *Ultrasonic Communication by Animals*. London: Chapman and Hall, 1974.

Speakman, J. R., and P. A. Racey. "No Cost of Echolocation for Bats in Flight." *Nature* 350 (1991):421-423.

Von Helversen, D., and O. von Helversen. "Acoustic Guide in Bat-pollinated Flower." *Nature* 398 (1999):759–780.

CHAPTER 4

Baker, R., (ed). *The Mystery of Migration*. Toronto: John Wiley and Sons, 1980.

Baker, R. R., (ed). *Fantastic Journeys: The Marvels of Migration*. London: Merehurst, 1991.

Davis, W. H., and H. B. Hitchcock. "Biology and Migration of the Bat, Myotis Lucifugus, in New England." *Journal of Mammalogy* 46 (1965):296–313.

Fenton, M. B. "Population studies of *Myotis lucifugus* (Chiroptera: Vespertilionidae) in Ontario." *Life Sciences Contributions, Royal Ontario Museum*, 77 (1970):1–34.

Stoddart, D. M. *The Ecology of Vertebrate Olfaction*. London: Chapman and Hall, 1980.

CHAPTER 5

Dumont, E. R. "The Effect of Food Hardness on Feeding Behaviour in Frugivorous Bats (Phyllostomidae): An Experimental Study." *Journal of Zoology (London)* 248 (1999):219–229.

Fenton, M. B., et al. "Foraging Behavior and Prey Selection by Large Slit-faced Bats (*Nycteris grandis*; Chiroptera: Nyctendae)." *Biotropica* 22 (1990):2-8.

Fleming, T. H. *The Short-tailed Fruit Bat.* Chicago: University of Chicago Press, 1988.

Kunz, T. H., and K. A. Ingalls. "Folivory in Bats: An Adaptation Derived from Frugivory." Functional Ecology 8 (1994):665–668.

Tuttle, M. D. "Africa's Flying Foxes." *National Geographic* 4, no. 169 (1986):54–58.

———. "The Amazing Frog-eating Bat." *National Geographic* 1, no. 161(1982):78–91.

———. "Bats: The Cactus Connection." *National Geographic* 6, no. 179(1991):130–40.

CHAPTER 6

Audet, D., and M. B. Fenton. "Heterothermy and Use of Torpor by the Bats *Eptesicus fuscus* (Chiroptera: Vespertionidae): A Field Study." *Physiological Zoology* 61 (1988):197–204.

Bhat, H. R., and T. H. Kunz. "Altered Flower/Fruit Clusters of the Kitul Palm used as Roosts by the Short-faced bat, *Cynopterus sphinx* (Chiroptera: Phyllostomidae)." *Journal of Zoology, London* 235 (1995):597–604.

Fleming, T. H. *The Short-tailed Fruit Bat.* Chicago: University of Chicago Press, 1988.

Koehler, C. E., and R. M. R. Barclay. "Post-natal Growth and Breeding Biology of the Hoary Bat (*Lasiurus cinereus*)." *Journal of Mammalogy* 81 (2000):234–244.

Kunz, T. H., and G. F. McCracken. "Tents and Harems: Apparent Defense of foliage roosts by Tent-making Bats." *Journal of Tropical Ecology* 12 (1996):121–137.

Thomas, D. W., and D. Cloutier. "Evaporative Water Loss by Hibernating Little Brown Bats, *Myotis lucifugus*." *Physiological Zoology* 65 (1992):443–456.

Thomas, D. W., M. Dorias, and J-M. Bergeron. "Winter Energy Budgets and Cost of Arousals for Hibernating Little Brown Bats, *Myotis lucifugus*." *Journal of Mammalogy*, 71 (1990):475–479.

Timm, R. M., and B. L. Clauson. "A Roof Over Their Feet." *Natural History* 3, no. 90 (1990):55–58.

CHAPTER 7

Crichton, E. G. and P. H. Krutzsch (eds). *Reproductive Biology of Bats.* New York: Academic Press, 2000.

Cumming, G. S., and R. T. F. Bernard. "Rainfall, Food Abundance and Timing of Parturition in African bats." *Oecologia* 111 (1997):309–317.

Fenton, M. B. *Communication in the Chiroptera.* Bloomington: Indiana University Press, 1985.

Hassanloo, Z., M. B. Fenton, J. B. DeLaurier and J. L. Eger. "Fur Increases the Parasite Drag for Flying Bats." *Canadian Journal of Zoology* 73 (1995):837–842.

Racey, P. A., et al. "Spermatozoa-Epithelium Relationships in Relation to the Time of Copulation in Little Brown Bats, *Myotis lucifugus*." *Journal of Reproductive Fertility* 80 (1987):44–54.

Scully, W. M. R., M. B. Fenton, and A. S. M. Saleuddin. "A Histological Examination of Holding Sacs and Scent Glandular Organs of Some Bats (Emballonuridae, Hipposideridae, Phyllostomidae, Vespertilionidae and Molossidae)." *Canadian Journal of Zoology* 78 (2000):613–623.

Trivers, R. *Social Evolution.* Menlo Park, Calif.: Benjamin/Cummings, 1985.

Watt, E. M., and M. B. Fenton. "DNA Fingerprinting Provides Evidence of Discriminate suckling and Non-random Mating in Little Brown Bats *Myotis lucifugus.*" *Molecular Ecology* 4 (1995):261–264.

CHAPTER 8

Fenton, M. B., D. H. M. Cumming, and D. J. Oxley. "Prey of Bat Hawks and Availability of Bats." *Condor* 79 (1977):495–497.

Fenton, M. B., et al. "Raptors and bats: threats and opportunities." *Animal Behaviour*, 48 (1994):9–18.

Marshall, A. C. *The Ecology of Ectoparasitic Insects.* London: Academic Press, 1981.

Ransome, R. D. *The Natural History of Hibernating Bats.* London: Christopher Helm, 1990.

CHAPTER 9

Acharya, L. "*Epomphorus wahlbergi.*" *Mammalian Species* 394 (1992):1–4.

Cloutier, D., and D. W. Thomas. "*Carollia perspicillata.*" *Mammalian Species* 417 (1992):1–9.

Fenton, M. B., and R. M. R. Barclay. "*Myotis lucifugus.*" *Mammalian Species* 142 (1980):1–8.

Herd, R. M. "*Pteronotus parnellii.*" *Mammalian Species* 209 (1983):15.

Hermanson, J. W., and T. J. O'Shea. "*Antrozous pallidus.*" *Mammalian Species* 213 (1983):1–8.

Hood, C. S., and J. K. Jones, Jr. "*Noctilio leporinus.*" *Mammalian Species* 216 (1984):1–7.

Hudson, W. S., and D. E. Wilson. "*Macroderma gigas.*" *Mammmalian Species* 260 (1986):1–4.

Kurta, A., and R. H. Baker. "*Eptesicus Fuscus.*" *Mammalian Species.* 356: (1990) 1–10.

Kwiecinski, G. G., and T. A. Griffiths. "*Rousettus egyptiacus.*" *Mammalian Species* 611 (1999):1–9.

Langevin, P., and B. M. B. Barclay. "*Hypsignathus monstrosus.*" *Mammalian Species* 357 (1990):1–4.

Navarro, L., and D. E. Wilson. "*Vampyrum spectrum.*" *Mammalian Species* 184 (1982):14.

Qumsiyeh, M. B., and J. K. Jones, Jr. "*Rhinopoma hardwickei* and *Rhinopoma muscatellum.*" *Mammalian Species* 263 (1986):1–5.

Watkins, L. C. "*Euderma maculatum.*" *Mammalian Species* 77 (1977):1–4.

CHAPTER 10

Brown, D. E., *Vampiro: the Vampire Bat in Fact and Fantasy.* Silver City, New Mexico: High-Lonesome Books, 1994.

Greenhall, A. M., G. Joermann, U. Schmidt and M. R. Seidel. *"Desmodus rotundus." Mammalian Species* 202 (1983):1–6.

Greenhall, A. M., and U. Schmidt, eds. *The Natural History of Vampire Bats.* Boca Raton, Fla.: CRC Press, 1988.

Greenhall, A. M., U. Schmidt, and G. Joermann. *"Diphylla ecaudata." Mammalian Species* 227 (1984):1–3.

Schmidt, U. *Vampirfledermaus.* Leipzig: Die Neue Brehm-Bucherei, 1978.

Turner, D. C. *The Vampire Bat.* Baltimore: Johns Hopkins University Press, 1975.

CHAPTER 11

Advisory Committee Immunization Practices. "Rabies Prevention: United States 1991." *Morbidity and Modality, Weekly Report: Recommendations and Reports* 40(1991):1–19.

Brigham, B. M., and M. B. Fenton. "The Effect of Boost Sealing as a Method to Control Maternity Colonies of Big Brown Bats." *Canadian Journal of Public Health* 78 (1987):47–50.

Childs, J. E., C. V. Trimarchi, and J. W. Krebs. "The Epidemiology of Bat Rabies in New York State, 1988–1992." *Epidemiology and Infection* 113 (1994):501–511.

Hunt, L. A., and K. P. Bhatnagar. "Human Rabies and Silver-haired Bats in the United States." *Bat Research News* 38 (1997):85–89.

National Association of State Public Health Veterinarians, Inc. *Compendium of Animal Rabies Control 1997.* Morbidity and Mortality Weekly Report, (1997)46/No. RR–4.

Tuttle, M. D., and S. J. Kern. *Bats and Public Health.* Milwaukee: Milwaukee Public Museum Press, 1981.

CHAPTER 12

Barbour, R. W., and W. H. Davis. *Bats of America.* Lexington: University of Kentucky Press, 1969.

Bates, P. J. J., and D. L. Harrison. *Bats of the Indian Subcontinent.* Sevenoaks, U.K.: Harrison Zoological Museum, 1997.

Bonaccorso, F. J. *Bats of Papua New Guinea.* Washington, D.C.: Conservation International, 1998.

Churchill, S. *Australian Bats.* Sydney, Australia: Reed New Holland, 1998.

Corbet, G. B., and S. Harris, eds. *The Handbook of British Mammals, 3rd ed.* Oxford: Blackwell Scientific Publications, 1991.

Corbet, G. B., and J. E. Hill. *A World List of Mammalian Species.* 2nd ed. New York: Facts On File, 1986.

Eisenberg, J. F., et al. *Mammals of the Neotropics, Volume 1: the Northern Neotropics: Panama, Colombia, Venezuela, Guyana, Suriname, French Guiana.* Chicago: University of Chicago Press, 1989.

Eisenberg, J. F., and K. F. Reford. *Mammals of the Neotropics, Volume 3: The Central Neotropics: Ecuador, Peru, Bolivia, Brazil.* Chicago: University of Chicago Press, 1999.

Harvey, M. J., J. S. Altenbach, and T. L. Best. *Bats of the United States.* Arkansas Fish and Game Commission, 1999.

Kingdon, J. *Mammals of East Africa: an Atlas of Evolution.* Volume 2A. *Insectivora and Chiroptera.* London: Academic Press, 1974.

Kiser, M., and S. Kiser. "Bayou Bats: Success in Louisiana." *The Bat House Researcher*, 7, no. 2 (1999):1–2.

Mickelburgh, S. P., A. M. Hutson, and P. A. Racey. *Old World Fruit Bats: An Action Plan for Their Conservation*. Gland, Switzerland: International Union for the Conservation of Nature, 1992.

O'Shea, T. J., and T. A. Vaughan. "Population Changes in Bats from Central Arizona: 1972 and 1997." *The Southwestern Naturalist* 44 (1999):495–500.

Payne, J., C. M. Francis, and K. Phillips. *A Field Guide to the Mammals of Borneo*. Malaysia: The Sabah Society with World Wildlife Fund Malaysia, 1985.

Redford, K. H., and J. F. Eisenberg. *Mammals of the Neotropics, the Southern Cone*. Vol. 2. *Chile, Argentina, Uruguay and Paraguay*. Chicago: University of Chicago Press, 1992.

Reid, F. A. *A Field Guide to the Mammals of Central America and Southeast Mexico*. Toronto: Oxford University Press, 1998.

Rosevear, D. *Bats of West Africa*. London: British Museum (Natural History), 1965.

Schmidley, D. J. *The Bats of Texas*. College Station: Texas A & M University Press, 1991.

Smithers, R. H. N. *Mammals of the Southern African Subregion*. Pretoria: University of Pretoria Press, 1983.

Stebbings, R. E. *Conservation of European Bats.* London: Christopher Helm, 1988.

Van Zyll de Jong, C. G. *Handbook of Canadian Mammals*, Vol. 2. *Bats*, 1984.

CHAPTER 13

Audet, D., M. D. Engstrom, and M. B. Fenton. "Morphology, karyology and echolocation calls of *Rhogeessa tumida* (Chiroptera: Vespertilionidae) from the Yucatan Peninsula." *Journal of Mammalogy* 74 (1993):498–502.

Barbour, R. H., and W. H. Davis. *Bats of America*. Lexington: University of Kentucky Press, 1969.

Barclay, R. M. R., P. A. Faure, and D. R. Farr. "Roosting Behavior and Roost Selection by Migrating Silver-haired Bats *(Lasionycteris noctivagans)*." *Journal of Mammalogy* 69 (1988):821–825.

Barlow, K. E., and G. Jones. "Function of Pipistrelle Social Calls: Field Data and a Playback Experiment." *Animal Behaviour* 53 (1997):991–999.

———. "Differences in Songflights and Social Calls between Two Phonic Types of the Vespertilionid Bat, *Pipistrellus pipistrellus*." *Journal of Zoology (London)* 241 (1997):315–324.

Barratt, E. M., et al. "DNA Answers the Call Pipistrelle Bat Species." *Nature* 387 (1997) :138–139.

Betts, B. J. "Roosts Used by Maternity Colonies of Silver-haired Bats in Northeastern Oregon." *Journal of Mammalogy* 79 (1998):643–650.

———. "Effects of Interindividual Variation in Echolocation Calls of Big Brown and Silver-haired Bats." *Journal of Wildlife Management* 62 (1998):1,003–1,010.

de la Cueva Salcedo, H., et al. "Energetic consequences of Flight Speeds of Foraging Red and Hoary Bats *(Lasiurus borealis* and *Lasiurus cinereus*; Chiroptera: Vespertilionidae)." *Journal of Experimental Biology* 198 (1995):2,245–2,251.

Fenton, M. B., et al. "Bats and the Loss of Tree Canopy in African Woodlands." *Conservation Biology* 12 (1998):399–407.

Fenton, M. B., and D. R. Griffin. "High Altitude Insect Pursuit by Echolocating Bats." *Journal of Mammalogy* 78 (1997):247–250.

Francis, C. M., et al. "Lactation in Male Fruit Bats." *Nature* 367 (1994):691–692.

Grindal, S. D., and R. M. Brigham. "Impacts of Forest Harvesting on Habitat Use by Foraging Insectivorous Bats at Different Spatial Scales." *Ecoscience* 6 (1999):25–34.

Hecker, K. R., and R. M. Brigham. "Does Moonlight Change Vertical Stratification of Activity by Forest-dwelling Insectivorous Bats?" *Journal of Mammalogy* 80 (1999):1,196–1,201.

Hickey, M. B. C., and M. B. Fenton. "Behavioural and Thermoregulatory Responses of Female Hoary Bats, *Lasiurus cinereus* (Chiroptera: Vespertilionidae), to Variations in Prey Availability." *Ecoscience* 3 (1996):414–422.

Jung, T. S., et al. "Habitat Selection by Forest Bats in Relation to Mixed-wood Stand Types and Structure in Central Ontario." *Journal of Wildlife Management* 63 (1999):1,306–1,319.

Kalcounis, M. C. et al. "Bat Activity in the Boreal Forest: Importance of Stand Type and Vertical Strata." *Journal of Mammalogy* 80 (1999):673–682.

O'Donnell, C. F. J., and J. A. Sedgeley. "Use of Roosts by the Long-tailed Bat, *Chalinolobus tuberculatus*, in Temperate Rainforest in New Zealand." *Journal of Mammalogy* 80 (1999):913–923.

Ormsbee, P. C., and W. C. McComb. "Selection of Day Roosts by Female Long-legged Myotis in the Central Oregon Cascade Range." *Journal of Wildlife Management* 62 (1998):596–603.

Parsons, H. J., D. A. Smith, and R. F. Whittam. "Maternity Colonies of Silver-haired Bats, *Lasionycteris noctivagans*, in Ontario and Saskatchewan." *Journal of Mammalogy* 67 (1986):598–600.

Simmons, N. B., and R. S. Voss. "The Mammals of Paracou, French Guiana: a Neotropical Lowland Rainforest Fauna. Part 1. Bats." *Bulletin of the American Museum of Natural History* 237 (1998):1–219.

Voigt, C. C., and von Helversen O. "Storage and Display of Odor by Male Saccopteryx bilineata (Chiroptera, Emballonuridae)." *Behavioral Ecology and Sociobiology* 47 (1999):29–40.

Vonhof, M. J., and R. M. R. Barclay. "Roost-site Selection and Roosting Ecology of Forest-dwelling Bats in Southern British Columbia." *Canadian Journal of Zoology* 74 (1996): 1,797–1,805.

Vonhof, M. J., and R. M. R. Barclay. "Use of Tree Stumps as Roosts by the Western Long-eared Bat." *Journal of Wildlife Management* 61(1997):674–684.

CHAPTER 14

Couffer, J. *Bat Bomb: World War II's Other Secret Weapon*. Austin: University of Texas Press, 1992.

Jarrell, R. *The Bat-Poet*. New York: Collier Books, 1964.

Murphy, H., ed. *Animals in Art*. London: Unwin Hyman, 1989.

Tupinier, D. *La chauve-souris et l'homme*. Paris: L'Harmattan, 1989.

William, C. A. S. *Outlines of Chinese Symbolism and Art Motives*. 3d rev. ed. New York: Dover, 1976.

INDEX

Page numbers in **boldface** indicate illustrations.